Sermons On The Gospel Readings

Series III

Cycle C

Cynthia E. Cowen
Frank Ramirez
Arley K. Fadness
Rick McCracken-Bennett
Scott Bryte

CSS Publishing Company, Inc., Lima, Ohio

SERMONS ON THE GOSPEL READINGS, SERIES III, CYCLE C

For more information about CSS Publishing Company resources, visit our website at www.csspub.com or email us at csr@csspub.com or call (800) 241-4056.

Cover design by Barbara Spencer

ISSN: 1937-1330

ISBN-13: 978-0-7880-2621-8
ISBN-10: 0-7880-2621-6

PRINTED IN USA

Table Of Contents

**Sermons For Sundays
In Advent, Christmas, And Epiphany**
Jesus Makes All The Difference
by Cynthia E. Cowen

Advent 1   **15**
　Don't Burn The Cookies!
　Luke 21:25-36

Advent 2   **21**
　Go, Johnny, Go, Go, Go!
　Luke 3:1-6

Advent 3   **25**
　The Coat Off Your Back
　Luke 3:7-18

Advent 4   **31**
　A Concert Of Praise
　Luke 1:39-45 (46-55)

Christmas Eve/Christmas Day   **37**
　Christmas Grass And Easter Tinsel
　Luke 2:1-14 (15-20)

Christmas 1   **43**
　Tradition Can Be Changed
　Luke 2:41-52

Christmas 2   **51**
　Fire! Fire!
　John 1:(1-9) 10-18

The Epiphany Of Our Lord   55
Jesus Makes All The Difference
Matthew 2:1-12

The Baptism Of Our Lord
Epiphany 1
Ordinary Time 1   59
Don't Touch Me With That Water!
Luke 3:15-17, 21-22

Epiphany 2
Ordinary Time 2   63
Only The Best
John 2:1-11

Epiphany 3
Ordinary Time 3   69
Love Walked Across The Field
Luke 4:14-21

Epiphany 4
Ordinary Time 4   75
Fit The Picture
Luke 4:21-30

Epiphany 5
Ordinary Time 5   81
The Ashes Of Our Lives
Luke 5:1-11

Epiphany 6
Ordinary Time 6   89
Risk Takers
Luke 6:17-26

Epiphany 7
Ordinary Time 7   95
Forgive As You Have Been Forgiven
Luke 6:27-38

Epiphany 8   **101**
Ordinary Time 8
   How Firm A Foundation
   Luke 6:39-49

Epiphany 9   **107**
Ordinary Time 9
   Bridge Builders
   Luke 7:1-10

The Transfiguration Of Our Lord   **113**
(Last Sunday After Epiphany)
   Go, Climb A Mountain!
   Luke 9:28-36 (37-43)

Sermons For Sundays
In Lent And Easter
You Are Here!
by Frank Ramirez

Introduction   **119**

Ash Wednesday   **121**
   There's Still Time
   Matthew 6:1-6, 16-21

Lent 1   **127**
   Hit Me With Your Best Shot
   Luke 4:1-13

Lent 2   **133**
   Oh, Jerusalem
   Luke 13:31-35

Lent 3   **139**
   The Tower Of Siloam
   Luke 13:1-9

Lent 4   145
   This Fellow Welcomes Sinners
   Luke 15:1-3, 11b-32

Lent 5   153
   No Pleasing Some People
   John 12:1-8

Passion/Palm Sunday   159
   No ... On
   Luke 22:14—23:56

Maundy Thursday   165
   Holy Ground
   John 13:1-17, 31b-35

Good Friday   171
   You Are Here
   John 18:1—19:42

Easter Day   177
   Another Mary, Another Martha
   John 20:1-18

Easter 2   181
   Believing Thomas
   John 20:19-31

Easter 3   187
   Low-Carb Christians
   John 21:1-19

Easter 4   193
   How Much Of An Honor?
   John 10:22-30

Easter 5   201
   Simple Enough?
   John 13:31-35

Easter 6   **207**
    Advocate And Redeemer
    John 14:23-29

The Ascension Of Our Lord   **213**
    The End Of The Beginning
    Luke 24:44-53

Easter 7   **219**
    That We May All Be One!
    John 17:20-26

**Sermons For Sundays
After Pentecost (First Third)
Veni, Spiritus Sanctus, Veni
by Arley K. Fadness**

The Day Of Pentecost   **227**
    Veni, Spiritus Sanctus, Veni
    John 14:8-17 (25-27)

The Holy Trinity   **233**
    Holy, Holy, Holy
    John 16:12-15

Proper 4   **239**
Pentecost 2
Ordinary Time 9
    Amazing Faith
    Luke 7:1-10

Proper 5   **245**
Pentecost 3
Ordinary Time 10
    Sit Up And Speak!
    Luke 7:11-17

Proper 6   **251**
Pentecost 4
Ordinary Time 11
    The Forgiven Love A Lot!
    Luke 7:36—8:3

Proper 7   **257**
Pentecost 5
Ordinary Time 12
    Liberating The Possessed
    Luke 8:26-39

Proper 8   **263**
Pentecost 6
Ordinary Time 13
    Keeping The Main Thing The Main Thing
    Luke 9:51-62

Proper 9   **269**
Pentecost 7
Ordinary Time 14
    Appointed And Sent!
    Luke 10:1-11, 16-20

Proper 10   **277**
Pentecost 8
Ordinary Time 15
    Checked The Ditch Lately?
    Luke 10:25-37

Proper 11   **283**
Pentecost 9
Ordinary Time 16
    Sister Act(s)
    Luke 10:38-42

Sermons For Sundays
After Pentecost (Middle Third)
Where Would You Go To Meet Jesus?
by Rick McCracken-Bennett

Proper 12   **291**
Pentecost 10
Ordinary Time 17
  Forgive Us
  Luke 11:1-13

Proper 13   **297**
Pentecost 11
Ordinary Time 18
  Stuff!
  Luke 12:13-21

Proper 14   **303**
Pentecost 12
Ordinary Time 19
  Don't Be Afraid
  Luke 12:32-40

Proper 15   **309**
Pentecost 13
Ordinary Time 20
  The Great Divide
  Luke 12:49-56

Proper 16   **315**
Pentecost 14
Ordinary Time 21
  What If The Disciples Had Email
    And One Of The Disciples Was A Woman?
  Luke 13:10-17

Proper 17   321
Pentecost 15
Ordinary Time 22
   But I Really Like The Best Seat In The House!
   Luke 14:1, 7-14

Proper 18   327
Pentecost 16
Ordinary Time 23
   Finish What You Start
   Luke 14:25-33

Proper 19   333
Pentecost 17
Ordinary Time 24
   Where Would You Go To Meet Jesus?
   Luke 15:1-10

Proper 20   339
Pentecost 18
Ordinary Time 25
   How Do You Know The Good Guys
      From The Bad Guys?
   Luke 16:1-13

Proper 21   343
Pentecost 19
Ordinary Time 26
   The Great Divide
   Luke 16:19-31

Proper 22   349
Pentecost 20
Ordinary Time 27
   When The Going Gets Tough ...
      The Tough Start Praying!
   Luke 17:5-10

Sermons For Sundays
After Pentecost (Last Third)
Knowing Who's In Charge
by Scott Bryte

Proper 23   357
Pentecost 21
Ordinary Time 28
   Can't Stay Away
   Luke 17:11-19

Proper 24   361
Pentecost 22
Ordinary Time 29
   Will He Find Faith?
   Luke 18:1-8

Proper 25   365
Pentecost 23
Ordinary Time 30
   Begging And Bragging
   Luke 18:9-14

Reformation Day   369
   Getting Back Into Shape
   John 8:31-36

All Saints   373
   Saint Who?
   Luke 6:20-31

Proper 26   377
Pentecost 24
Ordinary Time 31
   Just Deal With It
   Luke 19:1-10

Proper 27   381
Pentecost 25
Ordinary Time 32
  Trick Questions, Big Answers
  Luke 20:27-38

Proper 28   385
Pentecost 26
Ordinary Time 33
  Forecast
  Luke 21:5-19

Christ The King   391
Proper 29
  Knowing Who's In Charge
  Luke 23:33-43

Thanksgiving Day   395
  Not Just Being Polite
  John 6:25-35

Lectionary Preaching After Pentecost   399

US/Canadian Lectionary Comparison   401

About The Authors   403

Sermons On The Gospel Readings

For Sundays In
Advent, Christmas,
And Epiphany

Jesus Makes
All The Difference

Cynthia E. Cowen

Advent 1
Luke 21:25-36

Don't Burn The Cookies!

Today we enter the season of Advent. The countdown has begun as we once more anticipate the celebration of the birth of Christ. Advent is a time to prepare, not just our homes but our hearts. What joy floods our hearts as we sing "Joy to the world, the Lord has come!" The Son of God entered our world so quietly — no one, except those searching the heavens, saw the star that announced his birth. However, today's gospel tells us that when Christ comes again, it will be a like a hurricane or a tornado. The sun will be darkened, and the moon will not shine. Stars will fall from the sky. The seas will roar and toss with violence. People will faint in terror.

It's been over 2,000 years since Christ promised to return with power and glory. "Let ev'ry heart prepare him room" we are told in our Christmas carol. Are we prepared? Look around. You'll find complacent hearts, worldly hearts, hearts striving for popularity and success. Hearts that are anticipating a return on their investment of time and money, not anticipating the return of the CEO of the universe.

Christian believers also anticipate. They anticipate the return of Christ. Don't despair, but rejoice. That's what Advent is all about — looking forward to Christ's second coming when he will establish a reign of justice and peace.

- Anticipation — seeing a heavy snow fall and hoping school is closed tomorrow.
- Anticipation — seeing beautifully wrapped gifts under a tree and hoping they are for you.

15

- Anticipation — hoping that Tom will bring his tasty cheese and mushroom bread to the office party.
- Anticipation — smelling Christmas goodies and hoping to get the first cookie out of the batch.

In the weeks ahead we will be treated to goodies we wouldn't normally eat at other times of the year: Great-grandma's cut-out sugar cookies, iced and sprinkled; buttery Swedish spritz; delicate Norwegian krumkake and rosettes; Danish kringles; Italian macaroons or pizzelles with anise flavoring. Then there are those German Christmas braids, English plum pudding, and powdery Mexican wedding cakes. The list of the various ethnic delicacies goes on and on. Sweets prepared for us to feast on. And so it is with Advent as we anticipate a "foretaste of the feast" to come.

A lot of thought and time goes into the preparation of seasonal treats. Ingredients need to be purchased. Taking inventory of the pantry, we begin to make out a grocery list: powdered sugar, nuts, candied fruit, flavoring (almond extract for icing, rum flavoring for Grandpa's favorite rum balls), red and green food coloring, chocolate chips, sweetened condensed milk, and coconut. Oh, oh! The baking soda has expired — better not risk it. Don't be cheap, buy another. Time has to be set aside to bake — sometimes a whole day just for one item like sugar cookies. Anticipating using the Christmas cookie cutters, youngsters can't wait for dough to be rolled out, cut out, and baked. Ears are alert to the ring of the timer ... "brrrring."

"Mommy, Mommy ... they're done. Can we frost them now?"

"Not yet ... they have to cool."

Three minutes later, "Mommy, Mommy ... I touched one. It wasn't hot."

In anticipation of decorating snowmen, Santas, bells, and stars, little hands reach for the cookie toppings. As multicolored sprinkles roll across the floor, a voice cries out, "Oops! I'm sorry, Mom. The cap wasn't on tight." Mom smiles as she already anticipated this "oops" event. "Wash floor" was on her "to do" list.

One of the most important things in baking is timing. The oven has to be preheated, cookie sheets placed inside, and time calculated. My niece is one who is not very successful at baking cookies, but she tries. Setting the timer, she becomes sidetracked. Switching her focus from baking to laundry, she'll find herself in the basement, not hearing the "brrrrring" of the timer over the "chug, chug, chug" of the washer. Eventually her nose becomes aware of the aroma of burning cookies. "Drat," she mumbles as she races up the stairs to dump the first dozen into the garbage can instead of into the cookie can.

Preparing and baking Christmas goodies might be related to our Advent preparation. As we anticipate Jesus' arrival, we take stock of our pantry. Do we have all the necessary ingredients to enable us, as followers of Christ, to make a difference in our family, our community, and our world this season? Is our focus centered on a spiritual walk or on the hustle and bustle of the commercial world? Are we praying for a parking spot or praying for a tired check-out clerk? Do we pick up the Bible with as much anticipation as we do the sales flyers, hunting for "bargains"? Are we in worship as much as we are in retail stores?

The good news is that attention to our spiritual walk throughout the year will enable us to reap extra blessings during Advent. For instance, giving an understanding look and a smile to a frazzled mom with a very tired child in a shopping cart, instead of flashing a disapproving scowl. "Been there; done that." You remember having raised your own children.

Other things we can do as an Advent witness to others: dropping more than a dollar into the Salvation Army bucket, buying mittens for the Mitten Tree, making a special meal for a widower, caroling at a nursing home ... or even baking cookies for your pastor! I had to add a little humor to the list ... but I won't refuse them. Christ is coming again, so we need to be spiritually fit, taking advantage of the opportunities presented. As we set our eyes on others, we become the presence of Christ in our world. "Keep watch! Be careful!" Jesus reminds us.

We are entering a season of countdown the newspaper reminds us: 25 days to shop! We have our "list" and feel relief in checking off each item: Christmas cards, buying and wrapping gifts, decorating the house, inviting friends over for dessert, attending company dinners, dashing through the snow! But remember, "Keep watch! Be careful! Be prepared, stay focused ... don't let those cookies burn!" In other words, "Don't burn yourself out rushing around like a reindeer with his head cut off!"

The countdown to Christ's return began the day of his birth. An infant born in a Bethlehem stable grew up. Jesus walked this earth preparing its people for the greatest gift ever given. Salvation — a free gift to us but a costly gift from God. Following the giving of the gift, he returned to his Father with the promise to come again. When will that happen? No one knows the time, not the angels nor Jesus himself. Only the Father knows the time. The hour is not recorded anywhere in scripture when Jesus will arrive to take those who have prepared themselves home. However, the Bible does tell us that people will be buying and selling, eating and drinking, playing and working, marrying and having children, living and dying. The good news is that God has given us a "No-Fail Recipe" for a wonderful life here and now. Jesus purchased the key ingredient for you — his death on a cross for the forgiveness of your sin. Then he added the Holy Spirit enabling us to rise to life in power. Next he mixed in love for God and love for others. Stirring in fellowship, prayer, study, and worship, we bake until done, watching carefully, preparing ourselves for his coming once more. How many more Christmases will we celebrate? We don't know, but celebrate we will until that time when Jesus returns.

- Anticipate — Jesus' return through your Advent preparation.
- Anticipate — new life in Christ as you prepare yourself.
- Anticipate — his birth and celebrate his death.
- Anticipate — and enjoy his promises and his salvation now.

Don't wait until Jesus comes again. If you fail to add baking soda, your sticky buns won't rise. If you fail to add Jesus to your life, you will find that this "ill-preparedness" will be costly. If you forget to set your timer, your cookies will burn. It's guaranteed! If you put off following Jesus, you will live a life separated from the joy of your salvation and face a burning. "Be on watch. Be prepared."

As we anticipate the result from the oven, we anticipate eternal life with Christ. Set your dial correctly as you look forward to the final outcome. Expect his return at any moment. Experience him now. Anticipate as you enjoy this blessed Advent season. And remember, "Don't burn the cookies!" Amen.

Advent 2
Luke 3:1-6

Go, Johnny, Go, Go, Go!

Every Sunday, a church broadcasts a one-hour service over the waves of 1450 WMIQ, the local radio station. It begins with this announcement, "From the shores of beautiful Crystal Lake, we bring you Our Saviour's morning service."

One Advent season, the pastor had selected an "in the sandals" sermon series. The first biblical character to be heard from was John the Baptist. As John entered clothed in the prophet's clothing, a reader announced: "Prepare the way of the Lord. Make his paths straight" (Luke 3:4b).

Recently, there had been some problems. Another station had been broadcasting over WMIQ's airwaves. As the character playing John introduced himself to the congregation, the words of a golden oldie spilled out, "Go, Johnny, go, go, go!" Laughter went up reminding those listening that God has a sense of humor. He seemed to be saying, "Go, Johnny, go, go, go! Go out and tell the world that Jesus is coming; he's coming soon!"

"Heeeeeeere's Johnny," Ed McMahon used to announce as Johnny Carson came on stage to the applause of his television audience. Late night talk show hosts like Jay Leno, David Letterman, or Conan O'Brian can never replace the famed Johnny Carson or the man who prepared Johnny's way, Ed McMahon. "Heeeeeeere's Johnny!" On cue, the star of *The Tonight Show* entered, taking his place center stage. When the applause died down, Johnny assumed the starring role, and Ed McMahon's role decreased.

21

Jesus came onto the world's stage to unveil the greatest story of love the world would ever witness. While he was yet in the wings, there was one out front preparing the audience for his entrance, John, the son of Zechariah. As Jesus stepped forward to assume the major role in the drama already prepared for him, John, the supporting actor in this drama, cried out, "Here's the one you've been expecting ... the one I've been talking about ... the one who will take away the sin of the world" (John 1:29 cf). God had told John that he would see the Spirit come down from heaven and rest on a man.

In chapter 1 of the apostle John's gospel we hear confirmation of this event. He wrote, "I have seen this happen, and I tell you the truth: This man is the Son of God" (John 1:34 NCV).

And so, the end of Act One. In the first scene of Act Two, John the Baptist reappears. The audience sees Jesus passing by and hears John say to two of his disciples, "Look, the Lamb of God." The two disciples heard John and without looking back at their teacher followed Jesus, God's Lamb. Why? Because that's what John wanted them to do. He knew the script. Jesus was selecting his cast of twelve, whose roles in life would never be the same.

Disciple one, Andrew, knew what he had to do. He ran to tell his brother about his encounter.

"Simon, Simon ... come and see! We've found the one John told us would come — the Lamb of God, the Messiah — the Christ. John baptized him yesterday, and when we saw him today and heard what John said about him, we left John and followed him. He invited us to the place where he was staying. Simon, we spent the whole day with him. There's no question in my mind — the one they call Jesus of Nazareth is the Messiah! Come and see for yourself." And he brought his brother to Jesus.

But Andrew didn't have to do any introductions. Jesus simply looked at his brother and said, " 'You are Simon, son of John. You are to be called Cephas' (which is translated Peter)" (John 1:42).

John first appeared on stage as a rugged man, dressed in the prophet's wardrobe of camel's hair and a leather belt. His speech was direct and confronting. Luke tells us that God's word came to John in the wilderness. John was convinced he had been called by

God — not merely to reflect the moods and opinions of his time — but to speak the truth imparted to him by God. In his wilderness preparation, he prayed and meditated on his role. The word of God became forged into his very being, molding him into a fiery and dramatic figure that attracted crowds. When Jesus entered on cue, John was content to lower himself and to let Jesus take the higher place.

John the Baptist had a very important role to play in the first part of the story. With a booming voice, he fearlessly cried out to the crowds, "Repent! Turn from your sin and be baptized." Jesus was now stepping forward to assume the major role he had been chosen for. John had always known he was not the star of this unfolding drama. Jesus had top billing. But John's lines had been vital in the presentation. He was there to announce, "Here's Jesus! The Lamb of God, the one who takes away the sin of the world."

John realized that his role was about to come to an end. He had confronted too many, alienating the self-righteous, and the religious leaders of the day. He had condemned corrupt and ruthless political leaders such as Herod the Great, whom he rebuked for having taken his brother's wife. John never compromised his words, but a new act was to begin. The Son of God was on the move.

Act Three finds Jesus speaking about John to his attentive audience:

> *What did you go out into the wilderness to look at? A reed shaken by the wind? What then did you go out to see? Someone dressed in soft robes? Look, those who put on fine clothing and live in luxury are in royal palaces. What then did you go out to see? A prophet? Yes, I tell you, and more than a prophet. This is the one about whom it is written, "See, I am sending my messenger ahead of you, who will prepare your way before you." I tell you, among those born of women no one is greater than John; yet the least in the kingdom of God is greater than he.* — Luke 7:24b-28

John, the messenger who prepared the way for Jesus, had fulfilled his God-given role. Yet Jesus tells us that in the kingdom of God

23

all who came after John would have greater spiritual understanding because they would see the end of the drama: the purpose of Jesus' death and resurrection. Advent — a time to prepare our hearts for Jesus' second coming. We will see the heavens open and Jesus appearing as a warrior on a white horse.

John saw Jesus, God's perfect Lamb, the one who would be a sacrifice for our sins. John died before he saw that Lamb return as a conquering king, bringing judgment on those refusing to acknowledge him as Lord and Savior.

In the last chapter of the Bible, in the book of Revelation, we find the battle lines drawn. We engage in a round of applause as the curtain drops. But we know there will be a curtain call. The stage is set. Are you ready to call out, "Come, Lord Jesus, come!"

> *There will be signs in the sun, the moon, and the stars, and on earth distress among nations confused by the roaring of the sea and the waves. People will faint from fear and foreboding of what is coming upon the world, for the powers of the heavens will be shaken. Then they will see "the Son of Man coming in a cloud" with power and glory. Now when these things begin to take place, stand up and raise your heads, because your redemption draws near!* — Luke 21:25-28

Guess what? We are now the current cast of this long-running drama, the cast that announces to those who have ears to hear, "Here's Jesus! King of kings and Lord of lords! The star of the greatest show on earth!" Amen.

Advent 3
Luke 3:7-18

The Coat Off Your Back

Thanksgiving — cornucopias, fall harvests, turkey and pumpkin pie, corn stalks, and scarecrows — outward signs associated with the holiday we celebrated only seventeen days ago. Even before Halloween and Thanksgiving ended, holiday colors had changed. Orange pumpkin lights were replaced by white or multicolored twinkling lights.

A small town policeman looks forward every year to hanging his outside Christmas lights. His goal is to measure up to Chevy Chase's outlandish display in the movie, *Christmas Vacation*. So far his record is 18,000 twinkling lights — only 7,000 more to go!

Like John Grishman's book, *Skipping Christmas*, Frosties begin to adorn yards and rooftops. Let's not forget the Dr. Suess character, the "Grinch Who Stole Christmas." His inflatable green body, topped with a red Santa hat, sits a few feet away from a lighted, plastic Nativity scene. Retail stores remove Halloween candies from their shelves, replacing them with candy canes and red and green wrapped Hershey kisses. A new season of consumer buying is heralded with the seasonal shopping flyers. "Happy holidays!" we hear more often each year. But for many this is more than a holiday season that bridges the 25 days of commercialism. Christians call this season Advent — a bridge that announces the entry of God from heaven into our world.

Yes, many of us cringe when we see early Christmas decorations thrown up, or hear "Rudolf, The Red-Nosed Reindeer," "Frosty The Snowman," and "Jingle Bells" playing over the PA systems in stores. Excitement rises as the Sear's Christmas catalog arrives in many homes. As a child, I devoured every page. "Santa Mom" was busy "Makin' a list, checking it twice — what store is promising the bestest price?"

Wait! Let's not get riled up. Focus on the real preparation — the excitement of the celebration of the day the greatest gift arrived — God in human form. Jesus, the reason for the season. We give our thanks, along with Mary, his mother, "My soul magnifies the Lord, and my spirit rejoices in God my Savior, for he has looked with favor on the lowliness of his servant. Surely, from now on all generations will call me blessed" (Luke 1:46b-48). Mary was blessed because she surrendered to God's plan. The time had arrived! She was prepared to cross that bridge from being a humble servant to being the mother of the Savior of the world.

That Christmas Eve the world was full of blessings for a young public accountant finishing up his paperwork in a bank board room. Glancing out the window, he noticed a light snow beginning to fall. He and his partner had agreed to stop work at noon. Both had all their Christmas shopping to do. With a joyful heart, he began to shop the seven floors of a nearby department store. The hours passed quickly. His shopping concluded, the young man took the down escalator, arms loaded with just the *right* presents. This was going to be a really good Christmas. Success had brought him much in the way of material blessings.

Bracing himself for the cold, he pushed the store door open. Gusting winds blew delicate snowflakes over the sidewalks. Drifts had begun to pile up in doorways as he headed for the parking ramp. Glancing at his watch, he noticed it was already five o'clock. It'd be tight, but if the traffic was light, he'd make it home for that Christmas Eve feast.

The beauty of Christmas window displays caught his eye. Magical moments in winter wonderlands. Carols mingled with falling snow as sharp wind bit his ears. Hurrying down the street, his thoughts once again turned to his wife and young son, a warm home, and the delicious food that awaited him. "Blessed, you bet!" he thought shielding his face from the icy sting.

He began to sing "Silent Night." "Silent night, holy night. All is calm, all is bright." Entering the parking garage, his mood suddenly shifted. It would be a moment that he'd never forget — a moment that turned his life upside down.

Before him a man was supporting himself against a pillar — evidently one of the homeless, he assumed. Trying to avoid looking at the man's eyes, he turned his own down. That was when he noticed the man wearing worn out shoes but no socks. As he raised his eyes, he saw that the man wore "high water" pants. The accountant continued his upward glance, taking in the stranger's shirt. It had been white at one time; now it had yellowed. The old man pulled his coat together, trying to keep the biting chill out. It was apparent he hadn't shaved in days. His frail body showed his meals were few and far between. And those eyes ... they looked so empty. They were eyes without hope.

"Hey, mister, I'm hungry. Got a dollar?" he asked and reached out his hand. The question startled the young man. The warm fuzzies of Christmas disappeared in a poof. Before him was a man who did not fit in with the music ringing in the air or the pork pie and spiced egg nog awaiting him at home.

"What should I do?" he asked himself. He stared at the man and then walked away.

What should he have done? What would you have done? John tells us, "If you have two shirts, two coats, food or money to share, do it" (Luke 3:11 cf). That young man would remember the night he met Jesus, "Mister, got a dollar?" He had a dollar and more. He had a shirt and a coat on his back. He could have given them to the man. There were more at home. It's hard to be Thanksgiving or Christmas people — to consider all that one has as gifts from God — blessings from God to be shared with others.

God promised his servant Abraham: "Leave all — follow me — and I will make you a blessing to others." Like the young man who could list many excuses not to help the vagrant begging on the streets, Abraham could have listed his excuses not to do as God asked: "My wife won't like being uprooted. She's comfortable here. Nice tent, friends, family — a support system." But Abraham stepped out in obedience to God. The result? Blessings that have been given to all generations. His example of trust and faith in

God, who cares and provides for faithful followers, still stands before us. Abraham didn't look at the current situation, but looked forward to God's next move. He was blessed to be a blessing to all future generations. And we, in this future, are now blessed to be blessings.

Jesus fervently desires us to be thankful people — people "in the world" but not "of the world." Not people so distracted "by the world" that we fail to see the needs of those around us. We are called to be people willing to give in love and give whatever it takes to fill a need — people, who seeing that need (a person with no socks, no coat, no hope) won't turn the other way simply because it doesn't fit into their plans.

As Christians we are called to look beyond our own needs to the needs of others. The young accountant, so richly blessed, did not know at that time his "source of blessing." His life had been focused on living for number one, himself. But that Christmas Eve encounter changed his life. Six years later, he left his job to become a pastor, and he continues to reflect on that night he met Jesus in a Detroit parking garage, turned, and walked away — his coat still on his back.

Nora rushed into the gym. She was late. The women were already dishing up the soup. Items of used clothing lay in neat stacks on metal tables. White elephant articles from garages, basements, and attics were piled up at one end of the court. Craft items took up the tables along the bleachers. Jen had set up her candles and Tyler his unique split-wood carvings. They were selling at cost. The smell of spiced apple cider permeated the building as the community gathered for the local Christmas bazaar.

"Sorry I'm late, girls," Nora apologized. "But you know Roy. He wanted me to fix his lunch before I fixed it for someone else." Knowing Roy was a fuss-budget about his schedule, the girls smiled, shaking their heads in agreement.

As the afternoon progressed, the pile of clothes and treasures decreased. Finishing her meal, an elderly woman rose to leave. She had found a nice, wool coat — and it was red, her favorite color. She had just enough money to buy it. After paying for her "need" not "want," she discarded her worn, matted coat. She smiled as she slipped her arms into the warm, winter coat. Then she headed for the door.

"Nora! Hey, Nora!" a voice cried out. "Isn't that your coat walking out the front door?" Alarmed, Nora turned from clearing tables to see the old woman opening the front door. And that was her red coat she was wearing!

"Hey, wait a minute," Nora called out dashing to the exit. The woman abruptly stopped. Embarrassed and confused, she turned to see a woman running toward her. Seeing her fearful expression, Nora halted. "Please, wait a minute," she said. Stopping by a table, Nora picked up a red and black crocheted hat.

"This hat will go perfectly with your new coat."

"But I ain't got no more money," she answered, with downcast eyes.

"Consider it an early Christmas gift," Nora beamed and handed her the hat. "In fact, I think this scarf goes with the hat, too. Take them both."

The elderly woman smiled. "The hat will do me well. My momma always told me that you lose a lot of heat up there if the head isn't covered." She chuckled as she put the hat on. "And thanks for the scarf. I do look spiffy, don't I?"

"You sure do. Have a wonderful Christmas," Nora said. The woman smiled, turned, and went out the door.

Returning to cleaning up, Nora's friend asked, "Did you get your coat back?"

"No, I didn't, but no need to worry," Nora answered. "I happen to know that Roy put a big, fancy-wrapped box under the tree for me. I'm sure it's that black leather coat I've been hinting about."

"But that red coat looked so good on you. I could chase the woman down and tell her we made a mistake," her friend said.

"Don't get upset, Barb. You see, one of my Advent devotions asked how we might help our neighbor; how we, who are blessed, can be a blessing to others."

Barb smiled and said, "Well, God just answered your prayer."

In the remaining days of this Advent season, pray that God interrupts your plans and gives you the opportunity to be Christ's presence to others. I assure you, God will answer those payers.

Remember the young accountant who wouldn't take off his coat and give to someone in need? Remember the praying kitchen worker who gave the coat from her back to one who really needed it? Remember what God says to us, "Whoever has two coats must share with anyone who has none; and whoever has food must do likewise" (Luke 3:11). As people of hope and plenty, we must give hope as well as share from our abundance.

Advent: a time of blessing.

> *Come, you that are blessed by my Father, inherit the kingdom prepared for you from the foundation of the world; for I was hungry and you gave me food, I was thirsty and you gave me something to drink, I was a stranger and you welcomed me. I was naked and you gave me clothing, I was sick and you took care of me, I was in prison and you visited me ... Truly I tell you, just as you did it to one of the least of these who are members of my family, you did it to me.*
> — Matthew 25:34-40

When you encounter Christ, you will never be the same. Blessed we are called to bless others so go and do it — even if it means "giving the coat off your back." Amen.

A Concert Of Praise

The Christmas concert was about to begin. The professional musicians were ready. All eyes were on the band director as he brought down his baton. Softly, flutes began weaving a magical introduction, capturing the audience's spirit. An instrumental duet formed with clarinets adding their voices. Then more wind instruments came in. Finally, brass and percussion entered and volume and tempo increased. Each section's contribution melded into a harmonious voice. The rehearsals had been worth it; the time and labor had not been in vain. Dedicated individual practice paid off as a glorious concert was birthed. "Praise the Lord, O my soul; all my inmost being, praise his holy name. Praise the Lord, O my soul" (Psalm 103:1-2a NIV).

Corporate worship is like that. Those gathered are caught up in a symphony of wonder. Under the direction of the Holy Spirit, personal worship becomes part of the whole — a glorious chorus magnifying God.

Mary's song of praise, recorded in our text, is traditionally called the "Magnificat," a hymn glorifying God for what he is about to do. From the lips of a young girl comes a revolutionary declaration in three parts:

First of all, it is a bursting forth of a chorus of moral revolution: "He has scattered the proud, people who think great things about themselves." The theme is carried by the knowledge that only through death to pride are we able to lead a submitted life. Placing your life next to Christ's cannot help but tear down that pride. When our sin is revealed, we call out to God in shame.

31

O. Henry, not the candy bar, but O. Henry, one of the greatest writers of his day, used his gift to reveal the condition of the human heart. In one of his short writings, he holds up a magnifying glass to examine a boy growing up in a small village. In school he formed a strong friendship with a girl he sat next to. His admiration for her increased over the years. Her life reflected her convictions. What did his life reflect? Did he have convictions? He had at least one — he didn't want to live and die in this place. He felt trapped. The pressure became too much. The lights of the big city drew him. However, the temptations and influence of that environment trapped him in an unhealthy way. Soon he found it easier to make a living on the wrong side of the law. He became a successful pickpocket and petty thief. Having never gotten caught, he became proud of his cleverness.

After snatching an old woman's purse one day, he fled with a smirk of satisfaction on his face. As he turned a corner, he was confronted with his past. Coming toward him was that sweet, innocent girl he used to know. It was as if she held up a mirror to his soul. At that moment he really saw himself. Burning with shame he cried out, "God, I wish I could die." Pride has to die in order to truly see our real selves.

The second revolution Mary's song reveals is a social revolution. In a small town, a lakeside street became labeled "Millionaire's Road." The houses were grand, the yards were well-manicured, and flower gardens boasted a variety of expensive plants.

Between two massive houses on wide lots sat a small, tar-papered one on a very narrow lot. Though the owner did not have the money to side it for many years, he worked hard keeping his small yard mowed and tenderly cared for a planter alongside the entry. He was proud of his little "toe hold on the bay." He shared the same beach with his neighbors, and he enjoyed watching his children build immense sandcastles. The only ladder of success the children climbed was attached to a floating raft. The view of the bay was just like his neighbors. However, there was a difference in the contribution of each to the picture. On each side of his small beach area floated sea-doos, motor boats, and elaborate portable docks. In the middle of that picture was his old, metal dock with a rowboat tied up to it. Elaborate fire pits dwarfed his homemade rock circle. His neighbors were very proud of their elegant houses on the bay — feeling proud of their place in society. The man in he middle was humbled to live on that same bay — feeling blessed by what God had given him.

Mary raises her voice in praise to God, "He casts down the mighty — he exalts the humble." Mary recognizes her place in society. "For he has looked with favor on the lowliness of his servant" (Luke 1:48a). Mary understood that she was but a humble instrument under the direction of God. She recognized the honor the solo God had bestowed upon her.

Mary continued to sing her song of praise, "Surely, from now on all generations shall call me blessed; for the Mighty One has done great things for me, and holy is his name" (Luke 1:48b-49). This was not a statement of pride. Pride is refusing to accept God's gifts or taking credit for what God has done. Humility is accepting the gifts and using them to praise and serve God. What an honor God bestowed upon her, but that honor would lead to pain. The pain came even before her child was born. Small-town people can be mean. Mary would be gossiped about and ridiculed. She would be labeled as a girl with low morals. And even her fiancé Joseph considered leaving her. She remembered the comforting words of her cousin, Elizabeth, upon her earlier visit. Filled with the Holy Spirit, Elizabeth addressed Mary with these words:

> *Blessed are you among women, and blessed is the fruit of your womb. And why has this happened to me, that the mother of my Lord comes to me? For as soon as I heard the sound of your greeting, the child in my womb leaped for joy. And blessed is she who believed that there would be a fulfillment of what was spoken to her by the Lord.* — Luke 1:42-45

Mary hadn't even told Elizabeth she was with child, but God had. The knowledge of that filled Mary with her personal concert of praise.

A young maiden from a tiny village in Nazareth had found favor with God. She did not feel trapped. She did not run to the big city where she could get lost in the crowds. Raising God's Son in the shelter of a loving family brought Mary much happiness. Surrendering herself as an instrument of God, she had been elevated to a much higher level in the eyes of Elizabeth. But Mary still considered herself a lowly servant. When we realize what Christ did for all men and women, we are stripped of labels and prestige and find that social grades are eliminated. They are gone forever as equality for all is given by Christ. Our tar-papered lives of sin are covered by the blood of the Savior of our souls.

Finally, we hear God's plan for an economic revolution. "He has filled the hungry with good things, and sent the rich away empty" (Luke 1:53).

Amid a playroom filled with toys, a child twisted a figure until it broke. Then he tossed it away. His playmate complained, "Look what you did now! You took off Spiderman's head. I liked him best." Picking up another toy, the boy simply replied without any guilt, "Don't worry; my mom will buy me another one."

In a world obsessed with accumulating things, we have become selfish and uncaring. We ignore the cries of those in need. Like insensitive Ebenezer Scrooge we might state, "Are there no prisons? Are there no workhouses?" Like sensitive Jesus, we should say, "Come to me all of you who are tired and have heavy loads, and I will give you rest" (Matthew 11:28 NCV). Having lived among us, Jesus knew humanity's sinful, stubborn nature. That's why Jesus had to die to save us.

Harold had gone to church with his wife for 37 years. Stella had raised their two sons as Christians, but Harold remained somewhat committed to his Jewish faith. Over the years pastors invited him to join, but he would always say, "Not until Uncle Saul dies. He'd be really upset with me if I converted."

When Hurricane Katrina struck, a local owner of a restaurant challenged her customers to donate money for its victims. After collecting a goodly amount of money, she realized she did not know how to channel it appropriately. She approached her pastor, who made some telephone calls. Contact was made with a local church in Alabama. "Of course we'll accept your money, but what we really need is helping hands." That Sunday the pastor extended the challenge to his members to volunteer their hands in the relief efforts. Harold and others took up that challenge, and after his first experience, he went twice a year with the church's work crews.

Harold worked side-by-side with men and women from around the nation — people of different faiths — people making a difference in the lives of others — people whose work filled those who were hungry; hungry for rebuilt homes and rebuilt lives.

Every day the volunteers ate breakfast together, had lunch on the job, and came back to eat supper together. Every evening they met to share the events of the day, how it impacted them, scripture reading and prayer. Harold listened, saw Christ's love in those who surrounded him, and began to participate in his quiet way.

Each time Harold went back he found familiar faces and new ones. He looked forward to working with his partner from California, Bob the Roofer, appropriately nicknamed. Then there was Dr. Johnson, a neurosurgeon, and Dr. Baker, an opthamologist. Most of their time was spent clipping toenails of diabetics, irrigating ears, pulling out infected splinters, and treating rashes. As Harold continued to watch Christians in action, he grew in the faith they held to. He even began bringing a Bible to church and witnessing about the rewards of joining the next work crew. He was a very successful recruiter.

After his ninth trip, Harold approached his pastor. "Pastor Steve, I would like to be baptized." Their witness brought Harold to Jesus. He didn't wait for Uncle Saul to die but was baptized a year later.

God had used a gentle and humble man and done great things for him and for others. When Harold took communion for the first time, his heart was filled with thanks to God and his spirit rejoiced in his Savior.

Our society is often described as made up of "the haves" and "the have-nots." However, in a Christian society those who "have" dare not to share with those who "have not." God's formula is clear — we receive and then respond by giving. God began a revolution when he chose to come to us in Christ. The message Christ shared caused moral, social, and economic upheaval.

The door slammed as Austin rushed into the kitchen. "Mom, what color was Mary's uniform?"

"What are you talking about? Mary who?" his mother asked, trying to calm her agitated, young son.

"You know, Mary, the mother of Jesus. What color was her uniform? It was blue, wasn't it? That's what Christmas cards show. And it's blue on the plastic Mary in Mr. Olson's manger scene."

Mom smiled, "I never thought about the color of Mary's clothing. What's up?"

"Taylor is Mary in the school play on Friday. She told Mrs. Morgan that she was going to wear a pink costume because pink's the color for girls."

I've never seen a Mary in blue or pink uniform, but I do know that Mary wore a uniform of a surrendered life. She was an instrument played under the baton of the director of the universe. She sang a solo, and Elizabeth's voice joined her in a duet of praise, and down through the centuries others have joined in, individual instruments used by God in a symphony of praise: "My soul magnifies the Lord, and my spirit rejoices in God my Savior" (Luke 1:46-47).

Don't worry about what you will wear to worship on Christmas Eve or Christmas Day. Put on your uniform of surrender and join with others in a symphony of wonder and a concert of praise. Amen.

Christmas Grass And Easter Tinsel

I think there are two items that seem never to disappear. You might find them anywhere in your home — under the couch, adorning a plant, behind the hamper, on the bathroom floor, or imbedded in the carpet. Of course, you can try to remove them. A vacuum, a broom, or a feather duster might take care of them, but they are bound to return. Let me give you some clues to solving this mystery.

- Clue: One is metallic silver.
- Clue: The other comes in traditional green or in a variety of pastel colors.
- Clue: They are used during two different seasons.
- Song clue: "O Christmas tree, O Christmas tree, how pretty are your branches."
- Song clue: "Here comes Peter Cottontail, hopping down the bunny trail."

Can you guess what they are? Answer: Easter grass and Christmas tinsel.

When tinsel shows up in the holiday section of retail stores, you know Christmas is coming. When colored grass appears on the shelves, you know Easter is coming. Tinsel and grass — signs with meanings. Signs pointing to celebrations. First, let's look at these signs from a secular view. Christmas tinsel is a sign of tree decoration, of sending cards, and of buying presents. Easter grass is a sign to stock up on candy, to search for a new Easter outfit, and to dye those hard-boiled eggs. Though these items are commercial, they are also signs with spiritual meaning. They are signs of birth and rebirth. They are signs pointing to the moving of the Spirit on earth but also in the spiritual world. They are signs that reveal God taking the ordinary and making it extraordinary.

For instance, an ordinary Christmas tree becomes an extraordinary Christmas tree as tinsel is carefully dripped over its boughs. Notice I said "carefully." Impatient children ready for a bedtime snack, teenagers needing to call that special someone, and even Dad who has had enough of this decorating stuff should not be handling the job of tinseling. Picture the end result: globs of silver stringy things thrown thoughtlessly at a tree. Mom doesn't like that picture, so she takes on the job. Methodically hanging each delicate strand over each individual bough, she sings, "O Christmas tree, O Christmas tree, I'll make your branches pretty. O Christmas tree, O Christmas tree, it is a mother's duty." The ordinary has just become extraordinary. It has become a sign of commitment to excellence and a sign of caring.

Tweety the parakeet thought the Christmas tree was a feast to plunder. Attracted to that shiny stuff, the bird stuck his beak through the cage wires to grab a strand and got stuck. What a ruckus he made! Did he want to taste the tinsel or use it to decorate his cage? Who knows the mind of pets?

Baskets filled with colorful Easter grass are signs of expectancy. My mother had a tradition of putting jelly beans underneath our Easter grass and marshmallow eggs on top. Of course, "Daddy Bunny" better hide our baskets well, for Tucker, our dog, could always sniff them out. Oooh, the smell of milk chocolate. The evidence he had devoured a peanut butter fudge egg was not on his mustache or his breath, but on his coat — pink Easter grass on a background of black dog. Tucker could also be a means of spreading Easter grass around the house. Remember, Christmas tinsel and Easter grass are signs with a meaning.

Why do you think I'm concentrating so much on these two items for my Christmas message? Because you can't separate what they represent. I want you to understand that they are more than just flimsy, processed decorations. They are ordinary signs pointing to the extraordinary. What happens when we move two words around? What about Christmas *grass* and Easter *tinsel*? How's that for a switcheroo? Just think of a jokester swapping traffic signs, making a stop a go and a go a stop. Whoa! What an impact that would have on drivers and vehicles.

Our Christmas gospel tells us that when Joseph and Mary arrived at Bethlehem they could not find a place to stay. Someone must have had compassion on them, for we assume Mary gave birth in a stable. How do we know this is true? Check the story out in the Bible.

> *And because Joseph was a descendant of King David, he had to go to Bethlehem in Judea, David's ancient home. He traveled there from the village of Nazareth in Galilee. He took with him Mary, his fiancée, who was now obviously pregnant.*
>
> *And while they were there, the time came for her baby to be born. She gave birth to her first born child, a son. She wrapped him snugly in strips of cloth and laid him in a manger, because there was no lodging available for them.* — Luke 2:6-7 (NLT)

"She gave birth to her first child ... and wrapped him snugly in strips of cloth and laid him in a manger" (Luke 2:7 NLT). Did you hear any mention of a stable in this translation? I checked out other versions, but nowhere can it be found a stable was Mary's delivery room. However, we are told that Jesus' first bed was a manger. A manger is a place where animals were fed. It didn't contain fresh, tender grass. It probably was filled with harsh, dried out straw. A physically worn out Mary laid God's Son in an animal's feeding trough on a rough bed of hay. Have you ever slept on hay? It's rather prickly. Certainly not a Serta mattress with a hypoallergenic, memory foam, two-inch thick mattress topper. Aren't we spoiled today? Even campers have to have a pad to sleep on hard ground. But the King of kings on a bed of straw?

Because a manager is mentioned, a traditional belief grew up that Jesus was born in a stable. Stables were often caves carved into rocks with feeding troughs (mangers) carved into the rock walls. Christmas cards often depict those surroundings as warm, comfortable places, but in reality they were dark and dirty. Look at today's nativity scenes: a clean stable, clean sheep, clean donkey, a pious Joseph, reverent Mary, a visiting shepherd with a crook in his hand, and a picture-perfect baby Jesus lying upon a ceramic bed of hay. A neat decoration, but a sterile picture.

Let's get down now to a reality picture. How could any of you as fathers register at the Stable Inn with a pregnant wife? Wouldn't you ask where the nearest HMO hospital was? Mothers, how many of you could envision your husband as a doctor delivering your baby? Where was the anesthesia? Where was the hot water? The hand sanitizer? The lack of these items would be a definite sign to us today.

Scripture's recording of the birth story points to obscurity, poverty, and rejection. Luke portrayed the King of kings born into poor and humble circumstances — born as a human — born to serve. The ordinary that would become extraordinary. Signs pointing to a miracle that occurred on one ordinary, extraordinary night.

That night there were shepherds in nearby fields, guarding their flocks of sheep. Suddenly, an angel of the Lord appeared among them, and the radiance of the Lord's glory surrounded them. They were terrified, but the angel reassured them. "Don't be afraid!" he said. "I bring you good news that will bring great joy to all people. The Savior — yes, the Messiah, the Lord — has been born today in Bethlehem, the city of David. And you will recognize him by these signs: First, you'll find a baby. Second, that child will be wrapped in bands of cloth. Third, he will be lying in a manger." These signs pointed to a Savior, whose coming had been promised. "For a child has been born to us, a son given to us; authority rests upon his shoulders; and he is named Wonderful Counselor, Mighty God, Everlasting Father, Prince of Peace" (Isaiah 9:6).

Terri smiled with pride as she placed her nephew's birth announcement on her refrigerator. Dressed in a blue sleeper with puppies on it, lay Maksim John upon a warm flannel blanket adorned with paw prints. The picture card announced the birth of a son to Nick and Sara. Birth date: November 18, 2009. Place of birth: their town, USA. The first line said, "Mommy can't wait to share the joys; Daddy can't wait to share the toys!" Cute. Everyone who received this card was asked to celebrate the good news of the arrival of a special gift from God.

Skip back 2,000 years to another birth announcement. That announcement wasn't on a WalMart picture card and didn't go through the US postal service. It was sent by air, carried by angels in the sky. The recipients were not family members, but lowly shepherds. Birth date: Today! Time: This very hour. Place: the city of Bethlehem. Father? God! Mother? Mary. Invitation: Come and see. Come and see the one born to be Savior of the world. You'll find him lying on a bed of Christmas grass.

So how about Easter tinsel? What Saint Paul says of Christ crucified is also true of his birth: To the Jews he was a stumbling block, and to the Gentiles, utter foolishness (1 Corinthians 1:23). "This foolish plan of God is wiser than the wisest of human plans, and God's weakness is stronger than the greatest of human strength" (1 Corinthians 1:25 NLT). These are signs with definite meanings.

Another correlation between Christmas and Easter is that there was no room in the inn. It is symbolic of what was to happen to Jesus. The only place where there was room for him was on a cross. Jesus sought entry to the overcrowded hearts of men; he could not find it; and still his search — and his rejection — goes on.

We cannot think of jumping to the celebration of Easter without passing through Good Friday. Its symbols (cross, crown of thorns, and nails) are the ordinary made extraordinary. Tools of death, yet tools of life. The Christmas manger and Calvary's cross are twin parts of God's salvation plan. Whenever the two seem unrelated, it is because an uncomprehending, frail humanity has misunderstood these two "mighty acts" of God, and has tried to separate that truth, which cannot be separated. God chose to come to us in his Son, Jesus, born in a manger, God taking on human form. A sign of great love is a sign showing commitment. God entered through the door of the manger, left through the door of the cross, and opened the door of the tomb.

We celebrate Easter because of Good Friday. We celebrate Easter because of Christmas. We celebrate the ordinary becoming extraordinary. Christmas and Easter are signs of God's great love and promise. Christmas grass and Easter tinsel. Two things that stick around. A helpless babe and a crucified and risen Lord — signs of one who is always there — Jesus. The world tried to remove him, but they could not. He has not disappeared. Jesus is here among us! He's here right now! The signs are joy and celebration. Joy to the world, and thanks be to God! Merry Christmas. Amen.

Christmas 1
Luke 2:41-52

Tradition Can Be Changed

Tradition is defined as an inherited, established, or customary pattern of thought or action. Take for instance a cooking method. Sarah asked her mother, "Why do you always cut the turkey in half and put it in two small roasters?"

"Because my mother always did. It's a tradition handed down through our family," responded her mother.

"But Mom, did you ever think they didn't have big roasters back then?" Tradition — a customary pattern or action. But who said traditions can't be changed?

A family tradition concerning the Christmas tree in Ingrid's house was: The men cut the tree, put it in a stand, strung the lights around it, and watered it daily. The women unpacked the ornaments and decorated it — taking roads down memory lane.

"Here's Baby's First Christmas. You were so cute, Elsa."

"Look! Here's Grandpa's Swedish horse."

"Careful! That snowflake is very delicate."

It might take hours, but the result was breathtaking. Four weeks later — when the needles began to drop — the women undecorated the tree and carefully packed the ornaments up. The men unwound and removed the lights, lifted the tree from its stand, wrapped it in a plastic sheet, and hauled it out to the curb for pick up. Tradition — it's good, but tradition can change, and often for the good. This year it had.

Tonight Ingrid's Christmas tree lights twinkled brightly as she finally found time to sit and admire it. The Christmas season had been a blur for her this year. She watched it rotate on its plastic

43

stand, waiting for her favorite ornaments to come into view. Who cares if the twelve days of Christmas are over? Why hadn't she bought an artificial tree long ago? Answer? Because it had been tradition in her home to have a real tree. Of course, as dictated, it had to be a blue spruce. They smelled the best. "Never a black spruce," Grandpa had warned her. "They stink like cat urine!"

When her husband was in the army, a real blue spruce in Colorado almost "broke the bank" their first Christmas together. But tradition had to be observed. For over ten years now, they followed the custom of having a real, blue spruce Christmas tree. But a change in tradition was about to occur. In year eleven, her beautifully decorated blue spruce fell over — not just once, but twice! Then there was that strange odor — it smelled like cat urine. "How can that be? This isn't a black spruce," she wondered. Then she caught Tigger the cat using the water in the stand as a litter box. "That's it! I'm through," she yelled.

The after-Christmas sales found Ingrid purchasing a large artificial tree for next year. "Heck with tradition — it looks like a blue spruce, and if I buy some room spray, it'll smell like blue spruce!" Christmas twelve would be different, and it was because of change. And for Ingrid the change was good.

- Change — No more braving the elements to cut down a forest tree and string lights. The only thing to brave now was the cold of the attic where their new tree was stored. No need to check each strand of lights. This tree already had lights attached to its boughs. Artificial trees are a lot easier to handle and set up.
- Change — No need for a tipsy tree stand. This year we can drink all the 7-Up and not a gulping tree. Artificial trees don't drink, don't drop needles, and cats can't — well you know what I mean.
- And the last change? — No need to take the tree down early. Artificial trees can be enjoyed for a long time. I've even heard of artificial Christmas trees becoming Valentine trees!

"Tradition! Tradition!" Tevia sings out in *Fiddler on the Roof.* Yes, tradition is important. But traditions like cutting a turkey in half because your mother, her mother, her mother's mother, and so on have always done it can and should be changed. I bet Sarah didn't continue that tradition. Do you think Mom hung on to it? Tradition is also defined as the handing down of beliefs and customs by word of mouth or by example. As was their custom, Jesus' parents went to Jerusalem every year for the festival of the Passover. Passover commemorated the night of the Jews' escape from Egypt when the Angel of Death came, killing the firstborn of the Egyptians but passing over Israelite homes. At twelve years of age, Jesus was now allowed to attend the festivals. He and his family joined other families traveling to Jerusalem. It was quite common to caravan to keep one safe from robbers. Imagine entering the holy city for the first time, seeing the temple, and observing sacred rituals. How that would have fascinated Jesus.

Jesus was no longer a child. As a man he would follow the traditions observed by all Jewish men. Every Jewish male was required to go to Jerusalem three times a year to celebrate the three great festivals: the Feast of Unleavened Bread, the Feast of Weeks, and the Feast of Tabernacles. In fact, it was the aim of every Jew in the world at least once in a lifetime to attend the Passover feast. Following the Passover came the weeklong Festival of Unleavened Bread. The time had arrived for Jesus to fulfill the law by taking on the obligations of the law — becoming a son of the law.

This was an exciting time for Jesus as he attended his first Passover celebration. He enjoyed the ritual of worship and festival. At every opportunity, he went to the temple courts to hear from some of the greatest rabbis of the faith. He listened attentively to their words. He was not dismissed because of his age but was allowed to join in the discussions. His questions at times were confronting as they probed the depth of traditional belief. Jesus demonstrated wisdom beyond his age. "And all who heard him were amazed at his understanding and his answers" (Luke 2:47).

Packing up his reference books, his business journals, training manuals and the like, the young man looked at his framed master's degree in education with pride. It had been a long journey through

45

the academic halls, but it was worth it. He had just accepted a good career opportunity. Before packing to move, he had one more thing to do — replace his worn blue jeans and tennis shoes with more job-appropriate items. It was off to the Summerset Mall with his fashion consultant, Marissa, his wife. Too bad their young son had to come with them. The budget had no money for a sitter, and after this shopping spree it'd be tuna casserole and scalloped potatoes with Spam for some time.

Confining their toddler in his stroller, the couple began to sort through a wide selection of suits, pants, and sport coats. As her husband paraded out of the dressing room, Marissa would nod her "Yes" or shake her "No." After deciding on the navy blue sport coat with beige pants and a black suit, they turned their attention to shirts, ties, and shoes. Shopping completed, Tom followed the sales clerk to a register wondering if he worked on commission.

Breathing a sigh of relief, Marissa looked down expecting to see her son asleep. He'd been very quiet during their time spent searching for just the right outfits. At once her heart skipped a beat, and then another. The stroller was empty. Panic set in as she searched the aisles for her son. "Nathan! Nathan! Where are you? This is not funny! Tom, Nathan's gone!" Immediately, parents and clerk began a search. Store security was called. Was their son hiding? Had someone abducted him? Fear gripped father and mother. Nathan was nowhere to be seen. Then they heard childlike laughter coming from under a display of jackets. Parting the hangers they discovered their smiling son sitting on the floor beneath it. "I'm not lost, Mommy. I just been here," he said reaching out to her. Flooded with relief, Marissa pulled him out. Embracing him and then directly facing him she warned, "Don't you ever do that again! Your father and I were so scared we'd lost you." "Okay, I promise. Can we go now?" he agreed so innocently.

"Our son, our son ... has anybody seen our son? Has anybody seen Jesus?" The caravan was on the road early for the return trip home. Customarily, women and children traveled in the front with the men bringing up the rear. Joseph assumed Jesus was with Mary up front. Mary assumed he was with Joseph in back. Neither was concerned. A day's journey out the caravan stopped to strike camp. It was unusual for Jesus not to be there to help. They began to search for him, "Jesus, our son, Jesus, have you seen him?" He was nowhere to be found. The realization then hit them that he must have stayed behind in Jerusalem. "Why would he do that without telling us? Didn't he know we'd be worried?" Mary asked Joseph as they hurried back to the city to retrieve him.

Nathan's parents' journey to the mall had been abruptly interrupted with the disappearance of their son. Jesus' parents' journey back to Nazareth had been abruptly interrupted with the disappearance of their son. Nathan's parents found him safe under a coat rack right away. Jesus' parents found him safe in the temple court three days later. Nathan's mother scolded her son, and Jesus' mother scolded hers.

Can't you hear Mary saying, "Child! Why have you done this to us? Your father and I have been frantic, searching for you everywhere?" (Luke 2:48 NLT). Never had Jesus done anything without his parents' knowledge. However, this time he had become so absorbed in temple discussions that he hadn't given a thought about his parents or the return to Nazareth.

When Joseph and Mary found Jesus three days later, something profound had occurred. Upset but also relieved, Mary said with emotion, "Look, your father and I have been searching for you in great anxiety" (Luke 2:48b). I emphasize here the word "father." Jesus had always recognized Joseph as his father. He was a good father, providing for him and teaching him God's ways. A pivotal change was about to occur in his relationship with Joseph. "Why were you searching for me? Did you not know that I must be in my Father's house?" (Luke 2:49).

With these words, Jesus takes the title of "father" from Joseph and very gently, but emphatically gives it to God. His experience in the house of God had revealed much to him. Jesus now knew what his parents had always known — that he was truly God's Son. God was his Father, not in the spiritual sense but in reality. He was God's Son, not in the spiritual sense but in reality.

What we have heard today is a story of recognition — the day Jesus discovered who he actually was. "Then he returned to

Nazareth with them and was obedient to them ... Jesus grew in wisdom and in stature and in favor with God and all the people" (Luke 2:51a, 52 NLT). Growth occurred for Jesus in three areas. Physically, he grew from a child to a boy to a man. Spiritually, he grew in communication with God his Father and in the practice of his Jewish faith. Above all he grew mentally in the understanding of his mission as the Son of God on earth.

Setting out as an adult to fulfill that mission, he took with him tradition and the need to change peoples' view of it. The time for change had come. God's law was to be observed for God's law was given for the good of people. But there were those who abused God's law, using it for their own gain. Historically, by Jesus' time, the religious leaders had turned the laws into a confusing mass of rules. Jesus revealed the hypocrisy in the hearts of the experts of the law. They told others to obey God's law, but they failed to practice it themselves.

Jesus did not speak against the law. He wanted to bring the people back to its original purpose. "Don't misunderstand why I have come. I did not come to abolish the law of Moses or the writings of the prophets. No, I came to accomplish their purpose" (Matthew 5:17 NLT). Tradition was changing — and the change was good. Jesus presented a new way to look at the law — to live not just with words but with actions.

Tradition — traditions are good. Tradition — traditions can be changed for the better. Try it. What have you got to lose? Let Aunt Bessie instead of Cousin Alma, who's always done it, host the Christmas Eve gathering after church. Have Uncle Alfred bring the cardamon bread instead of sister Frieda. He'd feel so appreciated. How about saving a turkey by eating a chicken? Maybe you could fit four small birds into those two small roasters. Or you could save on scouring pots and pans by putting really big birds into that really big roaster your daughter just gave you for Christmas. They'd be a lot juicier, and Papa likes gravy.

How about that Christmas tree? Remember the question? Should it be the traditional, real tree or is it time for a change? No matter if the tree is real or artificial, there's a tree that cannot be replaced — the Calvary tree. For it was on that tree Jesus suffered and died for our sins. The rugged cross that became a tree of death has now become a tree of life. This is most certainly true. And this is not an "artificial" truth. It's the "real" thing! Amen.

Fire! Fire!

After this second Sunday of Christmas, the church will enter the season of Epiphany. Epiphany officially begins on January 6. Epiphany is the time the church commemorates the coming of the magi as the first manifestation of Christ to the Gentiles. The magi, traditionally called the *wise men*, had discovered a new star shining in the heavens. They believed it announced the birth of a divine being. After traveling thousands of miles using the light of the star as their compass, they stopped in Jerusalem, the seat of King Herod the Great. Can't you see the look on Herod's face as they inquired of him, "Where is the child who has been born king of the Jews? For we observed his star at its rising, and have come to pay him homage" (Matthew 2:2).

This news would have greatly disturbed Herod, because he was not the rightful heir to the throne. He was considered a usurper. If this child was the Messiah, the true heir to King David's throne, the Jews would possibly unite around him. Because Herod was a ruthless leader, many Jews hated him and wanted him off the throne. Because he was suspicious that he might be overthrown, Herod planned to rid himself of this so-called king of the Jews. Because he was cunning, he might be able to use these visitors. They might actually be able to find the child, so he promised to consult his advisors. Because they were aware of the prophecies about the expected Messiah, especially that of Micah, Herod got his answer: "But you, Bethlehem Ephrathah, though you are small among the clans of Judah, out of you will come for me one who will be ruler over Israel, whose origins are from of old, from ancient times" (Micah 5:2 NIV).

Most Jews expected the Messiah to be a strong political and military leader like Israel's mighty King David. Herod would fear a Messiah like this. He would allow no such man to take his throne from him. Therefore, he returned to his visitors with the answer that Bethlehem was the prophesied location of the birth of this new king. Herod instructed his visitors from the east, "Search the city and then send word to back to me, for I, too, desire to go and worship him" (Matthew 2:8 cf). Herod had no intention of worshiping this child. By using a lie, Herod hoped to trick the magi into returning to him. Then he could proceed with plans to rid himself of this threat.

The magi continued their journey to the obscure town of Bethlehem, about five miles outside of Jerusalem, still using the star's light to guide them. When they found the child, they were overjoyed. The bowed their knees in reverence and worshiped him. The light of the star had guided them to the light of the world. As John recorded in his gospel, the true light that would enlighten everyone had come into the world — a light that would set hearts on fire.

Carla loves candles. Her husband does not. Every time he sees her light them, he fears she'll burn down the house. But this year, they chose to purchase a new Christ Candle for their small church. That candle, wrapped in butcher paper, rested against a chair in the alcove off their living room. Tomorrow it would be dedicated, but tonight they were entertaining friends.

Carla looked at the time. Everything was set except for one thing — lighting the candles. She had to hurry before her husband saw the flickering lights. She was almost done when the doorbell rang. Quickly she struck the wooden match, but the tip broke off and dropped "somewhere." Frantically searching, she found nothing, so she successfully lit another. Calming herself, she smiled as she went to welcome the first visitor. "Merry Christmas, Gerry! What can I get you to drink? Hot apple cider, holiday punch, soda, or coffee?"

As Gerry sat sipping his cider, the doorbell rang again. Craning his neck to see who'd arrived, he noticed a flame in the other room.

"Fire! Fire!" he cried. Carla turned to see the butcher paper around her $200 candle on fire. Darting over to it, she extinguished it by beating it with a throw pillow. Her husband rushed to the scene and removed the charred paper. Shaking his head he said, "I told you she was dangerous. It seems to be okay, just some soot on one side — we'll just wash it off. Won't we, dear?" Zing!

The flame, that had burned so brightly for a moment, had been put out for now. Wiping the candle down, Carla said to herself, "I hope nobody notices that little smudge near its base." Still feeling guilty, she rubbed harder.

The Christ Candle, lit during the Christmas season until the Ascension of Jesus, reminds us of "the" light of the world John tells us about in our gospel: "The light shines in the darkness, and the darkness did not overcome it" (John 1:5). Jesus, the Word made flesh, brings light to all humankind. When his light shines upon us, our sins are exposed. But as we confess our sin, and receive God's forgiveness, we find ourselves unwrapped, and washed clean with forgiveness. The stain of sin is covered by Jesus' blood. Jesus lights our lives, and faith fans the flame in our hearts.

As Jesus was teaching in the temple one day, he spoke to the crowds saying, "I am the light of the world. Whoever follows me will never walk in darkness but will have the light of life" (John 8:12). We have two choices in this life: to continue to walk in the darkness, stumbling over the obstacles of grace; or to walk in the light, being guided by "the light" of God's love.

In a different translation, John tells us in these words:

> *In the beginning was the Word, and the Word was with God, and the Word was God. He was with God in the beginning. Through him all things were made; without him nothing was made that has been made. In him was life, and that life was the light of men. The light shines in the darkness, but the darkness has not understood it.*
> — John 1:3-5 (NIV)

As our Lord is the light "of" the world, Jesus calls us to be lights "to" the world. That is why we were created. There will be some who refuse to let Jesus light up their lives. They remain tightly wrapped up in themselves and the things of the world. But there will be others with hearts on fire, unwrapped by God's love and grace.

As we approach the New Year, let us join together in making resolutions that will draw us closer to the light: to pray, to worship, to read the Bible, to gather and fellowship with one another. If we do, we will find ourselves enlightened and radiate Christ's light to a very dark world.

This world needs your witness. Saint Paul reminds us in the book of Acts, "For this is what the Lord has commanded us: 'I have made you to be a light for the Gentiles, that you may bring salvation to the ends of the earth' " (Acts 13:47 NIV).

This is an awesome responsibility. Christians are called not just at Christmas to light candles and sing, but to light candles in the darkness as beacons to other travelers. Look around you. Embrace the light of hope, the light of salvation, and sing with joy!

Let us pray: Jesus, light of our hearts. Jesus, light of our lives. Shine into our world today. Jesus, light of lights. You are the light that came into a world that did all it could to put that light out. It failed. With your eternal flame, continue to light our hearts on fire. Shine, Jesus, shine. Fill our hearts with your holy presence. Amen.

The Epiphany Of Our Lord
Matthew 2:1-12

Jesus Makes All The Difference

Our gospel reading for this Epiphany Sunday is a marvelous story about confrontation. The wise men — more commonly known as the three kings today — were teachers of science and truth. They had been watching the heavens, searching for a sign of God's activity in the world, when they were confronted by a star. The poet, Henry Wadsworth Longfellow, was confronted while reading their story in the gospel of Matthew. The result was his poem, *The Three Kings.*

> *And the Three Kings rode through the gate and the*
> *guard,*
> *Through the silent street, till their horses turned*
> *And neighed as they entered the great inn yard;*
> *But the windows were closed, and the doors were*
> *barred,*
> *And only a light in the stable burned.*
>
> *And cradled there in the scented hay,*
> *In the air made sweet by breath of kine,*
> *The little child in the manger lay,*
> *The child, that would be king one day*
> *Of a kingdom not human, but divine.*
>
> *His mother Mary of Nazareth*
> *Sat watching beside his place of rest*
> *Watching the even flow of his breath,*

For the joy of life and the terror of death
Were mingled together in her breast.

They laid their offerings at his feet;
The gold was their tribute to a King,
The frankincense with its odor sweet,
Was for the Priest, the Paraclete,
The myrrh for the body's burying.

And the mother wondered and bowed her head,
And sat as still as a statue of stone;
Her heart was troubled yet comforted,
Remembering what the Angel had said
Of an endless reign and of David's throne.

Then the Kings rode out of the city gate,
With a clatter of hoofs in proud array;
But they went not back to Herod the Great,
For they knew his malice and feared his hate,
And returned to their homes by another way.[1]

Longfellow spoke of these kings, people searching for a sign
from God, people yearning for a king, a spiritual leader, a Savior.
Longfellow may have seen himself in these wise men when confronted with Matthew's account of their visit to the Christ Child.
This is not a story of a road trip by men who had no idea where the
path would take them. It is a revelation of the discovery at the end
of that journey. It began as they searched the heavens and found a
new star, a sign that something great had occurred. As wise men,
the kings set out following that star until it stopped over Bethlehem.

We, too, as wise people, are confronted as we desperately search
for signs of a king, a spiritual leader, a Savior who could make a
difference in our lives. Jesus is the one who confronts and makes
that difference. We are told by Matthew that the wise men, after
meeting Jesus, returned to their homes by another road. When
people encounter Christ they return to life along a different path,
for Jesus makes all the difference.

The wise men were searching for a king to give order to life, to
protect them, to give them guidance, and to be a leader to whom

they could turn. They presented their gift of gold, a kingly gift, to Jesus. We, too, are to be wise people looking for a king to give order and purpose to our lives and to our world, searching for a king who will help us to live together in peace. As wise seekers, we find in Jesus, he who shelters and directs us; he upon whom we can depend in all situations; he who gives meaning and purpose to our existence. Having met Jesus, we will return to daily life changed people, traveling a much different path than previously taken. For the king we have met makes all the difference.

The wise men were not only looking for a king. They realized their need for a spiritual leader, one to guide them in matters of the heart. They presented their priestly gift of frankincense. We, too, as wise people, are searching for spiritual meaning and wholeness in life. However, we seem to look in all the wrong places — pursuits of pleasure, physical comfort, and materialism, just to name a few. We indulge ourselves in satisfying the physical side of our being but ignore the spiritual dimension. That is why we find our young people absent from church after their "big day" — confirmation. That is why the numbers of active, baptized members keep decreasing in most mainline denominations. The paths people choose often lead away from Jesus not toward him. Yet the wisest continue to seek their spiritual leader and walk through life depending upon God. Encountering Jesus does make a difference in the listing of our priorities.

The wise men sought a king and a spiritual leader and a Savior. They, too, knew death's dark shadow. They presented to Jesus the gift of myrrh, the bitter perfume that covered up the stench of death. We, too, as wise people, in the face of our own mortality, search for a Savior, one who would free us from the bondage of sin and death. We find in Jesus the one who makes the difference. For it is the journey from the cross to the grave that opens the tomb. This tomb now becomes a tunnel through which we pass to meet our risen Savior, Jesus Christ, who makes all the difference.

The wise men found Jesus and presented their gifts of gold, frankincense, and myrrh because they had found their king, spiritual leader, and Savior. Then they left, following the path God's messenger told them to take — a "different road." Their choice was not an easy one for following a "different road" involved risk of capture and being killed by Herod. They returned to other lands changed men, but the places they left had not changed. Many were and would be hostile to the message of God's love.

We, too, as wise people have found in Jesus a king, spiritual leader, and Savior. God sent a messenger to us to deliver that good news of salvation. All stand at a fork in their paths and must choose which way to travel, for the places we enter are also hostile to God's message of forgiveness and love.

Robert Frost can help us to make a right decision with his famous verse from the poem, "The Road Not Taken."

> *Two roads diverged in a wood, and I —*
> *I took the one less traveled by,*
> *And that has made all the difference.*[2]

When people encounter Jesus, they return to life along a different path. Jesus makes all the difference. As wise people, choose your paths carefully — for one leads to life with a king, spiritual leader, and Savior, but the other leads to death. Yes, the road you take certainly does make a difference — an eternal difference. Choose it wisely. Amen.

---

1. *The Three Kings* by Henry Wadsworth Longfellow (1807-1882). In the public domain.

2. "The Road Not Taken" by Robert Frost from *Mountain Interval*, 1920. In the public domain.

The Baptism Of Our Lord
Epiphany 1
Ordinary Time 1
Luke 3:15-17, 21-22

Don't Touch Me With That Water!

"Fill the glasses with water, honey. Daddy's guests will be here soon," Mother said. Her young son carefully filled the fragile, crystal goblets. "How's it look, Mom?" Surveying the elegantly set table, she smiled and ruffled his hair. "You did great work, honey. Daddy will be so pleased." The boy grinned in anticipation of his father's approval.

The door bell rang. "Our guests have arrived. Let's go greet them. We're done in here." Opening the door, the boy took his father's hand. "Come and see! Come and see what Mom and I did." Entering the dining room, his father lovingly picked him up. "You certainly did do a great job, son." The boy's face lit up with his father's approval.

Today we celebrate the baptism of our Lord. The setting had been prepared. God had summoned John to prepare the people for the arrival of the Messiah. John told the people that *he* was not the Messiah — the one they expected. "I baptize with water; but one who is more powerful than I is coming; I am not worthy to untie the thongs of his sandals. He will baptize you with the Holy Spirit and fire" (Luke 3:16).

The last genuine prophet of God was Malachi, 400 years before Jesus' birth. Malachi's words form a bridge between the Old Testament and the New Testament. He warned the Jews that they had broken their relationship with God and that judgment and punishment would come. After chastising them, however, he offers hope and forgiveness if they repented. John's baptism of water was done for the forgiveness of sin. Jesus' baptism of the Holy Spirit

59

and fire would give the truly repentant, not only forgiveness, but the power to do God's will. But those who failed to honestly repent would receive God's judgment.

Every day the crowds at the Jordan River grew. They'd come to hear the powerful voice of the prophet. John dressed like a prophet, and he spoke like a prophet, "Turn from your sin! Do it now!" Like a sharp knife, his words went straight to the heart, dividing his audience in two. The hard of heart found themselves confronted. Repentant hearts found comfort and hope.

John's words took root in unexpected places — among the poor, the dishonest, and even hardened soldiers — those who were painfully aware of their need for forgiveness of sin. "What must we do?" they asked John. "Repent! Believe and be baptized."

Nicholas stood at his father's side. He watched as his baby sister was baptized. He listened to the pastor's words recalling the story of Jesus' baptism. He heard that water was a sign of cleansing and rebirth. "In baptism we have been set free from sin and death," the pastor said. Sin and death are scary words to a six-year-old. Pouring water over his sister's head, the pastor continued. "Rachel Paige Martin, I baptize you in the name of the Father, and of the Son, and of the Holy Spirit. Amen." The pastor then turned to Nicholas, who quickly grabbed his father's leg shouting, "Don't touch me with that water!" Unlocking their son's arms, his parents said with firm voices, "We present Nicholas Robert Martin for the Sacrament of Holy Baptism."

Nicholas' defiance toward baptism stemmed from fear and misunderstanding. He did not comprehend what God was doing through this sacrament. The pastor spoke words of reassurance as he touched him gently with the warm water. Nicholas and Rachel were now children of God, forgiven, anointed by the Holy Spirit, and marked with the cross of Christ forever.

Jesus was fully human and fully divine. The great English evangelist, C. H. Spurgeon, tells us that Christ was not a "deified man," neither was he a "humanized God." He was perfectly God and at the same time perfectly man. In his baptism, Jesus identified with us in all ways. He could have gone up to Jerusalem and identified with the established religious leaders, but he chose to go to the Jordan River and identify himself with sinners.

Jesus did not need John's baptism for the forgiveness of sin. He was sinless. On that day, he was just one of the crowd coming for baptism, one among many. In this act, he showed his obedience to the Father, and the Father showed his approval. Luke tells us that after he was baptized, he prayed. Jesus' first response was to communicate with his divine Father. And God responded, not only to his Son, but to those gathered with him. The heavens opened, and the Holy Spirit, in the form of a dove, came down on him. Then God showed his approval by saying, "You are my Son; the Beloved; with you I am well pleased" (Luke 3:22).

Can you imagine that moment? In recording this event, Matthew tells us that when Jesus came to John for baptism, John actually tried to prevent it. Looking at him he asked, "Why do you come to me for baptism when I need to be baptized by you?" Jesus answered, "Let it be this way for now. We should do all things that are God's will" (Matthew 3:15 NCV). So John agreed. When John heard the voice from heaven speak, he knew that Jesus was the Lamb of God who would take away the sins of the world. John the Baptist was to decrease; Jesus the Christ was to increase. The prophet's role as a spokesman for God was to be replaced by another, the promised one. The real baptizer had arrived!

God had a mission for John — to announce that the kingdom of God was at hand. God had a mission for Jesus — to announce that God's kingdom had arrived. God anointed Jesus for that mission through baptism.

The prophets of old stood in the gap for the sins of their nation. Jesus now stood in the gap knowing he would die for the sins of the world. In order to accomplish the Father's mission and advance God's work in the world, Jesus was anointed to fulfill righteousness, freeing us from guilt and sin. His baptism showed support for John's ministry and inaugurated his own public ministry to bring God's message of salvation to all people. He, who was without sin, fully identified with those who had sin. And so he came for the baptism of water, the baptism of repentance, to set the example.

61

On a beautiful Sunday morning, three youth from a local detention home stood before the baptismal font. The pastor asked them, "Robert, Charles, Tory, do you desire to be baptized?"

Each responded, "I do."

As they were baptized in turn, their names were repeated. In the congregation, a foreign exchange student turned to his host mother with a questioning look. "Didn't these boys have a name before this time?"

Smiling at Mauricio, she responded, "Yes, they did. At their birth they were named, but now they are given new birth through their baptism. They are now children of God who claim the name of Jesus, the name above all names."

As the boys lifted their heads, their faces shone. They knew their sins. They wanted forgiveness for the wrongs they had done. They knew their need to be forgiven. They wanted God's approval. As God spoke to his only Son, he now spoke to these three boys. Can you see it in your mind's eye? Turning to each one, the Father nods, smiles at them, his beloved and precious children, and washes them clean of sin. Hear God say with pride, "You are my sons, whom I love, and I am very, very pleased with you." As God touches each of us with baptismal water, he also touches us with his love so we can touch others. Amen.

Only The Best

In areas where wine is made, there are places many go to sample the different varieties offered by each vineyard. People who are connoisseurs of wine — those who are critical judges in the matter of taste — can tell a good wine from a poor wine. The chief steward in our text was one of those who knew the difference, as does the winemaker, Leigh.

After retiring from a career in special education, Leigh decided to take on a hobby, wine making. At first he bought grapes suitable for wine making. Then he fulfilled a dream by leasing land. There he planted, fertilized, and tenderly cared for his vines. After five years of maturity, Leigh had prime grapes to turn into wines.

Leigh did not sell his wines for profit — but donations to World Hunger were not refused. Leigh took pride in his hobby. He used wine-tasting parties thrown by friends to educate others in the appreciation of wine. These are some of the steps he takes guests through.

1. Open the wine bottle to let it breathe. Allow oxygen to enter it.
2. Clear your palette with water.
3. If using a chilled wine, the glass should be long-stemmed so that body heat will not warm the wine. If it is a red wine, use a short-stemmed glass with a wider bowl. If reusing the glass, rinse it with water and wipe it with a paper towel making sure no water is left. Never use soap!

4. Fill your glass with a small amount of wine.
5. Swirl the wine in the glass and look at its legs — the marks down the inside of the glass. If the legs are thin and few, the wine is so-so. If the legs are numerous and thick, it's a fuller and better wine.
6. Lift the glass of wine to the light to look for impurities.
7. Then put the glass under your nose (almost into it) and sniff its aroma.
8. Finally, sample the wine. Take a small amount of wine into your mouth and let it sit. Swish it around, and then *spit it out*! Imagine sampling ten bottles of wine and drinking a whole glass of each. Warning — gulping is hazardous to your health!
9. Saving the best for last, Leigh would serve a dessert wine that would cost about $40 a bottle followed by chocolates. It was his closing gift to friends. These parties were not a time to indulge, but times to celebrate.

Marriage festivals are times of celebration. How embarrassing it would be for the host to run out of wine. In Jesus' time, weddings were weeklong festivals, celebrating the life of the married couple. I'm sure that there were no party favors or long-stemmed goblets to give champagne toasts. The guests were many, since everybody in town was invited. It was considered an insult to refuse. Today we have a reception after a marriage ceremony and limit those invited. Imagine having to furnish food and beverage for a week for your guests! Arrangements had to be carefully planned. How embarrassing it would be for the host to run out of wine. It was not just a slip up, but it broke the laws of hospitality.

If this happened at one of our receptions, we would do all in our power to resolve the problem. So when Mary saw the distress of her host, she went immediately to Jesus to resolve it. She didn't expect him to do a miracle, but asked that he would find more wine to solve the problem. She trusted that he would do the right thing. Jesus' answer to his mother's request is hard to understand, "Woman, what concern is that to you and to me? My hour is not yet come" (John 2:4). Mary had no idea what Jesus would do, but she trusted him to do what she asked.

Mary knew her son would respond to a heartfelt need. Without further deliberation, she instructed the servants to do what her son told them. Looking around, Jesus spotted six ordinary stone water jars that were used in ceremonial washing. When full, each held twenty to thirty gallons. Jesus told the servants to fill the jars with water.

> *When the jars had been filled, he said, "Now dip some out, and take it to the master of ceremonies." So the servants followed his instructions.*
>
> *When the master of ceremonies tasted the water that was now wine, not knowing where it had come from (though, of course, the servants knew), he called the bridegroom over. "A host always serves the best wine first," he said. "Then when everyone has had a lot to drink, he brings out the less expensive wine. But you have kept the best until now!"* — John 2:7-10

Jesus saved the day. Like those at the wine-tasting party were surprised by the expensive dessert wine served last, the chief steward was very surprised when he tasted the batch of new wine. He knew that the poorer quality of wine usually was brought out last. By that time people's impaired taste buds and senses rarely knew the difference.

Three young women, all dressed up for an occasion, sat in the sandwich shop. "Hello, girls. Are you going to a wedding?"

"Yesh, we are. It's at Our Saviour's something church ... what's that name?"

"Oh, the one over on Crystal Lake?"

"Yeah, that's the one. The bride is a good friend. The reception is at that swanky golf club. We've heard that the food and wine are great."

"Enjoy. I'll see you there. I'm the pastor's wife."

The three invited guests were looking forward to attending their friend's wedding and the reception following. Good food, free drinks, and dancing! It'd be a fun night. At least these friends would attend the marriage ceremony. Most invited guests today skip the wedding and head for the reception, missing the real reason for celebration.

People look everywhere but to God for excitement. Jesus attended wedding celebrations. In fact, in today's reading he provided the wine. For some reason, people expect God to be dull and lifeless. God has a sense of humor and enjoys displaying it. God has fun at picnics and ice cream parlors. I've even seen him making hospital patients laugh. God is in everything. He gives us his best, so why not expect the best?

Taylor was excited. It was her thirteenth birthday — a milestone. After opening cousin Jenna's gift, a CD of her favorite singer, a gift certificate to her favorite clothing store from her older sister, and a card with $3 in change from her youngest brother, Billy (probably his paper route tip money, bless him), she hoped she had saved the best for last. With eagerness she unwrapped her parents' present, praying it was that new top she wanted. She laughed with glee as she found a box that contained a box that contained another box. "Oh, you guys are jokesters. This is too small for that top I wanted."

"Open it, honey," her mother encouraged.

"I think it will pass the school dress code," her dad chuckled.

Her eyes opened with surprise as she lifted out a velvet box. Opening it, she found a beautiful birthstone necklace. A gift so unexpected, a gift given in love. A gift that was the best she'd ever received. She hugged her mom and then her dad, "I never expected this. It's beautiful. I'll never take it off." It was a gift she was to wear every day of her life.

Think about the gifts you have received throughout the years. For a birthday, marriage, anniversary, a shower, the arrival of a baby, Father's Day, Mother's Day, Christmas, and other events we celebrate. Gifts given with a lot of thought.

Hoping for a special gift on Valentine's Day, Sonya was confused when she opened her gift and found an odd-looking golf club. "What is this?" she asked.

"They call it a power pod. It'll really help you improve your score," her husband exclaimed.

"You know I don't golf."

"Oh, that's right. I guess I'll have to use it," he said smiling as he went outside to practice.

On his birthday, Sonya gave a lot of thought to her husband's gift. She watched his face in amusement as he opened her gift — a certificate for a spa weekend — facial, manicure, and pedicure included.

"What is this?" he asked.

"Honey, it's for the best weekend of your life. If you don't want it, I'll use it," and she grabbed it with delight.

Jesus was at a wedding. The wine ran out. The guests would notice. The hosts would be embarrassed. What could be done? Jesus provided as he always did, and the gift of wine was appreciated, accepted, and used.

Back to our story of winemaker Leigh. He had a fond spot in his heart for his pastor's son. He'd watched him grow up in the church from fifth grade to graduation. During his college years, he'd kept tabs on him. When the invitation came to his wedding, he remembered that Justin had enjoyed a special white Sauvignon Blanc at one of his wine-tasting parties. Leigh decided that his gift to the wedding couple would be forty bottles of wine to be used in toasting their life together as husband and wife. A gift unexpected and a gift of only the best.

Only the best! A host gift of the best dessert wine to friends. Only the best! A wedding gift at that son's reception. Only the best! A gift at a Cana wedding. Only the best! A gift given to you and given to me for the forgiveness of sin. Only the very best! The gift of holy communion.

As Jesus and his disciples celebrated the Passover meal, he first passed a cup of blessing. Then he took a loaf of bread, gave thanks, broke it, and gave it to his disciples, saying, "This is my body, which is given for you. Do this in the remembrance of me" (Luke 22:19). He did the same thing with the cup shared after supper, saying, "This cup that is poured out for you is the new covenant in my blood" (Luke 22:20).

What a gift we have received. What a gift we celebrate. God gives only the best, and that costly gift is ours to share.

Open your hearts, allow Jesus to enter. Take an honest look at yourself, look at the impurities of your life, and ask God to cleanse you. Through Jesus' body (bread) and his blood (wine) you are cleansed. Only the best gift for his children, only the best God can give: "For God so loved the world that he gave his only Son, that everyone who believes in him may not perish but may have eternal life" (John 3:16). Thank you, Lord, for giving us only the best. Amen.

Love Walked Across The Field

The ministry of Jesus was on a roll. After his baptism and time in the wilderness, he went forth to proclaim God's gospel of love. Following his preaching in Galilee, he entered his hometown. Although born in Bethlehem, his parents had fled to Egypt to protect their son from the wrath of King Herod. When Joseph heard of Herod's death, he brought his family back to live in Nazareth.

As a young boy, Jesus attended the synagogue with his father where he participated in community worship regularly. Attentively listening to the scriptures read from the Book of the Law, the Psalms, and the Prophets, he grew in knowledge, wisdom, and understanding. Now the son of Joseph had returned, knowing that what he would say would not be received well.

As there were no permanent rabbis in the outlying villages, itinerant ones were always welcomed. When Jesus came to worship as was his custom, he was invited to read scripture and reflect on it. The scroll handed to him that day was from the prophet Isaiah. Unrolling it, he chose the place where it is written:

> *The Spirit of the Lord is upon me, because he has anointed me to bring good news to the poor. He has sent me to proclaim release to the captives and recovery of sight to the blind, to let the oppressed go free, to proclaim the year of the Lord's favor.*
> — Luke 4:18-19

69

Wrapping the scroll up, he handed it to the attendant and said: "Today this scripture has been fulfilled in your hearing" (Luke 4:21). His audience looked at him intently, amazed by his words. Then he dropped a bombshell, telling them that God loved all people, Gentiles and Jews. Infuriated, they turned on him. The son of Joseph dared tell them that God's love was for all people. "How dare he? He's one of us. We are God's people, the chosen ones." They demanded Jesus give them a sign of his authority, but Jesus refused. He could do no miracles there because these people lacked faith. Jesus had not come to his hometown to put on a show. Rage took them over, and the mob drove him out of town to kill him. But Jesus walked right through them, a prophet not accepted in his own hometown. The people he once knew best lacked love, and they had just rejected the Son of God's love. Jesus left Nazareth and never returned.

The gospel of love was first preached to Jesus' own countrymen. When it was rejected, it was presented to others. Miracles were done where faith existed. His words were received by those with open hearts. God's love was demonstrated in word and confirmed with action. With Jesus' death, God's love confirmed that love.

"God is love." In the words of 1 John chapter 4 we hear these words confirmed.

> *Dear friends, we should love each other, because love comes from God. Everyone who loves has become God's child and knows God. Whoever does not love does not know God, because God is love. This is how God showed his love to us: He sent his one and only Son into the world so that we could have life through him. This is what real love is: It is not our love for God; it is God's love for us. He sent his Son to die in our place to take away our sins.* — 1 John 4:7-10

"God is love." When John defined God as love, he was not just describing a characteristic or an attribute of God. If he were, he would have said, "God is a loving person." He didn't say that. Through prayer and faith, we come to understand just what he says:

"God is love!" That is, God's very life empowers us to love. God is love, a love revealed in Jesus.

God is not some Buddha sitting in cosmic space, gazing upon his navel, for love is not static. Love is not a warm, fuzzy feeling, here some days and vanishing on others. Love is action. Love is what you choose to do.

A pastor was sharing his thoughts about love with a young couple preparing for marriage. He told them that to love — really love — was to reach out to another with only the desire to care, share, comfort, encourage, or give hope. These words brought tears to the eyes of the young woman.

"You know, pastor, not everyone is loving if that is what it means to love, and that includes some pastors. My parents are loving people. They made sure that I made it to Sunday school and worship. Faith and the church were very important to our family.

"After I left home, my brother, Jimmy, was born. He was a change-of-life baby and was physically and somewhat mentally impaired. It was hard on my parents. They loved Jimmy so much. They wanted him to know God loved him, too. Every Sunday they took him to church. One afternoon their pastor came to visit and said, 'Jimmy is very disruptive in church. Wouldn't it be better for everyone if Jimmy stayed home on Sunday mornings?' he suggested. Jimmy was being rejected because he just didn't fit in. After that visit, my parents stopped going to church.

"That pastor left a few years later, and the church called another. As the new pastor was looking over the membership files, he noticed that my parents were faithful in sending in their offerings, but they never came to worship or participated in any congregational events. Asking the church secretary what the story was he learned all about Jimmy.

"That very afternoon the pastor walked across the field — our home is on the other side of a field behind the church. After visiting for some time with my parents, he invited them to come to worship on Sunday.

" 'Well, it's sort of hard, pastor, with Jimmy. It's just a difficult situation,' my mother replied. The pastor would accept no excuse. 'God loves you and your son. I've walked across the field to make sure you understand that and to ask you to come to church this Sunday, and to bring Jimmy, of course.'

" 'We'll see,' was Mom's hesitant response. Sunday came, but neither Jimmy nor my parents showed up."

Rejection — it's so hard to deal with, especially when it's done by people who espouse faith. Jesus was rejected because he *didn't fit* the role of the expected Messiah. The words he spoke comforted some, but confronted others, those who refused to reach out and show love to others.

Love is the action of reaching out to others — of walking across a field — of caring for someone besides oneself. Love — God is love; a love revealed to us in Jesus. Jesus walked into his hometown and was rejected because he was different — he didn't fit in.

When the pastor walked across the field that first time, he put his love into action, but there was no response to his invitation to come to worship. Jimmy's parents hadn't rejected his overtures; they did not know how they would be received. They didn't want Jimmy to be rejected again.

The pastor was not discouraged. Once again he walked across the field. He told Jimmy's parents that all three of them were expected to be in church this Sunday. If they weren't, he'd personally come and get them even if the service had to be delayed.

Next Sunday all three were in church experiencing the love God revealed in Jesus. That love came through a young pastor who cared enough and was persistent enough to walk across a field and share the love he, too, knew in Christ. That walk continued for a long time as he walked with Jimmy across that field to watch a baseball game, to rake leaves with the youth group, to have a glass of lemonade, and just hang out. Jimmy's parents once again became active. In fact, his father now serves as president of the church council. Jimmy was the first graduate from a special Sunday school class for the impaired that was started in that church. This class now has six students. His mom cried as she saw his eyes shine the day he received his little cross pin.

God is love, a love revealed to us in Jesus. Love is when we receive God's love and put it into action. Think about it. It's time to remove that prejudiced "R" word, rejection, and replace it with a better one, the "R" word, receive. It really will make a difference in your life and in the lives of others. Think about it. And while you're thinking why not take a walk today — walk across the field with Jesus and talk to him about it? Amen.

Fit The Picture

It was the History Day Parade at James T. Jones Elementary School. Each class picked a period of time to portray. The sixth grade chose the medieval days. Every student was to design a costume, and, of course, mom, auntie, grandma, or another family member — female or male — was to create it. Those who couldn't sew could make a placard or paper bag costume or wrap themselves in universal duct tape.

Teddy and Mike were to be the front and back of a horse, translated into a spirited, knight's mighty steed. There were jousters, ladies in waiting, robed friars, Robin Hoods and merry men, court attendants, innkeepers, and peasants. Everyone chose their own role, but the king and queen were chosen by the class. Students had preconceived ideas about royalty. Consequently, they chose the best looking and most popular boy and girl to lead them in the parade.

The next week family members, friends, and the curious crowded the streets. The classes marched twice around the school for the best effect. Everyone in the parade received a blue ribbon and a goody bag from downtown merchants. The school board awarded the sixth grade first place for best era depiction. Their prize — a pizza party! King Richard and Queen Stephanie won for best costumes. As the newspaper photographer took their picture, their highnesses posed regally, noses in the air, proudly arrayed in gold satin, purple velvet, jewels, and metal crowns — no Burger King cardboard crowns for them. As Teddy and Mike took off the horse costume, Harvey the blacksmith turned in his personal ballot, "You guys get my vote for the best outfit. You really fit the picture of a knight's horse; loved your '*neigh* ...'! You've got heart! Way to go!" The boys smiled, and the three friends gave each other a high-five letting out a loud "*neigh*...!"

Jesus returned to Nazareth, to the section of the city where he had been raised. As he approached his home, he was recognized. "Look who's here! It's Joseph's and Mary's son, Jesus. It's good to see you. Where've you been?" Slapping Jesus on the back, they greeted him heartily. Statements like, "My, how you've grown. I remember when you were only this high," and "Hey, Jesus, remember when we ..." and then compliments like, "Jesus, that chair you made us? It's still in good shape. Levi's weight hasn't broken it like so many before."

Little did these people know that when Jesus returned to Nazareth, he knew his true identity. He was not Joseph the carpenter's son; he was God's Son, descended from the royal line of King David. Yet Jesus did not fit the picture of royalty. He was a common man just like them; nothing extraordinary about his looks. In fact, he looked like them, dressed like them, and worshiped like them, but he did not talk like them. At synagogue worship he was invited to read from the prophet Isaiah. After rolling up the scroll, Jesus said, "Today this scripture has been fulfilled in your hearing" (Luke 4:21). With these words, Jesus was proclaiming himself the "anointed one," a king in David's line, the king through whom the promises made to David would be fulfilled. As the promised Messiah, Jesus' ministry would focus on calling God's people to turn from sin and return to God.

All Isaiah prophesied, Jesus would do: evangelize the poor, proclaim freedom, give sight to the blind, and release the oppressed. But the way he would accomplish it found many Jews unable to grasp. Those he came to save had a very different picture of their deliverer. Jesus did not fit the picture of a conquering king, one who would free the people from Roman occupation. Instead, Jesus was a conqueror who would free them from sin — the sin that had caused their captivity and oppression in the first place — and restore them to wholeness, to a right relationship with God.

The comments Jesus shared that day began kind words of God's favor and grace bestowed on all people. Luke tells us that those who heard them were amazed at his insights and wisdom. Their first impression was that God was with him, but then things abruptly changed. His words became challenging, and his listeners were scandalized. "Is this not Joseph's son?" (Luke 4:22b) they asked, surprised at his claims. Jesus did not fit the picture they had in mind of the Messiah.

First impressions are important. A person, interviewing for a high profile position, would want to make a good first impression — no blue jeans or white socks; no mini-skirt or revealing Madonna top. Luke records what was first said of Jesus: "He was a prophet, who said and did many powerful things before God and all the people" (Luke 24:19). To be a prophet one must be open to God working through him. A prophet does not do God's work under his own initiative; it is God who sends him and empowers him. The prophet's words were affirmed by signs and wonders. In this gospel scenario, the people didn't ask Jesus for a sign, they "demanded" one! When we adopt a demanding attitude toward God, we are trying to usurp his power. In this case, it wasn't that Jesus lacked the power; the people lacked the faith to let him use it. Too often we define how God is to work in our lives, so that when he wants to act we won't let him.

I once heard this comment, "I sometimes think that I could do a better job running the universe than God." That person has a skewed picture of God. When we decide how God should act, and he doesn't do as we prescribe, we don't recognize him when he is working. It is often said that a position of leadership should be filled by someone from the outside, not by someone from within or from the community. The outsider's advice would be accepted over the person who has been in the business or community for some time. Familiarity often breeds disrespect. Jesus said, "Truly I tell you, no prophet is accepted in the prophet's hometown" (Luke 4:24). The people, who knew Jesus as a child, a teenager, and a young adult, could accept his physical growth but not his spiritual maturity. Jesus of Nazareth did not come home to set up a carpenter's shop and follow in Joseph's footsteps. He'd grown way beyond their expectations. He did not fit into the picture of the hometown boy making good, so they drove him out.

God gives each of you gifts and talents to use in building his kingdom. However, you might think that God cannot use you because "you know you." You might feel incapable of doing a certain job. You might feel ill-qualified or lacking experience. Take for example, Moses, who was considered the greatest prophet of God. Listen to him making his excuses to God for not qualifying for the job God had called him to.

> *But Moses said to the Lord, "Please, Lord, I have never been a skilled speaker. Even now, after talking to you, I cannot speak well. I speak slowly and can't find the best words."*
>
> *Then the Lord said to him, "Who made a person's mouth? And who makes someone deaf or not able to speak? Or who gives a person sight or blindness? It is I, the Lord. Now go! I will help you speak, and I will teach you what to say." But Moses said, "Please, Lord, send someone else."* — Exodus 4:10-13 (NCV)

God didn't have plans for a substitute. God had plans for Moses. That plan included separation from his Hebrew family and inclusion into the royal family of Egypt. Only God could elevate a slave to a prince. God was in control, orchestrating a plan for the deliverance of his people. Then Moses' life was turned upside down. From a basket of reeds, to an elegant bed fit for a king, to a shepherd's mat. What in the world was God doing? However, this humbling experience prepared him to be a great leader. Even though he did not connect the dots, God was painting the picture into which Moses would be placed forever.

Moses, the son of slaves, was placed in Pharaoh's court as a prince of Egypt. He could have had an "attitude." God does not want his servants to be "puffed up." God is noted for taking that which the world says is of no use and making it useful for his purposes. God's power does not rest in the package in which it comes. Moses came in a basket of reeds; Jesus came in a manger of straw. You come wrapped up in grace to let God use you right in your place.

Remember, God wants to use you just as you are. It isn't that you do great things, but that God takes the small things you do and makes them great. And so, through a shepherd, God's power set those in bondage free — his vessel? His vessel was Moses. Through a lowly shepherd boy who killed a giant, a kingdom was built — his vessel? His vessel was David. Through a child born in a manger came the Savior of the world — his vessel? His vessel was his Son, Jesus Christ. Our ways are not God's ways.

[Jesus] was in the world, and the world came into being through him; yet the world did not know him. He came to what was his own, and his own people did not accept him. But to all who received him, who believed in his name, he gave power to become the children of God.... — John 1:10-12

"And the Word became flesh and lived among us ..." (John 1:14). Almighty God took on human form, entering our sinful world in order to save it. God's time line was perfect: a child was born, he grew in wisdom, he was rejected by his own, he was received by those who hoped, he preached a gospel of love, and because of hate the world rejected and crucified him. Jesus took our sins upon himself. To those who believe, he gives the right to become children of God. Does this scenario fit into your picture? If not, ask why? Then reexamine the picture:

Christ himself was like God in everything, but he did not think that being equal with God was something to be used for his own benefit. But he gave up his place with God and made himself nothing. He was born to be a man and became like a servant. And when he was living as a man, he humbled himself and was fully obedient to God, even when that caused his death — death on a cross. So God raised him to the highest place. God made his name greater than every other name. So

79

that every knee will bow to the name of Jesus — every-
one in heaven, on earth. And under the earth, and ev-
eryone will confess that Jesus Christ is Lord and bring
glory to God the Father.

— Philippians 2:6-11 (NCV)

Humanity did not expect this great act of God, a child born to be Savior of the world. God's ways are not our ways, but God's ways are the best. Jesus is not in a popularity contest. However, like choosing a king for a parade or a nation, you must choose a king in your life. Don't reject Jesus as so many have. Believe and receive. Amen.

The Ashes Of Our Lives

When she was a teenager, Cindy worked for her father. She and her sister and three other girls were hookers. Don't get excited now. They were paid to put a fishing hook and red flipper on a split ring, then attach it to fishing lure. She was often teased about her after school job, as well as about the job her father had. It wasn't until she was a freshman in college that she learned to say that her father was a fishing lure manufacturer instead of saying, "My dad makes the Swedish Pimple."

Cindy was proud of her father. Working as a salesman, Ed grew in relationship and business skills. Living near water, he had opportunities galore to fish. Early in the morning or late at night, he could be seen casting a line from his boat. He would fish until he caught enough fish for a meal. Perch and walleye were the best eating and abundant in the unpolluted waters at that time. He never realized his expertise and love for fishing would turn into a 45-year trade. Talking his two brothers and three of the Nyberg boys into investing in his dream to make a new fishing lure, he set up business in an old blacksmith shop off Main Street.

As a partner and business manager, he was not afraid to take risks. The *Wall Street Journal* became his business bible. He used his knowledge of fishing and manufacturing to create a worldwide lure known as the Swedish Pimple. Its success was due to the fact that Ed knew fish and knew how to successfully catch them. His commitment to making a good product was rewarded year after year, as the lure's popularity grew.

81

Growing profits enabled him to add another working area to his existing one. The hookers, machine operators, buffers, and platers were now under one roof. What about him? He had started off managing his business in an upstairs loft of his brother's appliance shop, moving over to the black smith shop sharing space with inventory, bubble packers, and, of course, his hookers. When he set up his own office space, it was in a small room in the back.

What had enabled his fishing lure manufacturing business to grow? Ed's love of fishing, his desire to satisfy customers, commitment to his product, and his ability to promote it, and a fire! That's right, I said a fire.

One night the furniture store two blocks away caught fire. As the flames jumped from building to building, Ed stood on top of the shop hosing its roof down. All he could see was his dream going up in smoke, and that's what happened. The old wooden structure, that had been the birth place of a dream, burned to the ground.

"And we know that in all things God works for the good of those who love him" (Romans 8:28). Ed had known God since he was young, and felt close to him in the outdoors, especially while fishing. This was his quiet time, a time to listen, a time to reflect. When he married, he faithfully worshiped with his family. He made sure his children received a good foundation in the faith. He knew God was present in the good times and in the difficult ones. He'd been in both, but he trusted God, learned to accept, and not resent. Yes, God works in all things for our good. From those ashes of that burned shop came another vision. A vision that came to reality. The Bay de Noc Lure Company would be well known for its quality and success throughout the nation. From the ashes of disappointment rose hope.

> We also boast in our sufferings, knowing that suffering produces endurance, and endurance produces character, and character produces hope, and hope does not disappoint us.   — Romans 5:3-5a

Ed understood the certainty of that promise.

A man had spent a fruitless day fishing. He didn't want to go home empty handed. He decided to stop at a local fish market. "I'd like three good sized fish," he said to the clerk. "But before you wrap them, toss them to me, one by one."

The clerk looked puzzled at his request, "Sir? That's a strange thing to ask."

Smiling the man said, "This way I'll be able to truthfully tell my wife I caught them!"

Jesus had been preaching to a large crowd on the shore of the Sea of Galilee. Needing more space, he noticed two empty boats at the water's edge. The owners were on the beach washing their nets. They recognized Jesus for they had heard his preaching and responded to his call to follow him. "Come, Peter and Andrew. Come, James and John. Leave your fishing business, and follow me. You will become fishers of men, helping others to find God." Jesus was calling these four fishermen from their productive trades to be productive spiritually. Jesus was calling them to fish for souls. That same call comes to us today. Like a fisherman who pulls fish into his boat with nets, we are to practice Christ's teachings and share the gospel with others, drawing those around us to him.

When we read about these two sets of brothers in the book of Matthew, we are told that Peter, Andrew, James, and John became Jesus' first disciples. When Jesus called them the first time, they knew what kind of man he was and were willing to follow him. So what happened between their first encounter and the second? Why do we see in Luke's gospel that they had gone back to fishing? It could have been because they trusted more in their own abilities to support themselves. In other words, to put fish on the table. After all, Jesus had been a carpenter but hadn't set up shop, and it seemed he was more concerned about feeding the soul rather than the body. They would understand much later that he was concerned about feeding both.

One day as Jesus and his twelve disciples were traveling around the area of the city called Bethsaida, crowds came out to hear him preach. Welcoming them, he spoke to them about the kingdom of God, confirming his words with miracles of healing.

The day was drawing to a close, and the twelve came to him and said, "Send the crowd away, so that they may go into the surrounding villages and countryside, to lodge and get provisions; for we are here in a deserted place." But he said to them, "You give them something to eat." They said, "We have no more than five loaves and two fish — unless we are to go and buy food for all these people." For there were about five thousand men. And he said to his disciples, "Make them sit down in groups of about fifty each." They did so and made them all sit down. And taking the five loaves and the two fish, he looked up to heaven, and blessed and broke them, and gave them to the disciples to set before the crowd. And they all ate and were filled. What was left over was gathered up, twelve baskets of broken pieces. — Luke 9:12-17

When you hear this story, you would think that after all the miracles the disciples had seen performed up to this time, they would have had more trust in Jesus than they displayed here. But they aren't alone in that boat. We are with them. Do you think God would ask you to do something that you and he together couldn't handle? Don't let the ashes of the past cover you so completely that you give up hope.

When Peter met Jesus that first time, he was cautious in turning over control of everything, from his heart to his trade. He approached commitment very cautiously and so should we. As Jesus said, "No one starts to build a tower or goes to war without first counting the cost." With the second encounter, Jesus continued to reveal himself.

Luke tells us that Peter and his companions had been fishing all night and had come back to shore empty handed. Fishing was not a hobby for them, it was their livelihood, and it was serious business. They were tired, frustrated, disappointed, and discouraged, like a salesman who has gone for days without a sale. Like a lawyer who cannot attract clients or like a qualified college graduate who cannot get a teaching job, the negative feelings run deep. When doors seem shut, know God can open them if we have faith, even if it's only the size of a mustard seed.

When Peter responded to Jesus' request to take his boat out into deeper waters and let down his nets, he shook his head with doubt. A carpenter they had known for only a short time was suggesting to these professional fishermen that they go back out, and they did it. They obeyed, and their obedience brought a reward beyond their wildest dreams. Their nets almost broke with the amount of fish taken; the boat almost sank. Did Peter jump up and down with excitement? "Halleluiah! Praise God! Wow!" Peter was awestruck at this miracle, but then he felt his own insignificance in comparison to this man's greatness. He responded, "Go away from me, Lord, for I am a sinful man" (Luke 5:8b).

This miracle of the fish was not the first Jesus had performed. Jesus drove out demons and healed the sick, even Peter's mother-in-law. But this one amazed Peter for it showed that Jesus cared about his day-to-day routine and understood his needs. This should not surprise us for our God is not only interested in saving us, but also in helping us in our daily activities. When Jesus came to call the second time, he met the fishermen on their level and helped them in their work. The result? They didn't look back but left their nets and remained with Jesus until his death. We must do the same. Leave the ashes of our past behind and commit our future to Christ. How rewarding that will be.

When Ed sold his partnership in the Pimple Shop, as it was affectionately dubbed by the town's people, he had almost approached his dream of making it a million-dollar business. He did not retire with mega bucks, and the money he did receive went to making the last years of his wife's life comfortable and memorable. Having been told she'd have six weeks to three months to live because of her cancer, she put her life in God's hands, knowing that he took all things and used them for his glory. God didn't select Marge to develop ovarian cancer, but he used that sickness as a witness of his personal concern for his children. Marge and Ed enjoyed six more years together. On the first Sunday after Easter, with the church cross adorned with Easter lilies, her life was celebrated with her death. "From dust we came, and to dust we will return."

I would like to share the words of a song written by a woman named Carmen. Carmen happens to be the Swedish Pimple maker's niece. It was Harold, her father and Ed's brother, who he partnered with in dreaming a dream. As Ed knew out of ashes came more, so Carmen knew it, too. Even though she suffered from a hereditary disease, retinitis pigmentosis, she was outstanding in high school forensics. At times though, judges deducted points for memorizing a speech, but hey! She used her special gifts to excel. She fell in love with a man named Stephen. Their story has been told in an award-winning documentary, *White Cane and Wheels*, which appeared on a premium cable channel. It was directed by her nephew, Paul. It was a reality film of two people rising out of the ashes of difficulty.[1]

Stephen was afflicted with muscular dystrophy. Carmen kept the commitment made to Stephen in marriage, caring for him daily in the good days and in the downers. "For better for worse, in sickness and in health." After his morning routine, Carmen left for work at the Braille Institute for the Blind in Los Angeles, a direct service organization for the blind and visually impaired. She also served as a technical advisor for actors playing blind characters in movies and television.

After the tragedies of September 11, like the rest of the country, Carmen felt angry and lost. Her feelings of sadness and depression soon gave way to her drive to do something. She had to find a way to express what she was feeling at the time. That is how her song, "Ashes In The Wind" came about. It was a catharsis for her to be able to express her feelings through music. The words came to her — a mixture of hope and despair. Her spiritual advisor, Bonnie, enabled her to express her feelings about this event as well as the feelings about her life. Hear her words from "Ashes In The Wind."

> *'Tis a simple thing to want to cry each day*
> *'Tis a simple thing to want to touch someone*
> *'Tis a simple thing to let the anger sway*
> *When the ashes, when the ashes are in the wind.*

86

'Tis a simple wish to sit alone and pray
'Tis a simple wish to want to phone someone
'Tis a simple wish to need to hide away
When the ashes, when the ashes are in the wind.

The eagle flies above us
As the sun goes down each day
In the crumbled steel and concrete
Other voices flow away.

Can we move that mountain tower
'Til the land is sweet again
While the ashes, while the ashes are in the wind?
While the ashes, while the ashes are in the wind?

'Tis a simple hope to want to heal the pain
'Tis a simple hope to want to find someone
'Tis a simple fear that life won't be the same
When the ashes, when the ashes are in the wind.

Oh, the eagle flies above us
As the sun goes down each day
In the crumbled steel and concrete
Other voices flow away.

Can we move that mountain tower
'Til the land is sweet again
While the ashes, while the ashes are in the wind?
While the ashes, while the ashes are in the wind?

Oh, the eagle flies, the eagle flies,
Oh, the eagle flies.[2]

From the ashes of fire (Ed), from the ashes of shame (Peter), from the ashes of tragedy (Carmen), and from the ashes of your lives, comes new life. Jesus says, "Come, come let me heal the pain. Come, come life won't be the same. Come, come the eagle flies again, while the ashes, while the ashes are in the wind." Amen.

1. *White Cane and Wheels*, directed by Paul Apelgren, University of Southern California. Award winning documentary; Cinemax 2004.

2. "Ashes In The Wind," vocals, words, and music by Carmen Apelgren, recorded at QP Sound, North Hollywood © 2001. Used by permission.

Risk Takers

"Louise, can you and Pastor Hal come to Thanksgiving dinner at our house this Friday? I have this really, really big turkey, and I don't want a ton of leftovers," Tracy implored her friend.

"Well, I'd love to, but we always invite a widower, Andy Vespa, each Thanksgiving. I don't want him to be by himself with his pork and beans. Of course, Steve and Vicki will be here, too," Louise replied. "Andy's always been a part of this family gathering."

"I know Andrew! I visited his wife, Della, at the VA Hospital when she dying. Bring him along," Tracy exclaimed. "Tell Steve and Vicki I expect them, too." Tracy took a finger count of her guests. "There's our family — Jimmy, me, Adam, Erin, Jacob — that's five; then Hal, Louise, Steve, Vicki, and Andrew. That makes ten. Two more would make it nice since I have twelve place settings." And more than enough food, she thought.

She put in another call, "Cindy, I have a problem that involves a big turkey. If you don't have any Thanksgiving dinner plans, would you like to come here?"

"That'd be great. I wasn't going to fix a turkey dinner for just Steve and me. Who all will be there?" she asked.

"You two, the five of us, the four Fausts, and Andrew Vespa. See you at six o'clock and don't bring anything except your appetite!"

Little did Tracy know that God was the maitre d' in charge of this dinner party, and he had used, of all things, a turkey and a snow storm to make the arrangements.

After everyone arrived and introductions were made, they sat down for their bountiful Thanksgiving feast. Bowing their heads for grace, Tracy peeked up at Andy. His big, gnarled hands were folded like a child's. "What a gentle man," she thought, "but he looks so sad." When they had finished two pumpkin pies, Tracy said, "This was such a nice time. We were supposed to be with our families in Minneapolis, but weather storm warnings changed that." Looking at her guests, she smiled her "Tracy" smile. "Thank you for being part of our family on this special day." Then came the question that would change lives, "Mr. Vespa, do you have any family?"

Andy's eyes teared, "No, I'm alone. My wife, Della, and I had no children. She died a few years ago. I miss her every day."

"Well, Andrew, we'll just take care of that. Since we don't have family around here, and you're alone, how about being my children's grandpa?"

This question took everyone off guard. What would he say? Andy finally broke the silence, "I think I could do that."

"Great! But there are conditions: You'll have to come to all their activities with me — band and chorus concerts, basketball, football, and baseball games, and plays. You know all that stuff. Will you do that?"

"I suppose I can," he replied as he considered his responsibilities of being a grandpa.

"And, of course, you will go to church with us! That's a given. The fourth pew up front is our spot each week, and there's room for one more. We'll pick you up around ten o'clock. Got it? Okay, anyone for a game of Risk?"

"Bossy, isn't she?" Andy smiled with a twinkle in his eye. Jesus said, "Blessed are you who are poor, for yours is the kingdom of God" (Luke 6:20b).

Tracy took a risk by giving Andy a challenge. Andy took a risk in accepting the challenge. Over the next six years the two built a special relationship. Tracy always called him "Andrew" as a sign of respect. And yes, she did boss him some, like the time she laid down the law about housekeeping. "Andrew, you will clean your house."

To which he replied, "I like it as it is."

"In that case, my sons can never come to a sleep over, and remember they're your grandsons. Right?"

He agreed, and Tracy and he tackled the job. When Andy's garage caught fire, Tracy decided it was time to move him to assisted living, where he would get good meals and care. There his bulletin board was covered with Post-it® Notes:

- Doctor's appointment — Tuesday. I'll pick you up; be ready after lunch. Tracy.
- Visitors, no sweets for Andrew! He's diabetic.
- Aides! Make sure Andrew practices giving himself his insulin shot. Oranges in the refrigerator. Needles in the cupboard.

And always the reminder, "Andrew, I love you. Tracy."

Tracy visited or called him every day. Once a month he attended Lydia Circle's Bible study. He enjoyed telling his stories about God taking care of him all his life. When it was time for dessert, Andy said the grace. Then he'd add, "Now don't tell Tracy that I ate this piece of apple cobbler. She won't like it." Everyone knew that Andy and Tracy's relationship was more like a father/daughter one. Both had been blessed by God. On his 95th birthday they celebrated at Tracy's with cake and ice cream. When Andy got home, he felt so blessed. Crawling into bed that night, his final blessing came as he slept — the blessing of eternal rest.

In our gospel today, we hear what is called the Sermon on the Mount as recorded by Luke. It is also recorded in similar form by Matthew. Some think that it is one long sermon. The majority, however, understand it to be a compilation of many teachings of Jesus. Even though there are differences between the two gospel recordings, one thing is sure — Jesus' words were revolutionary. They exploded like bombshells in an already charged atmosphere, upsetting the accepted standards taught by the religious leaders of that time, exposing fake piety by focusing on true humility.

Jesus' popularity was rising. His teachings had been confirmed with miracles such as healings and deliverance from demons. When people heard Jesus was in the area, they flocked to see him. So it was in our gospel story that an enormous crowd turned out to hear him. What Jesus laid out for them that day were the traits he looked for in his followers. The Beatitudes, as they are called, explain how to be "blessed." They may sound like contradictions, but God's way of life contradicts the world's. Indeed, we will not be blessed by following the world's standards, but by living according to kingdom's standards.

"I'm so blessed to have a comfortable house, food on the table, family and friends. They bring me great happiness," we often hear. Yes, it's nice to have all these things, but blessed means more than happiness. What about those who don't have them? Are they being punished? In the Beatitudes, those Jesus calls blessed don't seem to be. The Beatitudes don't promise us laughter, pleasure, or prosperity. When Jesus used the word "blessed" he meant experiencing hope and joy outside of our circumstances. We find hope and joy, the deepest form of happiness, by following Jesus no matter what the cost.

The Beatitudes should be looked at as a whole because they challenge the way we live out our faith on a daily basis. They contrast kingdom values with worldly values. For instance, "Blessed are you who are poor, for yours is the kingdom of God" (Luke 6:20) clashes with the worldly value of pride and personal independence. "Blessed are you who are hungry now, for you will be filled" (Luke 6:21a) clashes with pursuing personal needs. These two beatitudes can stand alone, but they are also connected to one and other. Those who only look to their own needs, overlook those who have needs. Their material possessions and financial security cause them to think they have no need — they lack nothing — and so they have no need for God. They seem to be "rich" in the sight of the world, but in reality they are extremely "poor" and do not even recognize it.

The parable of the rich fool exemplifies this.

> *The land of a rich man produced abundantly. And he thought to himself, "What should I do, for I have no place to store my crops?" Then he said, "I will do this: I will pull down my barns and build larger ones, and*

92

there I will store all my grain and my goods. And I will
say to my soul, 'Soul, you have ample goods laid up for
many years; relax, eat, drink, be merry.'" But God said
to him, "You fool! This very night your life is being
demanded of you. And the things you have prepared,
whose will they be? So it is with those who store up
treasures for themselves but are not rich toward God."

— Luke 12:16-21

In accumulating his wealth, this man probably took risks and felt rewarded because of his efforts. However, he had taken an eternal risk that was to be costly: "But God said to him, 'Foolish man! Tonight your life will be taken from you. So who will get those things you have prepared for yourself?' " (Luke 12:20 NCV). The poor are receptive to the good news found in salvation. The rich are deaf — closed — and go to ruin because they were the ones who made it. God was never in their picture.

The rich man used his wealth to enrich only himself. He was proud of his business sense and didn't depend on any other person — especially not God. His power and wealth were of his own making. He looked to his wealth for blessing, never to God.

"Blessed are the poor," Jesus says. Jesus did not exalt poverty, but made it clear that those who are poor would ultimately be blessed because they could count on Jesus. They know that their hope and trust can't come from the world, so they look to God for help. When we look to God for help, we will be blessed. Whether rich or poor, we are to rely only on God. When wealth, power, prestige, and position reflect our own self-importance, we are lost. When we take what we have and use it for others, we find true blessing. Using our possessions as agents of God's grace, we are set free to help others experience Christ's love.

"Blessed are you who are poor" might be reworded as "Blessed are those who realize that they can't depend on the things of this world for happiness and put their trust in God."

The rich fool endangered his life because of his focus on money, which gave him a sense of false security. He sought a firm foothold, not in God where it can be found, but in his wealth where it cannot be found. It is easier for us to enjoy our wealth and ignore

93

the things that are eternal. It is precisely when we think we have it all that death knocks at our door, and our wealth becomes meaningless.

Many view people in economically deprived countries as "poor" (lacking money) but "rich in the spirit" (having great faith). Does this mean we should not use our resources to help them because it might take away their so-named richness, which has been caused by being poor? This makes no sense at all. Face it. We have the resources to end poverty, to end world hunger. Instead, we hoard what we have instead of using it to bless others.

The poor have nothing but God on whom to depend. They realize they have nothing of their own to give to God and, therefore, must depend on his mercy. When we see our own poverty, we begin to glimpse what it means to be happy, truly blessed. Finally, we have placed our trust in the only place that we are sure of — Jesus Christ. Amen.

Nothing in my hand I bring;
simply to thy cross I cling.
Naked, come to thee for dress;
helpless, look to thee for grace;
foul, I to the fountain fly;
wash me, Savior, or I die.[1]

---

1. "Rock Of Ages," words by Augustus M. Toplady (1740-1778). Tune: In the public domain.

Forgive As You Have Been Forgiven

She stood peeking out from behind the curtains. As the jogger passed her house, he recalled the hurt she had inflicted upon his mother. At one time she had been the matriarch of the congregation. His memories of her were not fond. He recalled her wicked tongue and the way she used it to cut down others. He never forgot the day she used it against his mother making her cry. That incident caused their family to leave the church where he had been baptized and confirmed. Here it was fifteen years later, and now all he saw was a picture of someone desperately needing to be loved. Praying for the ability to forgive her, he stopped and went to her door. The curtain quickly closed as he rang her doorbell. Hesitantly she cracked the door.

"Hello, Mrs. Sko. Do you remember me? I'm Marge's son." Her eyes widened in surprise as a note of recognition appeared. "I live in Arizona now, and I'm here on vacation. I saw you in the window and just wanted to stop and say hello. May I come in?" She hesitated and then opened the door and asked him in. "Forgive, and you will be forgiven" Jesus tells us (Luke 6:37b).

Today's gospel lesson is a challenging one for us. "Love your enemies," Jesus instructed his followers. The Romans were the enemies of the Jews. They oppressed and persecuted them. There was no love lost between the two. The natural reaction toward those we consider enemies is to retaliate. If we have suffered injustice, if we have been wronged, we want revenge. "What you have done to me, I will do to you" (Matthew 5:38). However, Jesus is not just telling us to love a military adversary. He wants us to love those

95

who have caused us personal injury. The jogger considered Mrs. Sko an antagonist, a person who had sought to hurt, showed ill-will, and caused injury. Transferring to another church, moving to another town, and maturing did not eliminate how he felt about her. But on that day, he saw a bitter, old woman who needed God's love. Right there and then he made a conscious decision to forgive her for the past harm she had inflicted. Hopefully, she would receive it. Even if she didn't, he would be free.

When we refuse to forgive, we place a wall between us and God. Forgiveness is the cornerstone in our relationship with God. Because God has forgiven our sins, we must now forgive those who have wronged us. To remain unforgiving shows we have not understood that we ourselves deeply need to be forgiven. Think of some people who have wronged you. Have you made a conscious effort to forgive them? How will God deal with you if he treats you as you treat others? When Jesus taught his disciples to pray he included a very important line: "Forgive us for our sins, because we forgive everyone who has done wrong to us" (Luke 11:4a NCV).

Consider the actions of a young boy who has felt betrayed by a friend. He comes home slamming the back door loudly. "That does it!" he yells. "I'm never going to talk to Marc again."

"What on earth did he do to make you feel this way?" his mother inquired.

"He says he's my best friend, and then he doesn't pick me for his side in baseball. What kind of friend is that?"

More than not being selected for his friend's team is the attitude the child now has toward his friend. Their relationship has been broken and only forgiveness can mend it.

We must choose to forgive even if we feel wronged. We all fall short and need forgiveness. Precisely because God forgives our sin, we need to forgive others. Our prayer should be, "Lord, enable me to be more loving and forgiving of those who have hurt me."

Those who work with young people see the emotion behind this process. Jacob B. and Jacob C. were proud of their friendship. They were best buds outside the church and inside. They belonged to God Club, a weekly gathering of grade school children who spend time together eating, creating, exploring the Bible, and growing through faith in action. "Who's your best friend?" their leader asked. "Jesus!" the group responded. Closing for God Club always included prayer at the altar. Jockeying for position, Jacob B. and Jacob C. got into a scuffle. Jacob B. ran up to the leader holding his arm. "Jacob punched me in the arm." To forgive or not to forgive? That became the question. Only intentional forgiveness would restore their broken relationship.

Sin separates us from God. Because we cannot fix that broken relationship, we need a mediator, one who intercedes between opposing parties. Jesus is that mediator who enables us to forgive others. Are you able to relate to this example? Now let me appeal to the animal lover in you.

There are cats, there are birds. There are hamsters, there are goldfish. But I'd like to focus on dogs. Boris was a gift, not just a gift from friends, but truly a gift of love. He was a combination of cocker spaniel and poodle. For over twelve years he'd brought unconditional love to his owners. "Bobo dog, we were gone, but now we're back" became the litany between owners and dog. With tail a' wagging, he ran quickly to greet them. He was truly excited to have them back.

There were times though when Boris was in the dog house, one might say. When he chewed on Dale's new tennis shoe, when he piddled on the carpet, when he threw up in the dining room late at night. At those times he was scolded and spanked. He'd run and hide under the bed because he knew he had done wrong. Later, he'd appear with tail a' wagging, anxious to please, wanting to be forgiven. "You know you did bad, Bobo. But we still love you. Here's a Bobo treat to show you we forgive. Don't do it again, though." Rubbing his ears and kissing the top of his head, he accepted the treat.

Like Boris who seeks forgiveness for doing wrong, we seek God's favor not realizing that we don't need to do it right to get it. God already forgives us because he loves us. In that forgiveness and love, God asks us to treat others the same way he treats us. Now I don't know if Boris made a conscious decision to seek forgiveness for his actions or be forgiving and loving to those who

97

had punished him, but we must make a conscious decision to do both. If we don't, there will be consequences to our decisions.

One night Boris and his owner were walking home. He was given instructions so he'd enjoy the walk like: "Stop." "Sit." "Don't go over there." Not listening, Boris did his own thing. Dashing across the street, he ran smack into a car. The driver heard the thump but never saw the little black dog. Knowing he'd disobeyed, Boris ran into the backyard where his owner found him cowering under the steps. Grateful that the dog was alive, his owner stroked him and told him. "Don't ever do that again, Boris. You almost got killed."

Boris made a cognitive choice to disobey. He saw home and ran for it, never anticipating running into the side of a car. However, he knew he had done wrong, and the shame of it caused him to hide. The consequence of not doing what God wants us to do will eat us up inside. We all have a choice to be forgiving and loving. We forgive not to gain anything, but because we have already received forgiveness from God. The blessing in this action is that when we forgive, the burden of unforgiveness is lifted from us. Bitterness and hatred are taken away, and we begin to realize the wonder of God's grace that first forgave us.

As we walk with God, he tells us "Stop being unforgiving. Stop hating. Those actions have consequences." God invites us to be blessings to others, even those who we feel have harmed us. When we forgive, we become the ones blessed and set free.

Being a Christian is all about relationship — with family, friends, those we work with, those we worship with, and with God. The whole point of Jesus' death and resurrection was that sinners could come to know God and live with him forever. We can't earn our way to heaven. Building a personal relationship with God is a priority for each of us, and we need to remember that we are Christians under construction. Every day we try to do the right thing. So when we fall down, we need to get up. Being a Christian means asking forgiveness and giving it. Therefore, we should make allowances for each other's faults, forgiving those who offend us. "Forgive, and you will be forgiven" (Luke 6:37b).

A bonfire burned on a cool summer night. At the foot of a cross, campers warmed themselves in its glow. During their week at camp, they had eaten meals together and enjoyed the outdoors. They had laughed and cried, slept in cabins or under the stars, prayed, studied God's word, worshiped, and grown in friendship and faith. There had been many close moments and some far moments. There had been times of rest and times of struggle. Still, through each experience they had grown closer to each other and to Jesus. Yet there were those sitting around that campfire that still had issues. Sensing this, the director began to talk about God's love and his forgiveness. Reading from the Bible, he reminded those gathered that they should love one another, for love comes from God.

> *Anyone who loves is born of God and knows God. But anyone who does not love does not know God — for God is love. God showed how much he loved us by sending his one and only Son into the world so that we might have eternal life through him. This is real love. It is not that we loved God, but that he loved us and sent his Son as a sacrifice to take away our sins.*
> — 1 John 4:7b-10 (NLT)

He paused and then continued

> *Dear friends, since God loved us that much, we surely ought to love each other.* — 1 John 4:11 (NLT)

In the stillness of the night, God came to that place and sat among those campers. As the fire bathed them with its warmth, his closeness bathed them in love. They were quiet, basking in the moment. Then they joined their voices as one singing a familiar camp song, "Be ye kind, one unto another; tenderhearted, forgiving one another. Even as God for Christ's sake has forgiven you ... Do, do, doodlely do, Ephesians 4:32."[1] Another silence, and then these words, "Go and do likewise. Amen."

1. "Be Ye Kind," words by an unknown spiritual author. In the public domain.

**Epiphany 8
Ordinary Time 8
Luke 6:39-49**

How Firm A Foundation

Every night after work and on weekends, Eric worked on building his cabin. It was not on his lot in Waterford Township, but in his own backyard. It was sort of prefab — constructed with cedar, a section at a time. On Sunday afternoons, accompanied by his family, he loaded up his trailer with completed sections and hauled them up to his property. The camp became known as Shaky Cedars. As each wall was placed side by side, the sections soon became a whole.

When we buy a house, we carefully look at the construction. Before approval of a loan, it has to be inspected. But who looks at inspecting a tiny cabin in the woods made out of cedar? In spite of mice and weather, Shaky Cedars still stands after fifty years. Is it because of the materials? Is it because of the construction? No, it's because of its foundation. What Eric did was to lay a firm foundation of cement blocks. Next he put a solid floor over it. Then came linking each panel of wood. Completion was a framed roof. Travel backward now: roof to panels to flooring to blocks. The cabin stood for all those years because of the firm foundation laid by its builder.

Jesus taught using simple stories to illustrate a moral truth. They are called parables. I've just told you a story. Jesus' parables were fictitious short stories used to set forth a teaching. It is estimated that the number of parables in the gospels is as low as 35 and as high as 72. The variation arises from the difficulty in classifying them. Yet one thing is certain, the parables come from Jesus himself. In order to get a real picture behind the parable of the two

101

foundations recorded by Luke, we need to read Matthew's version of it as well.

> *Anyone who listens to my teaching and follows it is wise, like a person who builds a house on solid rock. Though the rain comes in torrents and the floodwaters rise and the winds beat against that house, it won't collapse because it is built on bedrock. But anyone who hears my teaching and ignores it is foolish, like a person who builds a house on sand. When the rains and floods come and the winds beat against that house, it will collapse with a mighty crash.* — Matthew 7:24-27 (NLT)

To appreciate this parable, we should understand that where Jesus was preaching, rains come seasonally. In recording this parable, we must remember that Luke was not a native of Palestine so consequently did not have a clear picture of the circumstances described. Whereas, Matthew did. Being a Palestinian, he knew just what the picture was. During the dry season, there is prime real estate to be had. But buyer beware! When the summer rivers dried up altogether, they left a sandy bed of empty water. In the winter, after the September rains had come, the empty river bed became a raging torrent. Those inviting stretches of sand may have looked good, but after the rains they may be fifty to sixty feet under water.

Jesus said that the wise man searched for rock upon which to build. It may have been harder to build on, but it was worth it. When the storms of winter came, he would be rewarded for all the hard work. His house stood strong and firm and secure. In form, Luke's or Matthew's, this parable teaches the importance of laying the right foundation for life; the understanding that the only true foundation is obedience to the teaching of Jesus. "So why do you keep calling me 'Lord, Lord!' when you don't do what I say?" (Luke 6:46 NLT). Obeying God is like building a house on a strong, solid foundation that stands firm when storms come. It doesn't seem to matter when life is calm, but when crises come, our foundations are tested.

The winds blew; the water rose. Paul stood at the window and sighed, "Oooh, Oooh!" The water slowly began to surround his

102

house. His wife lay in their bed fighting cancer. He had just suffered a heart attack. His car had been hit in the parking lot. The winds of crises were blowing. When the storms of life come, only the person who builds their life on the strong foundation of Jesus Christ will be able to stand firm. It doesn't seem to matter when life is calm, but when the crises come, the foundation is tested.

Why would people build a house without a foundation? Maybe to save time and avoid hard work. Possibly because the waterfront scenery is more attractive or because beach houses have higher social status than cliff houses. Just look at the east coast and the west coast. Houses there often don't have good foundations, and when the winds of hurricanes come or slippery mudslides move, houses are washed into the oceans. At those times we shake our heads and wonder if people had made wise decisions on where to build. Thus, this parable reminds us of the necessity of laying a good foundation.

For some reason people who build their lives on weak foundations assume that disaster can't happen to them. A man bought a house that looked great, but when the rains came, his basement flooded. He should have listened to the inspector and examined the foundation better. Warning! He didn't listen because he wanted a house in a prestigious neighborhood.

Have you ever thought that doctors might fire patients? Otis didn't. Dr. Olson had diagnosed his problem and given him a prescription, telling him to take the medication daily, and to schedule an appointment in two weeks. Otis returned, angry that his stomach was still a pool of acid, his throat was raw, and his persistent cough continued.

The doctor asked, "Have you been taking the medication I prescribed?"

"No. I decided I didn't really need to."

"So why are you coming to me for treatment? Why ask my advice if you won't take it?"

Ask any doctor, and they'll tell you that this is a truth. Patients, who will not do as asked, should be fired. They really don't want to get well. "Exercise and diet. It'll bring down your blood pressure." Not a prescription we eagerly want to fill. Yet, how often do

Christians profess Jesus as Lord and ignore his voice? We call him Lord and then refuse to do what he asks. It's foolish to see a doctor and disregard his instructions. Wouldn't you fire a worker when they did the same? Someone who wouldn't listen and obey?

Our Lord's commands are clear: Love God. Love one another. Treat others as you want to be treated. Be forgiving and have compassion for others. Don't settle for sand. Build on the rock — Jesus Christ.

Paul's beach house was built on a good foundation. When the waters came and surrounded it, they did not destroy it. He had shored it up for support. In his distress, he had also shored up his faith in his reliance on God. His physical and spiritual construction brought him through his time of crisis.

There are two favorite hymns I'd like to use as illustrations. The first is a hymn originating in the South. It was a favorite of such American leaders as Theodore Roosevelt, Andrew Jackson, who asked that it be sung at his bedside shortly before he died, as well as Robert E. Lee, who also requested it for his funeral hymn "as an expression of his full trust in the ways of the heavenly Father." The name of this song is "How Firm A Foundation."

How firm a foundation, O saints of the Lord,
is laid for your faith in his excellent Word!
What more can he say than to you he has said,
who unto the Savior for refuge has fled?[1]

Finally, "My Hope Is Built On Nothing Less." The refrain says it all.

On Christ the solid rock, I stand;
all other ground is sinking sand,
all other ground is sinking sand.[2]

Only those who have built their lives on Jesus and his teachings will stand the test. Though storms may buffet us, we will not cave in. The foundation of a life in Christ is our only flood insurance, for "On Christ the solid rock we stand, all other ground is sinking sand."[3] Amen.

1. "How Firm A Foundation," words by "K" in Rippon's *Selection of Hymns*, 1787. In the public domain.

2. "My Hope Is Built," words by Edward Mote, 1834. In the public domain.

3. *Ibid.*

Bridge Builders

As the three cousins ran through the woods, jumping over fallen trees, zigzagging through knee-high ferns, and pushing branches out of their way, a chorus of laughter rose in the still air.

"Don't be so pokey, Michael," teased his older cousin. "Watch out for that rock on the left," Sam warned the boys. A yelp went up as Jeremy stumbled. "Come on, come on. We're almost there," Sam hollered. "I can hear the river now and there's the bridge to Uncle David's camp."

The boys lined up along the edge of the cliff. "You expect us to walk across that creaky, old thing?" Michael whined. "No, way! It's swaying, and it's a long way down."

"It sways because it's a swinging bridge. See the cables attached to that big pine tree and then attached to those posts over there?" Sam asked. "They hold up the bridge. It's safe. I'll show you," and he stepped out. Carefully he began to cross on the wooden footboards. "Come on you cowards. Have a little faith. I'll stand right here and wait for you."

Cautiously Michael and Jeremy moved onto the bridge. "Keep your hands on the cables and your eyes on me," Sam directed.

As the boys neared him, Sam said, "That's good. Stop a minute and rest, but keep your hands on the cables."

Michael and Jeremy obeyed, sneaking a glance at the rushing water below. "Has anybody ever fallen from here?" Michael asked.

"Not that I know of," Sam replied. "Are you ready to start again?"

"Okay. Just take it slow," Jeremy pleaded.

"Do as I say and you'll be fine," Sam said with a mischievous grin on his face. Then he began to rock the bridge.

"Stop that! Stop that! You'll make us fall!" Jeremy cried out in fear.

"Hey, it's a swinging bridge, so let's sing and sway," Sam laughed and began singing a campfire favorite, "Do, Lord, O do Lord, O do remember me. Do, Lord, O do Lord, O do remember me...."[1]

"Ahhhh!" the cousins screamed out in unison as Sam swayed the bridge in time with the song.

The central character in our gospel reading today is a Roman centurion who had a need. He wanted Jesus to remember his servant who was sick and near death. Because of the authority of his military rank, he was no ordinary man. When he issued an order, he expected it would be obeyed. But in this story we find him not ordering Jesus to do what he wanted but imploring him to heal his slave.

Roman centurions were considered the backbone of the army. The historian, Polybis, says of the centurions: "[They are] men who can command, steady in action, and reliable.... When hard pressed they must be ready to hold their ground and die at their posts."

But this centurion was unlike his peers. First of all, he had an extremely unusual attitude toward Jews. In a time when other Romans treated them with scorn and disrespect, he held them in high regard. Next, he had a completely unusual attitude toward his slave. Luke tells us that he cared deeply about him.

According to the Romans, slaves were living tools. They had no rights, and a master could treat them as he wanted — he could beat them or even kill them if he chose. In fact, it was normal custom when a slave was no longer able to work that he was thrown out to die. Therefore, the centurion's attitude toward his slave was not normal for he would go to great lengths to save him.

Finally, this centurion was a sincerely religious man. Even though Emperor Augustus encouraged religion from a cynical motive that kept people in order, this centurion was no administrative cynic. An example of this can be seen when he assisted the Jews in building a synagogue where they could meet and worship.

Even though he was religious, he approached faith from his own experience of God. Having become disenchanted with the worship of so many gods, he looked to the wisdom of philosophers, but failed to find answers to his religious yearnings. Witnessing the Jews' strong faith in the one God, he began to embrace Judaism. He joined in Jewish worship, followed its moral laws, and expressed his love and dedication toward God with good deeds. Because he built bridges of genuine concern and love for the Jews, he was highly respected by them and had friends among them. He was numbered among those who feared God and sought the salvation God offers.

The centurion had heard about Jesus and his power to heal. He might have even heard how Jesus had healed a Roman official's son (John 4:46-54). Because of the signs and wonders attributed to Jesus, the centurion believed that Jesus enjoyed a special relationship with God, but he did not believe that Jesus was the Son of God. Instead, he believed that Jesus had authority and power to make things happen. When he sent for Jesus he had perfect confidence that Jesus could heal his servant.

Because of his own position of authority, the centurion was accustomed both to obeying and to being obeyed. His authority came from the Roman emperor. He saw that Jesus' power and authority must come from God. Therefore, when Jesus spoke, God spoke.

> *When he heard about Jesus, he sent some Jewish elders to him, asking him to come and heal his slave. When they came to Jesus, they appealed to him earnestly, saying, "He is worthy of having you do this for him, for he loves our people, and it is he who built our synagogue for us."* — Luke 7:3-5

After being encouraged by the man's friends to accompany them to the centurion's house, Jesus agreed to go. As he was nearing the house, Jesus received this message from him.

> *"Lord, don't trouble yourself, because I am not worthy to have you come into my house. That is why I did not*

come to you myself. But you only need to command it,
and my servant will be healed." When Jesus heard this,
he was amazed. Turning to the crowd that was follow-
ing him, he said, "I tell you, this is the greatest faith I
have found anywhere, even in Israel."
— Luke 7:6-7, 9 (NCV)

The centurion understood his need to fully depend on Jesus' power. Without a doubt, he knew that Jesus could do the impossible. It was this faith that both astonished and pleased Jesus. A bridge now existed from God to this humble man.

What does this mean for us today? Our faith calls us to believe that Jesus has the power to accomplish what he says he will do. He came to be our Savior, to do for us what the law could not do. Jesus came to restore our broken relationship with God. When we personally know Jesus and understand his power then we can trust the bridge he has built for us.

A pastor, returning from a visit to his congregation's companion church in Tanzania, Africa, shared many stories about this trip. One of them concerned a bridge. It seems that on a beautiful, sunny afternoon, he and his wife accompanied their host pastor to see the house he was building for retirement. After driving for almost three-quarters of an hour from Dar es Salaam, their driver, Deo, turned off the paved main road onto a dirt side road much like the two rut roads on the African plains. About ten minutes later, they arrived at a gully or wadi. During the rainy season, this gully was filled with much needed water. However, because it was currently the dry season, it was bone dry.

Across this fifteen-foot deep gully was a bridge made of branches and small trees woven together. Before crossing it, the driver and his three companions got out of the car to inspect the bridge, perhaps too gracious a name for what stood before them. Since the bridge looked like it would not support the weight of the car, Deo was to stay with the vehicle, and the other three would walk the half mile to the pastor's house. As the trio turned to cross the bridge, they noticed an African waving at them. They waved back but didn't stop. As they neared the pastor's house they heard the sound of a car driving up behind them. They turned to see Deo with a broad smile on his face. "Deo, why did you drive across that bridge? It was so dangerous," the pastor said in alarm.

Deo responded, "The man who waved at us? I knew him, and he built the bridge. He told me it was safe to drive over. Since I knew the builder, I knew I could trust the bridge."

I know a bridge that doesn't swing and sway like our first one. I know a bridge that isn't made of woven branches and small trees like our second one. It is a bridge that God made in the form of a cross. It is a bridge that was built by the sacrifice of his Son upon it. What does this mean to us? When we personally know the builder of our salvation, we can trust the bridge he has built for us. Amen.

---

1. "Do, Lord, Remember Me," words of an African-American spiritual. In the public domain.

111

The Transfiguration Of Our Lord
(Last Sunday After Epiphany)
Luke 9:28-36 (37-43)

Go, Climb A Mountain!

The plane from Amsterdam to Africa was crowded. As three passengers stood in the aisle, you could tell they were hikers. Awkwardly, they stuffed heavy backpacks into already overloaded bins. Excitement seemed to emanate from them. Their conversation was animated as they laughed and focused on their climb up the fourth highest mountain in the world.

As the plane flew over the Alps, they strained their necks to catch a view of the majestic mountains. Clouds enveloped the tops of their summits. Soon they would stand at the foot of Mount Kilimanjaro, straining their necks at another cloud covering that summit. Weary after the long hours spent in the air, they found it hard to sleep as their dream soon would become a reality. They were ready — prepared in body, mind, and spirit. What was next? Putting their lives into the hands of a qualified guide to take them on the climb of their lives.

In today's reading we find Peter, James, and John at the foot of a mountain. It may have been Mount Hermon or Mount Tabor. When referring to a mountain in the Bible, there is an association often related to the closeness of God and a readiness to hear his words. It is recorded in the Old Testament that God appeared and spoke to Moses and later to Elijah on mountains. In the gospels of Matthew, Mark, and Luke we find Jesus inviting his three closest followers to come with him up the mountain to pray. What an honor to be singled out for that experience. As prepared as these disciples were after spending time with Jesus, they had no idea what awaited them. This mountaintop experience would be the climb of their lives. It definitely would change their lives.

Have you ever experienced a life-changing moment? I'm sure you have. It may have been being able to ride your first two-wheeled bicycle. After the trusted training wheels were removed, you shakily mounted. You were probably not alone. A trusted someone was at your side, hands on yours as you tightly gripped the handle bars. Confidence increased knowing someone was there to keep your balance or catch you if you fell. As the bike gained momentum, he let go. You were on your own. The destination was in sight — your house was just a block away. Anticipation built as you continued to solo.

Looking back you realize your achievement didn't come in one day or even two. I bet your journey had its ups and downs. There might have been humiliating moments like falling off the bike in front of friends. Or leaping from the toppling bike onto the grass. Mom wouldn't appreciate the grass stain on your jeans. What about those skinned knees? Out came that stinging orange stuff and Band-Aids™. Ouch! That part really hurt! But you kept at it. You could hear your partner's words along side of you, "I'm right here. We'll keep trying. It'll happen." His confidence built up yours. "Ready! Set! Go!" he called and you were off again. This time, when he let go, you were ready and set, and bicycling down the sidewalk on your own.

"That's it! You're doing it. Just keep your eyes on the goal," a shout from behind came. Then your helper surprised you by running ahead. You saw him there — grin on his face. "You did it! You did it!" What a rush! Victory over fear! Victory over past failures! Victory! Yes, there was victory.

That's what it's like in our relationship with Jesus, the one we can trust to be at our side, the one whose hand holds yours, the one who takes away your fear, the one who sets you free to solo, the one watching over you. He promises, "I will never leave you or forsake you" (Hebrews 13:5).

Peter and his friends had a life-changing experience on that mountain, you might say it was an "Aha! moment." Oh, those "Aha! moments" — times that impacted your lives. "Aha! moments" like passing a swimming test and not drowning, jumping over track hurdles and not knocking any down, or challenging the first chair saxophone and winning! "Yes! You did it! You made it to the top of your climb!"

At his fortieth class reunion, Jim told of his journey up that African mountain. "My friends and I were as prepared as we could be, but it was the experienced guide who made it possible for us to reach our goal." Jim had climbed Mount Kilimanjaro. He had braved the elements, accepted the challenges, and rejoiced in the foot-by-foot trek over the rocky ground. He'd been encouraged by his friends and his guide. Yes! He did it! Because he had successfully hiked the path others had taken and had identified with every aspect that they had endured, he was ready to encourage others to climb their mountains.

Our gospel lesson tells us that while Jesus was praying, the appearance of his face was transformed, and his clothes became dazzling white. Then Moses and Elijah appeared and began talking with Jesus. What a glorious moment! A moment the disciples did not want to end. Peter blurted out, "Master, it's wonderful for us to be here! Let's make three shelters as memorials — one for you, one for Moses, and one for Elijah" (Luke 9:33 NLT). As he was speaking, a bright cloud overshadowed them, and terror gripped them. Then from out of that cloud a voice said, "This is my Son, the Chosen One. Listen to him! When the voice had spoken, Jesus was found alone" (Luke 9:35-36b NLT).

Peter, James, and John heard God clearly state that Jesus was his Son and that they were to listen to him and not to their own ideas or desires. The same applies to us as we follow Jesus, our guide on life's path. As Isaiah the prophet reminds us, "Whether you turn to the right or to the left, your ears will hear a voice behind you saying, 'This is the way; walk in it' " (Isaiah 30:21 NIV). We listen and step out with confidence for — "Jesus is the way; listen to him."

When the glory of that mountaintop experience disappeared; when the cloud went away and the conversation with heaven was over, Jesus was alone with his disciples. Jesus, their teacher and friend, was really the Son of God. What a confidence builder! If you believe Jesus is God's Son, if you have confidence and trust in that belief, then surely you will listen and obey.

On top of that mountain, three disciples experienced God's presence. When they came down, their spiritual vision had drastically changed, improved, and helped them to arrive at their destination. Jesus knew his destination — Jerusalem and a cross. He had to follow the path of suffering and what seemed like defeat in the eyes of others. It was only by obedience and the knowledge that God was at his side that he could accomplish the plan of salvation. "Not my will, Father, but yours be done." God's will, giving up his life, but only by dying could he give us life here and for eternity.

As the hikers looked out from Mount Kilimanjaro, they knew they had experienced the most memorable time of their lives. They remained silent, basking in the accomplishment, letting it all sink in. They understood that when they came down, their story would not sound as exciting to others. They had not personally experienced the thrill of victory.

When Peter, James, and John came down from the mountain, Jesus told them not to tell others what they had seen. It would be hard for they had seen and experienced God's kingdom and its mysteries. It really was an "Aha! moment."

It is time for each of us to embark on our own personal journey with Jesus as our guide. Are you ready? Are you spiritually fit and equipped? Are you willing to listen and obey the voice of God? Then ready, set, go! And don't be surprised when God sends you out to share the good news with everyone in our homes, our communities, our nation, and yes, even the nations of the world. Do not fear for he will be with you. Who knows? You might even get to climb to the top of a mighty mountain. And when you return from your own Kilimanjaro — your personal mountaintop experiences with the Lord — you will want to tell others that they, too, can experience victory in Jesus!

So, let's go and climb a mountain today! The Lord is with us. Amen.

Sermons On The Gospel Readings

For Sundays In
Lent And Easter

You Are Here!

Frank Ramirez

To Roger and Eleanor Weist,
good friends,
different communions,
same faith.
Thanks for all your kindness,
fellowship,
and friendship.

Introduction

The poet Dante begins his epic, *Divine Comedy*, with the words

Midway upon the journey of our life
I found myself within a forest dark,
For the straightforward pathway had been lost.

Three epic poems and 100 cantos later, including a journey from Hell to Heaven, and the earth between the two, Dante gives us a glimpse, the briefest glimpse, of the glory of God before he admits the subject is too mighty even for his pen.

Here vigour failed the lofty fantasy:
But now was turning my desire and will,
Even as a wheel that equally is moved,
The Love which moves the sun and the other stars.
                                              — Longfellow translation

Dante has a lot to say, and from the beginning it is always personal, always real, and he makes certain that we, his readers, are aware that it's happening to us. There is nothing theoretical about this journey. From the vestibule of Hell to the mystery of the Great Rose at the center of Heaven, rest assured — you are here!

That's what I love about his magnificent poem, which describes a journey crucial to our life here and hereafter. And the same thing is true for our annual Lenten journey, which takes us from the depths to the heights, from the cry on the cross to the shout of the resurrection. There is nothing theoretical about it. Our way begins in ashes and ends in glory, but there's this cross planted right in the middle of the path between the two, and there's no getting around it. You are here!

There's a fellow preacher who works out with me at the same gym, and we've both made the same observation — Lent and Easter are among the toughest times to preach, because everyone knows the story. There are no surprises. This is very familiar territory indeed. That's what makes this season such a challenge. That's what makes it so much fun.

In this collection I have endeavored to share the feeling that we are present in the Bible story, that what has happened is not theoretical, but true not only in the sense that this all literally happened, but also because the echo of the gospels in our lives confirm these words have the power to move us, guide us, grip us, and strengthen us. We recognize the deeper truths within.

In these messages I have not hesitated to use examples from my own faith tradition, the Church of the Brethren, rooted in our history as one of the Plain People. I have also not hesitated to bring in my own experiences as a Hispanic and a citizen of the United States. Although these may sometimes seem too particular for repetition, I hope they are universal enough that those who intend to preach these sermons will be able to immediately recognize similar and parallel experiences of their own.

The messages are fairly uniform in length, except the one for Good Friday. I think most Good Friday sermons are too long — less is more, creating a bigger impact.

Our Lord lives. We're going to live with him. But to truly be blessed we must walk this Lenten highway behind him. We follow with our own cross. This cannot be an adventure that happens to someone else. Your entire congregation, along with you, must be able to proclaim in truth — we are here!

The Lord bless you and keep you. I remain Christ's servant and yours.

Frank Ramirez
Everett PA

There's Still Time

Nowadays the cost of a dinner and a movie keeps going up, and a vacation can be especially expensive, but if I really want to go somewhere I just take the change out of my pocket and lay it on the desk. It's like a time machine. Each coin has a year stamped on it, and just thinking about the year helps me travel back in my memory.

1979 is the year my first son was born and the year I started in ministry. 1981 and 1983 are the years my daughter and second son were born. 1988 is the last time the Dodgers won the pennant. 1990 was when I moved to Indiana from Los Angeles. 1994 and 2004 were the years I turned forty and fifty. 2002 was when I moved to Pennsylvania. And it's getting harder to find, but any coin with 1954 is my birth year.

I enjoy laying out the change in my pocket and just glancing at the dates. It's nice to carry these little reminders of important events, good and bad. But they're just one kind of reminder. We carry all sorts of reminders around. One of the most obvious is our date book, which we use to remind us of important events that are not in the past but in the future. We especially need a reminder for Ash Wednesday. It comes in the middle of nowhere. It's not like Christmas or Independence Day that fall on the same dates every year. Ash Wednesday is all over the map, from early February to sometime in March. What usually happens is that we notice someone with a smudge on their forehead and suddenly realize: was that today? Really, it's not very convenient. The least Ash Wednesday could do is fall on a Sunday.

It is an interruption. And it's an unwelcome reminder of an unpleasant fact. Dust we are and to dust we shall return. The grass withers and the flower fades....

Folks in the middle ages didn't need Ash Wednesday to remind them of this unpleasant fact. Instead of the coins that jingle in our pocket, they carried around a medallion on their person somewhere that was called a *memento mori*, Latin for "Remember, you will die."

The phrase supposedly had its origins in the Roman empire. When a conquering general would parade through Rome, with all the people shouting his name in acclamation, it is said that a slave would walk behind the general, calling aloud, "*Memento mori*" as a reminder that nothing lasts, and that he too would die.

Carrying the *memento mori* brought about a change of perspective. Instead of assuming one will live forever, it made it necessary to remember that our time here is limited, that we don't know how much is left to us, and that we need to make the most of the day that is given to us.

Take a look at some of the portraits of the nobility during the Renaissance and after. The subject of the portrait sometimes holds a skull, or there is a skull on a desk or close at hand. The skull functions as a *memento mori* as well. Just like Uncle Sam pointing out at you from the old recruiting poster, grim death wants you.

That's the bad news. But this rather startling service meant to be a reminder of a rather unpleasant truth, is also the first step on the road to recovery. And that first step requires a change of perspective.

In today's passage Jesus sends us a message — stop doing things for show — do them because you mean them. He said, "And whenever you pray, do not be like the hypocrites; for they love to stand and pray in the synagogues and at the street corners, so that they may be seen by others. Truly I tell you, they have received their reward" (Matthew 6:5).

After all, you are going to die.

Jesus uses the word *hupocrites*, which is actually the Greek word for "actor," or "answerer" in the ancient world of theater. Outdoor Greek theaters seated tens of thousands of people, and the

122

acoustics were nothing short of amazing. Even today tourists sit in the far reaches of the stadium seating while tour guides crumble pieces of paper on stage. The tourists can hear the crumbling throughout the vast expanse of the theaters.

Although the acoustics were fantastic, the actors stood far away from the audiences. As a result it was not possible to see their facial expressions, so they wore very tall masks that exaggerated human features so that everyone near and far could see the emotion the actor was supposed to be projecting. The *hupocrites* wore masks as a matter of course.

That's good for actors — actors are supposed to project an emotion so clearly that everyone can see it. But people are not supposed to put on a show of false emotions that belong to someone else.

That's why Jesus warns us:

> *Beware of practicing your piety before others in order*
> *to be seen by them; for then you have no reward from*
> *your Father in heaven. So whenever you give alms, do*
> *not sound a trumpet before you, as the hypocrites do in*
> *the synagogues and in the streets, so that they may be*
> *praised by others. Truly I tell you, they have received*
> *their reward.*   — Matthew 6:1-2

The image is funny, but there is also something comic — and pathetic — when people do things because of what they imagine others will think. It is a source of embarrassment to me, but when I wore ashes as a little child I tried to imagine what people thought when they saw them. I imagined that they saw what a holy and pious child I was. However, I was the kind of child who always came home from school disheveled, wearing stains from the playground, my shirt untucked, and my pants dirty. So when they saw ashes on my forehead most adults probably thought I'd just been playing outdoors.

This is why Jesus says,

> *And whenever you pray, do not be like the hypocrites;*
> *for they love to stand and pray in the synagogues and*

123

at the street corners, so that they may be seen by oth-
ers. Truly I tell you, they have received their reward.
But whenever you pray, go into your room and shut the
door and pray to your Father who is in secret; and
your Father who sees in secret will reward you.

— Matthew 6:5-6

Note that this is not an excuse for cowardice. When it is no longer easy to be a Christian, then it is important that we stand up. Fear can make it difficult for us to live out our faith. Not long after the Japanese attack on Pearl Harbor in 1941 the irrational fear arose that loyal Japanese-Americans were somehow a danger to the country. A presidential executive order issued on February 19, 1942, evicted Japanese-Americans from the western states into internment camps. Over 110,000 people were relocated, many with only 48 hours to sell their homes and possessions.

It was not an easy time for Christians to stand up for what was right, but two school teachers from East Los Angeles, Ralph and Mary Blocher Smeltzer, were shocked by the sight of army jeeps with machine guns driving up and down the streets of their city, all the while ignoring the looting that was taking place in the Japanese-American homes.

Although they were threatened and harassed by others, they dedicated themselves to serving the needs of the evacuees. They began that day by serving breakfast to them and later ministered to them in the horse stalls of the Santa Anita Race Track and the LA County Fairgrounds, where they had been taken. They went on to work as teachers at the Manzanar camp, a lonely and cold place along what is now Highway 395, sharing the difficult conditions. They made themselves even more unpopular when they worked to relocate Japanese-Americans to Chicago and New York. History vindicated their stance, as it did again later when Ralph Smeltzer worked with Dr. Martin Luther King Jr. during the Civil Rights era.[1]

When it is dangerous to act like a Christian then it is important to pray in public and to live the gospel in public. It is only when it is easy to do so that the Lord Jesus advises us to pray in private.

124

When we engage in public piety in order to impress others, then we are only impressing ourselves. This is the type of behavior that Jesus warns us against.

Our ashes are a sign that we recognize our mortality, understand the danger of our hypocrisy, and the need for a true relationship with our heavenly Father. It all begins with repentance.

The Greek word for "repentance" is *metanoia*, turning around, turning away, turning back, and beginning the journey toward spiritual health. When Job truly understands the glory of God and his own position, he says that he would "repent in dust and ashes" (Job 42:6). That's how we repent in the face of God's wrath — and mercy. It is not too late for us to repent as individuals, as the church, as a nation, and as a world. In their name we rend our hearts and not our clothing. We return to the Lord, our God, for he is gracious and merciful, slow to anger, and abounding in steadfast love.

Finally, Jesus gives us a needed, even welcome reminder. When he tells us to lay up for ourselves treasure in heaven, where neither moth nor rust corrupt, and where thieves do not break in and steal, he is reminding us that there is a worthwhile reason for turning away from the world's temptations. There is something better!

One of my favorite movies is the 1966 film *The Trouble With Angels*, featuring Hayley Mills and Rosalind Russell. It marvelously chronicles a call to ministry, demonstrating the way God seeks out — and claims — the least likely. Set in an all girls' boarding school, it centers around a headstrong, young girl named Mary Clancy who proves she's tougher than all the teachers and Mother Superior combined.

Time and again Mary Clancy clashes with the Mother Superior, and by her final year at the school it's not clear who is winning. However, one night Mary Clancy watches as the Mother Superior rescues a hapless student who is simply unable to complete a sewing assignment. Working until dawn while the student sleeps, Mother Superior creates a wonderful dress from scratch, while telling Mary about how, as a child, she had worked for one of the finest designers in Paris, and dreamed of creating her own line of clothing. Indeed she admits she probably had the talent for it.

Aghast, Mary asks her how she could have left a promising career as a fashion designer. The reply: "I found something better." Where your treasure is, there your heart will be also.

Back in 1975, Dr. Graydon F. Snyder, known to his students simply as "Grady," wrote an article with the dry title "Sayings on the Delay of the End" in *Biblical Research* in 1975. The basic message is simple: When prophets talk about the coming end, they're not only reminding God's people that this day could mean bad news, they also talk about a delay — a delay just long enough for us to repent, and to go forward in God's mission.[2]

That's certainly what the prophet Joel is telling us. While God's people look forward to the end as a day when their enemies will get what's coming to them, Joel challenges them to look within their own hearts, to repent, and reinstitute justice and righteousness in the land.

This is the heart of Ash Wednesday. Perhaps you will attend a service today where you will receive ashes on your forehead as a symbol of your mortality and repentance. Perhaps this will be a day of private meditation. Perhaps you will start a personal fast or join others in sharing prayer or spiritual disciplines.

No matter how you observe this day, whether you receive ashes on your forehead as a symbol of your mortality and repentance or make it a day of private meditation, engage in a personal fast, or join others in sharing prayer or spiritual disciplines, what matters is that today you begin a journey for Jesus and with Jesus, through death and beyond to resurrection.

While there's still time. Amen.

---

1. For information on the Smeltzers see *A Cup of Cold Water*, by J. Kenneth Kreider (Elgin: Brethren Press, 2001), pp. 399-401.

2. Graydon F. Snyder, "Sayings on the Delay of the End," *Biblical Research* 20 (Chicago: Chicago Society of Biblical Research, 1975), pp. 19-35.

Hit Me With Your Best Shot

Harry Houdini (1874-1926) was an expert at sleight of hand, a skeptic when it came to the spiritualists and other psychic phonies of his day, but he was best known for his ability to escape from what seemed to be impossible situations. Straitjackets, chains, ropes, jail cells, strange devices such as a milk pail filled with water — he managed to escape from one situation after another in full view of his audience.

What did him in, however, was the blow he never saw coming. While reclining on a couch backstage after a performance he was asked by a couple of college students if he could withstand a punch to the stomach. When he answered that he could, one of the students surprised him by actually punching him several times. These blows caught him off guard, and seem to have ruptured an already aggravated appendix. Houdini died a week later.

The blow you never see coming is the one that can be the most dangerous.

The temptation of Jesus might have been the blow he never saw coming.

In a way it doesn't seem fair. Jesus had shown he could be obedient even when it didn't suit his wishes. He seems to have been surprised, for instance, when at the age of twelve his folks had been so worried about the fact he'd stayed behind to discuss the scriptures with the priests in the temple rather than follow them home after Passover. But follow them home he did.

The obedience of Jesus is also seen in his baptism. The humility he shows in descending into the water is rewarded with a

127

pronouncement from heaven: "You are my Son, the Beloved; with you I am well pleased" (Luke 3:22).

He answered the call of the heavenly Father. He made the right choice.

When we make the right choices, do the right things for the right reasons, most of us feel that the world owes us a reward, or at least a little slack.

But in response to his obedience Jesus was led into the desert by the Holy Spirit to fast for forty days, and after this he was tempted. Couldn't the temptation come at a time when he was stronger? Shouldn't Jesus get a break?

The fact is that there is never a perfect time for us to face the temptations of this world. We're never ready. In this time of Lent let us make no mistake: We will be tested — and it will never be the right time. We will be tempted to do things according to the way of the world, for a good cause, and it will be easy to ignore the means so we can achieve what we imagine are the goals of God.

Here is the cross, long before the cross. We see the cross in the temptation of Jesus and in our own temptation. The first Sunday in Lent reminds us of how vulnerable we can become to sin, how tempting it can be to cut corners and choose the easy road, and why the best landmark in the wilderness is a cross.

For Jesus the greatest temptation was power — to become the thing he was meant to be — the ruler of the world. He is, after all, the Son of God, but what does it mean to be the Son of God? Was it the aim of his ministry to put himself first, to help himself, to elevate himself, to preserve himself?

After forty days of hunger Jesus was about to learn one thing. It is possible to resist temptation. And he would need that knowledge later in the Garden of Gethsemane. Resisting temptation teaches us to endure.

In some ways the first temptation seems harmless. Jesus is famished. Why not turn a few stones into bread? It's not like he's going to do it every day. After all, some may wonder, didn't he multiply the loaves and fishes? What was so wrong about turning one lousy stone into a loaf of bread?

128

The difference, I think, is that in turning loaves and fishes to more loaves and fishes Jesus was quickening what was a natural process in order to feed others. The future kingdom of God, in which all will be filled, was demonstrated through this miracle.

Moreover, Jesus performed this miracle for others, because he had compassion on the people. The word compassion is reminiscent of the words used for how Moses felt about the children of Israel in the desert. In quoting from Deuteronomy 8:3 Jesus deliberately called to mind the words of Moses to the people in the wilderness:

Remember the long way that the Lord your God has led you these forty years in the wilderness, in order to humble you, testing you to know what was in your heart, whether or not you would keep his commandments. He humbled you by letting you hunger, then by feeding you with manna, with which neither you nor your ancestors were acquainted, in order to make you understand that one does not live by bread alone, but by every word that comes from the mouth of the Lord.
— Deuteronomy 8:2-3

The passage goes on to say that it was God who cared for them, though they did not trust him. Jesus was making it clear that even though he had not yet been cared for (and he would at last when the angel came to minister to him), he trusted in his heavenly Father to do so.

Knowing your Bible is very important. It means that people can't misquote it to you. Some may recall how, some decades ago, a group of well-meaning pop singers came together to sing "We Are The World," to raise money for children. One of the lines always galled me — "As God has shown us," they sang, "by turning stones to bread." Ah, that's not what Jesus did. Someone had failed to check a Bible.

In contrast to the natural process of loaves and fishes begetting more of the same, turning a stone into bread is a dog and pony show. It's a magic trick. And it would have meant Jesus had performed magic, if you will, to benefit himself and not to put others first.

The second temptation was the offer of a shortcut. It was through the cross that Jesus came to his throne — and Satan shows him an easy way. He would be recognized as the ruler of all the kingdoms — *if* he will bow to the lord of darkness.

This is the temptation to all dictators. Think of the abuses of the communist governments during the late and unlamented Cold War. They proclaimed a vision of a worker's paradise, where everyone would receive according to their need, and everyone would work according to their ability. But in order to establish such a glorious worldly vision it proved necessary to institute the gulags, to murder millions in prison camps, to rule by terror and deceit. And for all that, European communism almost melted away all at once at the end of the '80s. They sold their souls to an imagined future and the devil's vision of the kingdoms of the world turned out to be a mirage.

Nor is this all ancient history — what is to be said about the current state of fear that drives some to think that it is okay to torture and destroy civil rights in order to preserve civil rights? What claim have we to being called a people of faith if we act faithlessly?

In response to Satan, Jesus echoes two passages from Deuteronomy:

> *The Lord your God you shall fear; him you shall serve, and by his name alone you shall swear.*
> — Deuteronomy 6:13

> *You shall fear the Lord your God; him alone you shall worship; to him you shall hold fast, and by his name you shall swear.*
> — Deuteronomy 10:20

We serve only God. That means we abide by God's commandments. We dare not worship Satan.

In the final temptation, Satan seems to acknowledge the special protection that the Father has given to the Son. Jesus has only to cast himself off the pinnacle of the temple, because, as scripture points out, God will send angels to bear him up and not allow him to be harmed.

Satan quoting scripture. Well, what he said was in the Bible. Psalm 91:11: "For he will command his angels concerning you to guard you in all your ways."

It seems obvious but it bears saying, and then repeating — just because someone quotes scripture doesn't mean they're telling the truth. The false prophets of this world, the ones who try to tempt us with the easy way, can quote scripture as well as anyone.

I suspect that one of the reasons it is so easy to quote scripture out of context to mislead, intentionally or otherwise, is because some translations print each verse as if it were a separate paragraph. This gives an individual verse more weight than it sometimes deserves.

If you ever have a chance to take a look at an ancient biblical manuscript, regardless of whether you can read the language, you should be able to notice one thing — there are no spaces between the words, and no punctuation and paragraphs as we know them. Chapters were added later. Verses were not added until around 500 years ago.

Chapters and verses are invaluable reference tools, helping us to find our place in the Bible within a few moments, but they are not part of the text. They create artificial divisions in the Bible passages.

When you hear someone quoting a verse and the result doesn't sound consistent with what you know of God and scripture, remember that the larger context of a passage is always important, and that we interpret what we read through the mind of Christ.

Jesus responds with a scripture passage — "It is said, 'Do not put the Lord your God to the test' " (Deuteronomy 6:16). Note that the devil did not depart permanently, only "until an opportune time" (Luke 4:13).

When it comes to temptation, our own temptation, the trouble is that we see most clearly the things that tempt others — we deny most vociferously the things that tempt us. Other peoples' sins are more attractive as a target. Can we name and claim what tempts us?

Maybe the temptations that attract Jesus, or others, have no lure for us. Well and good. But that should not make us feel smug. For each of us there is something, perhaps different than others we know, but something, that calls to us. How are we to resist?

First, recognize that we are most vulnerable when, like Jesus, we are stretched to our limits. Exhausted, hungry, weak, beaten down by deadlines, stressed out by the demands that pull us in every direction — if we cannot keep our lives in order, if we do not put Christ on the throne in the center of our lives, if we neglect the rest that God has given us in the sabbath, we are asking for trouble. Even the King of kings and Lord of lords had to face temptation when he was famished and exhausted. Why should we think we'll get a free pass?

Second, if you know what you are tempted by, flee those situations. If you're a diabetic you can't be tempted by the cheesecake in your freezer if there is no cheesecake in your freezer. If you struggle with a gambling addiction then don't go to stores that sell lottery tickets, or only go in the company of a good friend who will give you strength to get through the checkout line.

Have we been hit with Satan's best shot? Do we know if we can resist? We should not go out and seek temptation, but it never hurts to rehearse — what's the worst that can happen — and what would be our best response? Think it through in advance. Make a plan.

Harry Houdini, after he had been hit by the college student, insisted at the time that if he'd known the punch was coming he would have strengthened his abdominal muscles and received the blow without damage. You know a blow is coming. You know that only rarely are our temptations presented as obviously evil. More often we're tempted to imagine we might do good if we take a moral shortcut. Don't kid yourself. If Jesus wasn't exempt, none of us will ride free. But as we learn from the temptation of Jesus, it won't last forever, and if you stand upon the rock of your salvation, you have a much better chance of weathering the storm. Amen.

Oh, Jerusalem

Nowadays we have 24-hour news stations, satellite radio, email alerts, and other ways of finding out breaking news pretty much the instant it is happening. But it wasn't always so.

When John Adams acted as an ambassador to Europe during the Revolutionary War he could go for months without hearing from the Continental Congress. He arranged loans of millions of dollars to help the fledgling nation, but no one back in America knew.

The Battle of New Orleans was a decisive victory for the new nation in the War of 1812, and it catapulted General Andrew Jackson into national prominence and eventually the presidency. The battle, however, took place two weeks after the peace treaty was signed and the war was over. The news arrived too late to prevent the bloodshed.

The first news event to travel almost instantly along the telegraph wires to most of the western world was the explosion of the volcano known as Krakatoa in what is now Indonesia. Some have said this was the beginning of the modern world.

There are times, though, we can get news too fast. Sometimes there is simply too much news, so that we can't absorb it all. There is suffering around the world. In one sense we have the information that allows us to respond to disasters almost immediately. However, because we have more information than ever we find ourselves able to tune it out.

That's when we can get overwhelmed with something that's called compassion fatigue. It happened to me when I'd been a pastor in Los Angeles for twelve years. Our church was located at a busy intersection in a large city, and we lived on the church grounds. There were constant demands on our time and decisions to be made — and always someone who needed help, with a story, possibly a true story, possibly well rehearsed and totally false. It got too easy to be cynical.

When the time came for a move we chose a rural portion of the state of Indiana, which helped ground us again. Some of the cynicism wore away. But even there it was still possible for compassion to be overwhelmed.

Jesus lived in a time of slow and unreliable communication — yet even he seemed overwhelmed at times, retreating to a hilltop to get away, to pray. This was important, because compassion was at the heart of his ministry. When Jesus fed the multitudes the gospels say that he felt compassion — using a root word that echoed the feelings of Moses in the wilderness, filled with compassion for a people who had lost their way.

The second Sunday of Lent finds Jesus on a hillside, filled with compassion for the problems of a big city that has lost its way. He is lamenting the hillsides of crosses that will dot the Jerusalem landscape when the city finally falls to the Romans. He sees the destruction that lies in store for Jerusalem. He longs as a mother hen to draw in the people and protect them. And he admits that because of the free will granted to all of us by God, there may be some people he cannot help.

Today's passage immediately follows a parable of judgment, complete with the gnashing of teeth. He reminds us that there can be losers, if we insist on making bad choices. Then, when he is told that Herod wants to kill him, he dismisses Herod's power — but still there is compassion.

When people choose a toxic lifestyle, how can we help them redeem the cross they have chosen? How deeply do we feel the sufferings of others, whether or not it's their own fault?

This is perhaps the flaw of the incarnation. There is no longer a great distance between God and humanity. God, having taken on human form, cannot deny that the divine knows intimately our flaws, our failings, our fears. God now thinks like us. That link

134

deepens even more the compassion we find in the prophets for doomed people.

Jesus lamented how little difference he was making at the core problem of those who lived in Jerusalem. As we lament with Jesus over the problems of our own toxic society, how can we continue to strive for the things that make for peace?

The essential thing, demonstrated by Jesus when he went to the extreme of accepting the cross in the face of our sinfulness, is that we must be as persistent as our Lord in the face of the world's stubbornness.

Like the proverbial squeaky wheel, our persistence must remain heroic until we finally get the attention of a world intent on ignoring the good news. Our example comes not only from the cross, but from God's world.

Take the birds. Birds can be persistent when it comes to making a nest. Last year a robin was persistent in using my porch light as a base for a nest instead of a tree. When that happens we feel like we have to use the garage door instead of the front door to enter and exit our home, and we can't use the light either. So for several days we would take off all the dried grass, string, twigs, and weeds that the mother robin painstakingly placed on the lamp. After about a week we had to go out of town for a couple days and that's all it took. The nest was made, the eggs were laid, and we were using the garage door as an entryway once more. Would that we were as persistent in working for God's kingdom as that robin was in making her nest.

In addition to persistence we must never set ourselves apart, so that what happens in the world seems to happen to someone else. Jesus was filled with compassion for the people. That compassion is part of the tie that binds.

"Blest be the tie that binds" — the words of the hymn remind us that we are one. But what binds us together? Shared experience and table fellowship. I have found over time that events involving food and the natural world really bind us together, and I think that's part of the insight contained in this parable. If we do not break bread, literally or symbolically, with our brothers and sisters close at hand and around the world, we will not be one.

135

Over the years of my ministry I've found it remarkable how richly church members recall those trips taken together into the natural world. Jeep trips, camping expeditions, long hikes, whether these are regular events or one-time occurrences. They call to mind with laughter the difficulties and privations and most of all the differences from the way they normally live life. Families — grandparents, parents, and children — often took these trips together and this strengthened the bonds within and among families. The backdrop of natural wonders only added to the bonding. I think the Hebrew Feast of Booths, for instance, which is a feast of tents, is nothing more nor less than a form of family camp, a crucible in which families leave the comforts of home to rediscover the essentials and each other.

At the heart of everything church is food. Most churches consider their cooks the best, their meals the best. Seriously, can there be anything better than warm, fresh bread? Perhaps that is why Jesus uses the image of yeast and bread making. Some churches send home a loaf of homemade bread as a gift for all visitors. And of course bread is integral to communion. The yeast that transforms the loaf is similar to the transformation that churches may experience with the new life in Christ.

Transformation — transforming events such as church camps, revivals, special guests, and camping trips are part of the yeast that leavens the whole fellowship. When a group member travels to a special event, a workshop, or a conference, are we ready to receive their enthusiasm upon their return and act on it. When a child comes back from camp singing old and new songs and filled with a strange enthusiasm for Christ and the church are we ready to receive, affirm, and channel that energy?

We must be connected and remain faithful in our connectedness. And not only with humanity. The parable of the mustard seed is a naturalistic image. The tree in the ancient world represented the interconnectedness of all things. The ecology of a tree included the birds, animals, and insects who made it their home, as well as the people who benefit from its fruit, its shade, its presence. In a larger sense the tree stood for the kingdom, or even the king, in biblical imagery. Faith in God's kingdom, faith in God's creation, can bind all together in a rapidly growing, transforming relationship.

Compassion fatigue can dull our memory. It's easy to forget. Oh, Jerusalem. That's right. People forget. The plight of inner-city schools may attract our attention for a day or a week, but sooner or later that becomes someone else's problem as our minds are focused on the glut of news that leads us to choose celebrity scandals over the true ills that beset us.

We know so much and we need to forget so much. There is a cross imprinted in the world around us — and a long memory. Nancey Murphy, in her book *Reconciling Theology and Science*, connects science and faith in one cohesive system. She reminds us that we live in a cruciform world, a world built around the cross.[1] The death of plants feeds the animals, animals die for our table, we die, and enrich the earth, and what has died feeds the plants. It's not a dog eat dog world, it's a life feeding life world.

This story of the ages is imprinted, if not in the memory of humans, then in the rocks, the earth, the trees. You can find out what happened in ages past by core samples taken from the ice in the Antarctic and in samples from the rings of trees. You can find out what happened in the words of scripture, your newspaper, and the magazines you've been ignoring. Where's the cross? It's there. So is life.

In the chapter that follows this passage Jesus heals a sick person. When questioned about this by the religious authorities, Jesus attempts their healing through parables he hopes will wake them up, cause them to look at their own sins, repent, and be transformed. It could happen. At least Jesus seems to think so.

The boundaries of our days are picketed with current events, events of such magnitude for good or ill that they cannot be forgotten. In my life, events such as the assassinations of John F. Kennedy, Dr. Martin Luther King Jr., and Robert F. Kennedy, the explosion of the space shuttle *Challenger*, the destruction on September 11, 2001, are defining moments. The pain and sorrow may lessen with time, but never fully fade.

This glut of news, these national tragedies, and the complications may lead us to say, "Woe is me." And for some people that's what Lent is all about — looking inward to bemoan our sinful nature. The solution may be to look out, and beyond, and toward God's suffering world. We may not have all the answers. Our answers may not work, but Jesus tells us to get back into the ball game. If we cannot forestall the destruction of Jerusalem, we may yet rescue one soul.

Oh, Jerusalem. That's right. It's still out there. And if Jesus is filled with compassion for them, how dare we fail in sharing his heart for a lost world. Amen.

---

1. Nancey Murphy, *Reconciling Theology and Science: A Radical Reformation Perspective* (Kitchener, Ontario: Pandora Press, 1997).

Lent 3
Luke 13:1-9

The Tower Of Siloam

It was over forty years ago, in the middle of December 1963, when my aging father retired from the Navy. He was only 37 years old at the time, but to a nine-year-old that sounded pretty old! He and mom packed us into the car and we moved from Norfolk, Virginia, back to our native California, taking the old Highway 66, a two-lane highway that could really cause motion sickness at times!

Dad made sure we stopped at important places from the sights of Washington DC to the austere majesty of mountainous Silver City, New Mexico, which is where our family settled after we crossed the Mexican border in 1910.

The stop I remember best lasted only a few minutes. My father stopped the car in the middle of Dallas and pointed to a window on the sixth floor of the Texas Book Depository. Less than a month before, a man had leaned out that window and killed a president. Nearly a half century later, we still argue about what that event means.

Probably most of us remember the school assignment known as "current events." We were asked to cut out an article from the newspaper and write about it. Nowadays one suspects that students can go to a newspaper website and do their cutting and pasting electronically, but it's the same thing.

In some ways it is futile. We know what happened but it's way too soon to know what it all means. It takes time to know if a "current event" is as significant as we think, and it takes perspective to understand what they mean. Today's passage involves Jesus

139

tion about a current event. Instead of giving a snap judg-
shall see that Jesus brought some real perspective to the

When people asked Jesus his opinion of one current event, he responded by giving perspective to a political event — the rebellion of some Galileans, a common enough event in that time. He did this by pointing to another current event, the fall of a tower and the death of those who randomly stood near it when it fell. Although both were big news at the time, neither was significant enough for historians to record, and we know nothing beyond the bare references in scripture. But in the parable that followed, Jesus made it clear that regardless of the peaks and valleys in the age we share, the time is so urgent that our shared life of faith in Christ remains most important. Jesus gives some perspective.

Perspective is not so easy to get, especially when you live in flatland. I've been a city boy much of my life, so what I see in the country still amazes and amuses me. I think back to the time when I lived for twelve years in rural Indiana. One autumn I was particularly amused by a raccoon who lived down the road from me. He was a bit of a genius and had learned to climb up telephone poles in order to get a better look. There was no food up telephone poles as far as I could tell, but this raccoon regularly climbed up and I want to believe it was for better perspective.

The years have gone by, but there is still a tremendous amount of national trauma, and rightfully so, surrounding the events of September 11, 2001. To some extent that raccoon had more perspective than most of us in the United States, sadly enough, and that goes for the churches of Jesus Christ, the Prince of Peace. People in the church failed to listen to the words of Jesus, to take the long view, or at least to take a long breath. We had no perspective.

In this way we are no different than the ancients who believed that the earth was at the center of the universe. It's hard to imagine how we can continue to believe in this conceit. When the *Voyager* space probe looked back and took a snapshot of the solar system, the Earth appears as a small blue dot. From a larger perspective we know we are on a small planet circling an average-sized star orbiting near the edge of an ordinary spiral galaxy that is part of an undistinguished Vegan Super Galaxy.

Even so, we are tempted as adults to consider ourselves the center of the universe. It's normal for children to feel that way. Indeed, one of the major stages of development is the recognition that there are others, these others have feelings, and are individuals with as much right to happiness and success as ourselves. One of the first ways children acknowledge that others matter, one of their first gifts, is potty training. Later they will give gifts without thought of what they will receive in return. At some point we hope that we come to value God and others more than ourselves.

However, some individuals — and churches and nations — never reach that point. Consider the United States. There is a tendency to consider what happens in that country as more important than anywhere else. The events of September 11, 2001, were horrifying and criminal — but the loss of around 3,000 souls pales to the evil involved when a few years before nearly a million Rwandans were killed one by one, largely with machetes, while the world at large did nothing. Westerners buy diamonds at artificially inflated prices without a care as to whether they are "conflict" stones, stolen by thugs who routinely hacked off the limbs of their victims. To even suggest that there is a larger evil than what has happened to our nation, however, can incite American churches to the flaming point.

I call it the "idolatry of current events." What happens to us now is more significant (in our minds) than anything else. One problem is that we get caught up in current events. If the news is followed religiously, there's a danger of it becoming a separate and idolatrous religion. That idolatry is demonstrated in Luke 13:1-9. Jesus and his listeners begin talking about current events. Some people bring up the topic of rebellious Galileans (whether they were freedom fighters or terrorists depended on your perspective) who were murdered by Pilate. Jesus responds that their fate was no different than those who died when the Tower of Siloam fell. According to Jesus the crucial fact was whether the individuals in question had repented in a timely fashion. His parable of the fig tree was a reminder for all of us that first and last things have priority over even the most compelling events of the present.

It all comes down to this. If a thing was right before September 11, it is still right, and if a thing was wrong, it is still wrong. We are Christians first. Christianity is not a convenient means of explaining or justifying our wars. Peace is the natural lifestyle of a committed follower of Jesus Christ, one who recognizes that the life, death, and resurrection of Jesus are real and saving events that change lives now.

The apostle Paul speaks of righteousness, which is properly defined not as a standard of outward morality, but the state of seeking to live in God's peace, a shalom that was intended to include all nations, all individuals, all of creation in a perfect reflection of God's will for our lives. This peace is not strident or self-justifying. It is not achieved by isolation from the world. It does not put itself on a pedestal to condemn others. It does not bend to the whims of current events.

As a matter of fact, it is not arrogant or rude. It is not jealous or boastful. It does not rejoice in the wrong but rejoices in the right. It bears all things, believes all things, hopes all things, and endures all things. It's a lot like love in this regard.

In addition to our longing for our human needs, there is a longing for justice with regard to the crimes, which have been committed that mirrors the biblical call for that same justice. Anyone who reads scripture from beginning to end recognizes that justice, the balancing of all scales to achieve God's righteousness on the earth in the form of shalom, is a constant thread that runs through the biblical tapestry. From God's law, through the claiming of the land, the struggles with judges, prophets, and kings, through the writings of the psalmist, there is the recognition that God's justice is an objective standard, and that we are all called to live that justice. In the New Testament, Jesus proclaims scriptures of justice, and the vision of Revelation is a strong reminder that ultimately, God's will shall be done.

Rather than seek revenge, would it not be better to take the biblical view and seek justice? Justice scalds the pages of the Old and New Testaments. When the Old Testament scriptures speak of an eye for an eye, it is with the aim of limiting vengeance. Jesus goes a step further and invites us to put transforming love at the heart of our lives.

Look again at the scripture text. Jesus said, "Unless you repent, you will all perish ..." (v. 3). Notice the "all"? It's not just the ones who don't repent who perish. We're all in the same boat. If we don't all repent of the heresy of wealth and power, we will all perish. Everyone around the world. If we don't all repent of our indifference to global warming, we will all perish, both those who practice green lifestyles and those who listen to self-appointed experts who fly in the face of established facts. If we don't all repent of the hardness in our hearts, we will all perish — everybody. It's not you and me, us or them. It's all or nothing.

Finally Jesus speaks to another major misconception with regard to the current events in Galilee and at Siloam. There's no escaping it. Some people think that only good things happen to good people and that bad things only happen to bad people. When disaster strikes they begin to try to figure out what people did wrong, rather than accept the fact that this is a broken world, bad things happen, and somehow we survive. Especially if we stick together.

Woulda, coulda, shoulda; Jesus doesn't play this game. In today's scripture text some folks call to mind the recent murder of some Galileans, possibly guerillas, who were murdered by Pontius Pilate, and Jesus insists they were no worse than anyone else. He goes his questioners one better — how about those killed when the Tower of Siloam fell? Were they worse than those who stepped out of the way just in time? No, the real question remains — are we ready to meet God?

The people you are serving did not deserve what has happened to them. Especially the children.

Every disaster, every act of terrorism, every genocide, every war, whether justified in our minds or not, is an invitation to see the world through God's eyes. God is not willing that even one should perish. And it is God's hope for humanity that all are ready, never knowing when we might be called, or when we might fall into a pit created by evil people. The apostle Paul says that whether we live or whether we die, we are the Lord's (Romans 14:8). That makes it imperative that before we are confronted with the unpredictability of life or death — we choose the Lord. Amen.

This Fellow Welcomes Sinners

In the old Soviet Union it was common for people who had fallen out of favor with the communist regime to also fall out of photographs. Long before digital photography made it easy to change our memories, a little air brushing could remove an inconvenient commissar who had been purged since the last worker's holiday. Indeed, Soviet watchers would study every photograph published in newspapers and journals to determine the rise and fall of cold warriors.

The Soviet Union didn't have the corner on the removal of inconvenient people. How many people grew up in our own country not knowing some basic facts about our country's founding? Four decades ago, my parents took us to historic Williamsburg where reenactors sought to bring Colonial America to life. Funny thing — there were no African Americans. Visitors who went to Monticello and Mount Vernon to learn more about Jefferson and Washington at one time would never have guessed they were slave owners. Histories might occasionally make a reference to Crispus Attucks, a black man who was the first to fall in the Boston Massacre, but how many knew about the exploits of the First Rhode Island Regiment, composed largely of African Americans?

Sometimes there's a reason someone is missing from the picture. One time our three children had their photographs taken with their fiancés in front of a historic building. A frame featuring all three photos hung on our walls. One of the weddings never occurred, however, and it became necessary to replace one of the photos with someone new. There, at least, it was obvious that the third photo was taken at a different place. In that instance it was pain and separation that led to the change, but we never made a secret of it.

The nice thing is that with computer programs we no longer have to resort to simply tearing out a former spouse from a photo. You may not even know someone is gone. So it's always important to ask who is missing from the picture we're given.

Which brings us to today's scripture text — the familiar story of the prodigal son. Maybe it is too familiar. In the passage Jesus is accused by religious leaders of being one who eats with sinners. This was a big deal by the society's standards. Sharing a meal — breaking bread — meant you approved of that person on some level. Social climbers wanted to be seen eating with people above their station. Those worried about what others thought would not want to be seen eating with those they imagined were beneath them.

In first-century Palestine there was no air conditioning, so buildings tended to be built with windward facing windows. The windows were large, and of course there was no glass. That meant people walking by could look in the windows and see who you were eating with. Nor did they have to glance out of the corner of their eyes. It was socially acceptable and even expected that people would stand outside and stare in to see who was eating together.

So everyone knew whose invitations Jesus had accepted. They assumed that Jesus was motivated by the same things they were, so when they sought to discredit him they assumed that accusing this fellow of eating with sinners would cause him great discomfort.

Jesus isn't embarrassed in the least. He proceeds to tell two parables about a lost coin and a lost sheep to explain why he was more than willing to eat with those accused by sinners of being sinners. People could understand immediately how lost property could make us change our behavior and how suddenly the missing thing became more important than all the things never lost.

We are not embarrassed to scramble around for a lost coin. He's not embarrassed to go to any lengths to save us lost sheep.

After sharing these two examples Jesus raised the stakes. He told the story of the prodigal son and put a human face on the topic of lost and found.

I said earlier that perhaps we're too used to the story. We know the main characters — the father, the prodigal son, and the brother. We may not realize that there is someone missing from the picture.

Jorge Maldonado, a family counselor, wrote a book called *Even in The Best of Families*, which alas is out of print.[1] Maldonado looked at seven familiar biblical stories through the lens of family systems. Keeping in mind (as the author does) that no one interpretation exhausts the depth of a story from the Bible, the author asks a thought-provoking question about the story of the prodigal son.

Where is the mother in this story?

A missing person can change history. Think of what happened in the story of Jacob after Rachel died. He was left with one son, Benjamin, whose birth had caused his favorite wife's death, and another son, Joseph, who he did not blame for his mother's death, not to mention ten other sons who he seems to ignore pretty completely. As a consequence, Jacob treated Joseph with a favoritism that outraged his other sons, who felt slighted. That coat of many colors changed history, in some ways for the better, but also caused decades of pain and separation because a mother was missing.

The prodigal's mother is missing. Is it because she has nothing to say? Or was it because she was dead? Certainly life expectancy was much shorter in Jesus' day. Childbirth as well as ordinary illnesses and injuries could kill that today barely slow us down. A car won't go far with three wheels, but families have to struggle along even when someone important is gone.

Maldonado suggests that many families are unbalanced because someone is missing, in this case the mother. If the mother had died there are probably many grief issues left unresolved. Perhaps one reason the father was so permissive toward the younger son was to try to make up for the loss of his mother. One reason the older brother might be such a hard worker, never allowing himself time off, is that he has become the missing person, the mother figure who is taking it upon himself to make everything right, not leaving room for anyone else's efforts because it is all on his shoulders. Maldonado wonders if the younger son is so irresponsible because he can never measure up to the older brother's standards

147

and has stopped trying. He simply wants to get as far away from a grieving father and an overbearing brother.

Of course this is Maldonado's interpretation and he does not want us to suppose this was all in the mind of Jesus or his listeners when the story was first told, but he wants us to think about unbalanced families — and we're all unbalanced. We're all grieving about something or someone. We're all trying to compensate, or we're backing off, making ourselves absent. Maldonado suggests that the father's overwhelming love may yet make things right, but the story is open-ended. Jesus doesn't tell us what happens the next week. Like any good storyteller Jesus draws us in, then leaves us with a cliffhanger that challenges us to put ourselves in the story. At different times in our lives we may find ourselves as the father, the older brother, and the younger brother. Or we may even find ourselves absent, though quite alive.

Keep in mind, of course, that this is a story. It's a sacred story, it was told by Jesus, but he was telling it to illustrate a point. One of the reasons for storytelling by the teachers in first-century Judea was that we take the story home with us, that we think about it, chew on it, retell it in our own way, see something new, ask questions, and find our own answers. Stories can have more than one meaning.

Most of us think of the changes that happened for the prodigal himself. He demanded his inheritance, squandered it, returned, and was not only forgiven but restored to the family. The love of the father for the son in this story is meant to mirror the love of the heavenly Father, who is determined to seek for the lost, even if it means that Jesus eats with sinners. It creates an example for us — to seek the lost and unloved, because they are part of the family.

But there's more. Dad and the other son need to change, too.

The story of the prodigal son demonstrates abundant love, abundant forgiveness. There are also abundant possibilities for transformation. It's time for Dad to be less of an enabler and for the older brother to loosen up and finally give himself permission to enjoy. What's the use of all this work if there is never any reward?

The older son is not an employee — he is an owner, in stark contrast to the situation when Laban "hires" Jacob. There are

148

consequences for what the younger son did. He will not be getting back the property he squandered. The older son is going to inherit everything. Everything already belongs to him.

We are not employees of God's kingdom — we're part of the family. That means we may not expect a regular paycheck, but we've got an inheritance that no one can beat. If we try to cash in now, as did the prodigal son, we're only hurting ourselves.

There's the old joke about a man who was finally rescued after being stranded on a remote island for ten years. He kept sane, he said, by constructing an entire town out of palm branches. His rescuers were astonished to discover a home, an apartment complex, a movie theater, a grocery store, and two churches, one at each end of the town. Why, they asked, did he build two churches?

"Well," the man replied, "I never lost my faith. The church was my symbol of faith and community."

But one of the rescuers persisted. "Why two churches?"

The man shrugged. "Well, the one church was where I went to worship. The other was the church I wouldn't be caught dead in."

It seems sometimes as if church members find it just as important to exclude others as they find it necessary to worship God. The older brother doesn't want to be in a family that accepts a prodigal that squandered perfectly good cash while others work hard all the day long. And sometimes it's hard not to think that the older brother is right — who wants to deal with a reformed younger brother who has spent all his money, puts on a good face, and is getting a party to boot? Give me a stranger any old day. But the cross is written in the face of each one of us. We've had a rough life, a tough life, and yet we're surviving. Let's see the Jesus who has been revealed when all the baby fat has been cut away, and we start marking our journey in the lines around our eyes and in our faces. Let's treat each other, sinners all, like old friends.

We may not like prodigals and they may even make us a little afraid. When Jesus healed the Geresene demoniac they wanted him out of there — the demoniac was scary enough — but a redeemed crazy man, one who was sane and whole, now revealed as their neighbor, once lost and now found — they were going to have do something about him. Before, they could skirt the graveyard and avoid him. Now he was one of them.

I work weekly with a jail ministry and lead a Bible study behind bars. The attendance is good. There's not a lot going on. What interests me is the strong skepticism expressed by many Christians about jail ministry. Trust me, all of us involved are mildly skeptical about jailhouse conversions. We have had enough experience with losing track of individuals once they leave the four walls of the jail, but just the chance, just the possibility that God might succeed in battering down a shuttered heart makes the work worth it.

So what happens when the prisoners get out? One pastor in our community was approached by the chaplain of the program about the possibility of a released prisoner attending his church. The pastor paused an uncomfortable moment and replied, "I don't think we're set up for him right now."

Contrast that with the attitude I encountered at another church. There were three or four members of that congregation in jail. When our church met with theirs for a joint Bible study there was a time each week during prayer in which these individuals were lifted up, and it was obvious that it was assumed they would one day return and be a part of the fellowship.

Jesus welcomes sinners. That includes us — and it also includes those others, including the missing in action, and those missing in our hearts. We will be made whole, and our cup will run over — in time, in God's time.

This task of welcoming sinners is too much for one person, or even one church, but we're not meant to be acting alone. One way to help is to get more people involved. Getting back to our original image of people missing from a picture, it's important to ask if we have excised people from the picture without even knowing it.

Take the family structure itself. It was only in the twentieth century that we developed the concept of the "nuclear" family: Dad, Mom, and children. Family in most eras and even in most of the world now includes many branches — grandparents, cousins, uncles, aunts, all vital parts of one unit. But we have lopped off

150

those branches, defining down the size of the family and the community, instead of stretching the boundaries. It really does take a village to raise a child. Remember the old days when everyone watched everyone else's kids?

Nor are we meant to see ourselves as one self-sufficient congregation — for many of us there is a larger denomination and beyond that the body of Christ consisting of all the Christian communions. We are meant to work together in communities, and as a national and global church, to reach out to the prodigals.

Finally, congregations need to strive to achieve a balance, remembering that the prodigal's family was unbalanced. We do not go off the deep end. We need all kinds — including those driven away by one event or another. Treating sinners like old friends is important, because they *are* old friends. We have missed them. We need to balance each other's lives and seek balance in our own.

It's worth noting that Jesus does not give us the end of the story. The father and the prodigal's brother are still standing out in that field. There's been no answer yet. We don't know what's going to happen, at least until we decide. The end of the story is up in the air. Our story is up in the air. How will you decide? Are you a prodigal who needs redeeming love? Are you a prodigal's brother, who need not fear eating with sinners and who needs to get off their high horse, get over their snit, and come join the rest of the human race and God's family? Will you bend? Will we reconcile with each other?

This Sunday in Lent brings to life loss and gain — the forgiveness that comes from the cross, visible in the story of the prodigal son. We once were lost but now are found.

The story of the prodigal son is not about one of those attractive sinners that we don't know, those symbols that are easy to support because we don't have to deal with them after they're redeemed, except perhaps with a check.

Remember the words of Jesus: "Just so, I tell you, there will be more joy in heaven over one sinner who repents than over ninety-nine righteous persons who need no repentance" (Luke 15:7).

Lost sheep, lost coins, lost lives. Found in every case. It's the word of Jesus. It should be our word as well. Amen.

1. Jorge Maldonado, *Even in the Best of Families: The Family of Jesus and Other Biblical Families* (New York: World Council of Churches, 1994). Out of print.

No Pleasing Some People

Secretly I'm on Judas' side on this one. You probably don't want to admit it, but so are you. He points out that 300 days' salary had just been cracked open and wasted on Jesus. Well, not wasted. Yeah, wasted. Because once that expensive perfume was used it couldn't be used again. It was a limited, one time resource. Can you imagine the good that could have been done for the poor? Try to imagine what our church could do if someone donated one year's worth of salary out of the blue! That's why I say that many Christians would find themselves on Judas' side if they were honest with themselves.

What was Mary thinking? A jar of perfume worth 300 days' wages? Take away the sabbath and that's pretty much a year's salary. Do you own something worth a year's salary — some piece of jewelry, a book, a car, a boat? What sort of use are you getting out of it?

Mary, the sister of Martha and Lazarus, offers a one time only gift for Jesus. Because once it's opened you can't use it anymore.

I don't know about you, but the longer I own something valuable, the less I want to part with it and the less I get out of it. Do you know people who can't bring themselves to use the good china for themselves? Or anyone? Is there a treasured antique car that never goes out on the road anymore for fear of a scratch or a patch of mud? Is there an outfit you refuse to wear because you're too sentimental and it has become too valuable?

In our society we have eliminated the sense of smell. We don't want strong odors. We mask them, eliminate them.

Mary lived in a society that was not afraid of smells. Perfume was handy, especially with the need for quick burial in a warm climate. But then, in most societies people love strong odors. They love thick perfumes. They burn incense. The woman who washed the feet of Jesus knew exactly how much that oil was worth. This extraordinary item was being saved for a day in the future. Probably her own funeral or the funeral of a loved one.

Suddenly the future is now. Mary is the one who sits at the feet of Jesus and listens. She gets it. Unlike the disciples, she knows what lies in store for Jesus. He is going to die. Evidently Mary is the kind of person who buys flowers before a person dies instead of sending them to the funeral home out of guilt. Mary anoints Jesus for his funeral while he is still alive and can enjoy the thick, rich perfume.

In response to those who criticized Mary, Jesus takes time to quote Deuteronomy 15:11: "Since there will never cease to be some in need on the earth, I therefore command you, 'Open your hand to the poor and needy neighbor in your land.' "

Some people think when the gospel quotes Jesus as saying that we will always have the poor among us that suggests there is no use in trying to work against poverty since we will never solve the problem. But that ignores what Jesus was saying.

Sometimes people don't study their scriptures quite enough. I've often heard people quote the words Jesus spoke after his feet were anointed with expensive perfume (John 12:8: "You always have the poor with you") as justification, somehow, of leaving the poor to their lot. They suggest that even Jesus was saying it's no use trying to keep up.

However, those who heard Jesus speak those words knew what he was talking about. They were used to the practice of quoting only the beginning of a passage. The listener was expected to know the rest.

Look at the larger context. In the Deuteronomy passage, Moses was talking about the Year of Jubilee. "Since there will never cease to be some in need on the earth, I therefore command you, 'Open your hand to the poor and needy neighbor in your land.' " This verse was quoted by Jesus when the woman washed his feet and some criticized her for wasting the gift. Jesus said, in reply, that the poor would always be with us and some have taken that to mean we'll always have the poor so there's nothing you can do about it. You can see however that Jesus was quoting the law to say that since we will always have the poor, we must never cease giving. The people who were criticizing the woman for what she did needed to mind their own business and set about helping the poor with their own cash instead of worrying about hers!

That had to make some of the listeners angry....

It's not easy to serve some of these populations. How do you choose who is really in need? We've all heard stories about people holding up signs reading "Will Work For Food" who have been unmasked as frauds, for instance. I remember well the compassion fatigue I suffered after serving a congregation in Los Angeles for over a decade. There were always calls for food and money, and it was tough to decide who needed it when there wasn't that much on our table in the first place.

This doesn't get us off the hook. Nor does quoting Jesus when he said, "You always have the poor with you, but you do not always have me." You know that now.

Sometimes it's in the interest of those in power to deride the poor. Stories about "Welfare Queens," who grow rich off the system (and these are rare, trust me) are blown out of proportion by the conservative media as justification for denying aid to many who desperately need it. The depiction of black faces supposedly engaged in fraud is designed to instill fear in those elements of a white population who want justification for their lack of sympathy.

Fortunately most Christians, even while practicing some measure of discernment in their stewardship, are more likely to err on the side of charity than sensibility.

If you want to know the truth, sometimes it is the people who have the least who are the most generous. I know people with very little money, limited mobility, and difficult lives, who practice effortless discipleship and limitless charity. For them it's the most natural thing in the world.

There's a ghastly — and funny — scene at the beginning of the movie *Monty Python and the Holy Grail*, which is a send up of every King Arthur movie you've ever seen. The plague is rampant, people are dying, and a man pushes a cart through the muddy streets of a decaying town shouting out, "Bring out your dead!"

One man comes forward with his father over his shoulder ready to throw the body on the cart. There's just one problem — the father says, "I'm not dead yet." In the end his son clunks him over the head and throws him in.

Jesus is not dead yet. But there are some who want to clunk him over the head and speed up the process. What are they thinking? Jesus just raised Lazarus from the dead. He doesn't fit their preconceived notions of what a prophet ought to be, where he ought to come from, and what hoops he should have jumped through. He is not one of them!

So what is Mary really doing? She is giving him flowers before he dies. Think of the funerals you've been to with all the wonderful flowers. Don't people say, as they ooh and ah, "Oh, she would have loved them." Wouldn't it have been nicer to give the flowers before the death?

Mary takes out the funeral perfume, worth 300 days' pay, and uses it on Jesus. This is her final gift to her Lord. She is not saving the good stuff. She is getting out the good china, the good silverware. Her home is not a museum and neither should ours be one. Our lives are lived behind glass.

In effect Mary tells Jesus she knows he must die, but the comfort begins now. She is present.

Are we present with the dying? Yes we are. We are all dying. Living is dying. We need to comfort each other and bring hope.

How can we lift the sufferings of others — as Mary of Bethany ministers to Jesus even as she anoints him for the tomb — he is not yet dead. Neither are we, yet if our path is set irrevocably in the direction of death it should be aiming directly at life eternal.

Actually things are worse than they seem. Mary breaks all sorts of barriers in the society and shocks people when she ministers to Jesus. There are social, cultural, and religious taboos that separate them — but Jesus reaches across all barriers to touch our lives, and we are called to take some risks to bring the gospel to those on the margins, those who are suffering, those who are lost.

156

There is no pleasing some people. Yes, she could have given that money to the poor. It's an argument that makes sense. But as pointed out before, instead of worrying about what other people are doing with their money, and giving it away for them, we ought to look in our own wallets and purses and take it upon ourselves to give more. As Jesus said, you will always have the poor with you — do something about it. Don't look to others to do something.

They don't like anything that Mary has done here — touched Jesus, wept on his feet, spent money. No one says, "Okay, there are poor here, so I'll spend my own money on them." It's all about her money.

Mary is using the good china. She is living the resurrection.

You will know Christ in the poor. You will know Christ in your giving. You will know Christ in your relationships. You must have Christ at the center. It is what makes all other things possible and gives them meaning.

This week plan someone's funeral — okay, maybe not that. But we're not dead yet! Let's do wonderful things for the living — and let's do wonderful things for the living Lord.

Remember as you go about the business of the Lord, there is no pleasing some people. Trust me, we can always find something wrong with everything. Jesus is quoting from a Deuteronomy text that makes it clear that rather than criticize others, we ought to get busy ourselves. We ought to pick up our own crosses and follow — it's a parade. The party starts now. It's time for the big show. And the parade continues past palms to crosses and beyond to glory. Amen.

No ... On

I've tried to get a handle on this Holy Week thing. How can Jesus be hailed as the one coming in the name of the Lord on Palm Sunday, delight the crowds with his wisdom, only to be condemned a few days later by the crowds who shouted "Crucify him!" and then mocked him as he hung in agony on the cross?

I believe that it happened, but what influences crowds to do the right thing — and the wrong thing? The same crowd.

There's a new statistical concept called the Information Cascade, and it just might explain things. There's a messy mathematical algorithm attached to it, but that doesn't concern us here. Just these few facts.

Statisticians and sociologists have come up with a theory that explains our herd mentality. It's called Information Cascade. It is the effect that we have on each other, an effect that can multiply a correct or incorrect response. If we all take a test in which we keep our answers from each other we have an opportunity to put down the right or wrong answer. If someone asks a question in public, however, the answer the first person gives out loud affects the answer of the second person. Regardless of how that second person might have answered on their own, their answer is influenced by the first person. If the second person agrees with the first person, then the third, fourth, fifth, and sixth person in the room is more likely to give the same answer, too.

The answer can even be affected by what other people are saying, whether we agree with them or not.

In Los Angeles they used to talk about the Tom Bradley Effect. Tom Bradley was the successful multi-term African-American mayor of Los Angeles. When he ran for governor of California the polls showed him winning by a large margin — but he lost the election to a white opponent. What studies showed was that white voters were reluctant to admit they would prefer to vote for a white candidate instead of a black candidate so they went along with the answer they thought the pollster wanted. But, in the privacy of the polling booth, enough citizens voted their racism to throw the election the other way.

How many times have you found yourself with a group of people when someone said something outrageously racist, but then discovered that others were agreeing? Some people will say nothing, or even give the appearance they agree, because they care about what other people say. But if someone was to stand up for justice, people would go along with that, too.

Information, bad or good, cascades, creating more good or bad information. Rumors get started, and they're hard to dislodge. That's why studies show that many jurors assume that if someone is arrested they must be guilty — after all, someone thought they were guilty enough to arrest. Where there's smoke, there's fire.

So maybe we're seeing information cascade going in two directions. When Jesus sent his disciples to get a colt he acted like a king. He instructed the disciples to tell whoever might protest when they commandeered a beast of burden that the master had need of it. Perhaps word got around — the king is coming! And the more people shouted, the more believed, until everyone was shouting, despite the protests of the religious authorities.

The word spread through Jerusalem on this Passover season that the king was in their midst and that his answers confounded the wise and cowed the powerful and brought low the rich. Bring the jubilee!

How, then, did the cries for his crucifixion get started? We know there were those who were paid to be false witnesses — why not a few who cried aloud for his blood? Others would follow. They always do. Soon the information was cascading and people were deriding the one who had stood so high in their estimation.

Isn't it the truth that the public loves to watch the meteoric rise of a person from obscurity to fame, and they love even more the spectacular fall?

So that's how people act when they know others are watching. But how did they really feel? How would they have felt if they'd paused a moment, examined Jesus for who he is, who he claims he is, how he acts, and what he does?

The same goes for you. Close your eyes. Forget we are here together, the church of Jesus Christ, and think about what you have heard and read about this man, Jesus. Think about how you have encountered him in your life. Consider what the Lord has done for you in the high moments and the low moments.

How do you feel about Jesus? Will you hail him as your king? Or will you cast him from the throne of your life?

What's the real answer? What's the real answer you give in your heart of hearts? Not an answer you give because other people are watching. Which side are you on?

Let's go back to the familiar scene of Jesus entering Jerusalem in triumph, which we associate with Palm Sunday. Picture the triumphant entry in your mind. What do you see?

Maybe you see the donkey. Maybe you see animals and children — actors know to avoid them. They take away the focus. People can't help but look at animals and children. There are plenty of animals in the familiar nativity scene — fortunately there's also a baby, or we'd never hear about Jesus.

Yet oddly enough in this scene the donkey doesn't overshadow Jesus. The donkey is essential to the story. If you were there you'd be surprised to find out that people are not surprised by a king riding a donkey. They rather expect it. What does this mean?

It means they knew their Bible. Especially their Zechariah. He was one of the most popular prophets of the day, and he'd been involved in a little Information Cascade over 500 years before. The people of God had been taken away into exile, into Babylon, their temple destroyed. They saw their nation destroyed — but even though they were taken away from the land, they did not lose their identity. They learned to be faithful without land, without a temple,

161

without a king — because they still had a God who was not tied to a land, to a building, or to any human conception of power.

Nevertheless, they remembered the glory of their temple, and when the Babylonians were conquered by the Persians and the people were sent back home, their dreams came true. At last, they were going to rebuild their temple. Soon. But first they needed to get settled again, to till the land, build houses, and raise families. The restoration of the temple was put off a month, a year, then many years.

Sixteen years went by with no work done. They had no king. They were depressed. Then God called out two prophets, Haggai and Zechariah, who called the people back to this great task and worked side by side with them to begin the restoration. It would be a long project that would ultimately take centuries to complete, but it was starting that mattered. Zechariah's words were part of the Information Cascade that got the people out of their tracks and back to work until suddenly everyone was involved.

Zechariah was a very popular prophet. His words were so well known that people could quote them from memory. In addition to encouraging the people to get back to work on the temple, he also spoke about a coming king, an eternal king. And Zechariah is quoted by the gospel writers more than any other Hebrew prophet in their accounts of Holy Week.

Here's what Zechariah said about the coming king, and this is why it was no surprise to the people that he rode on a donkey:

"Lo, your king comes to you, triumphant and victorious is he, humble and riding on a donkey, on a colt, the foal of a donkey" (Zechariah 9:9).

The conqueror comes, not on a war horse, but a donkey. He is a bringer of true peace. Everything is unfolding as God intends.

That's a lot harder than it looks.

Look at the donkey. Hallelujah. The people see their Savior, their meal ticket, their way out of their misery. They see the one who has all the answers. Hooray!

It probably looks different from on top of the donkey. We have no way of getting inside the mind of Jesus; yet he told us enough in his gospel discourses for us to guess what he saw looking out from on top of the donkey. Beyond the cheering crowds and the waving palm branches, sure signs that they saw him as a conqueror.

Jesus saw controversy, Gethsemane, and Golgotha.

No ... on.

There are times when we must grit our teeth and go just a little longer. The curtain will lift, there will be a silver rain, and a quick sunrise. There will be a dawn. Weeping may tarry for the night but joy will come with the morning ... on.

The temptation is to stop just a little short. The resistance gets greatest the further we go. There are barriers right before we reach glory. In *The Divine Comedy*, the poet, Dante, places a wall of burning glass right before the Earthly Paradise. He must walk through the fire before the glory. Every athlete knows there's a place in every contest where we struggle to go on. That's why the Greeks called it the *agon*, the word from which we get agony. There's a barrier before us that we must plod through before we get to glory. No ... on.

Regardless of what happens, say no to despair. Go on.

From where will we find this strength? How can we keep going when for now we see through a glass darkly, when we live with hope and to all appearances our hope is unfounded because the way is so dark.

The play, *Waiting for Godot*, by a then-obscure writer, Samuel Beckett, was first produced in France in 1953. It was soon famous worldwide, despite the fact that in its two acts nothing seemed to happen. In Act 1, two tramps met on a road to wait for a man named Godot. They mark time by discussing the scriptures, art, and their situation. At the end of the first act, a boy comes to tell them that Godot will not come today but will surely come tomorrow. The same thing happens at the end of the second act.

Though the play, which seemed to many to mirror the emptiness of the postwar years, seemed infused with despair (as well as a great deal of laughter) most of those who watched were nevertheless filled with a strange sense of hope. No matter how senseless the situation, we go on.

Hope. It's what we have.

163

On Palm Sunday, we see beyond the cross to the king — but which king do we proclaim? How self-serving is our image of Jesus? Certainly those who proclaimed Jesus the king on that first Palm Sunday had their own ideas of who he is.

Jesus has been seen differently in every age, and oddly enough Jesus ends up looking just like us. The Jesus I know, we hear, would never stand for us. But the Jesus we follow uncomfortably refuses to fit under any political or theological placard. He is the Lord, not our follower. We cannot simply pick and choose those parts of the gospel that confirm our pet notions. We must follow.

Proclaim Jesus as Lord — but not as convenient, easy, or clearly on our side. Follow, to find out if you're on his side. Don't wait to see which way the Information Cascade is flowing. Go against the tide. Stand up, whether you are standing with the crowd or not. Don't wait to see what others are saying or doing. Make up your own mind — for Jesus, for the cross, and for the resurrection glory.

It's going to be a rough week — but in the end it will be glorious. Amen.

Holy Ground

The Bible — under $10 if you do a little shopping.

Energy — read under natural sunlight and your only cost is the overpriced floofy coffee you bought from that boutique coffee bar — what? $5 or $6.

Reading John 13 and living like Jesus — priceless!

Post-Civil-War America was a country anxious to read about how the other half lived. There was a great appetite for reading, and the many periodicals of the era filled their pages with breathless accounts of what other people were doing.

Phebe Gibbons was a well-known writer for women's magazines, and her series on *The Plain People*, describing groups such as the Amish and the Mennonites who even back in the nineteenth century were living differently than the rest of society, was very popular.

When Gibbons caught a train to Lancaster County in 1871 to visit a Dunker Love Feast she prepared herself to enter what she thought would be a strange world. As a reporter for a major magazine she intended to write about what would no doubt be a strange, perhaps even bizarre, practice by an obscure religious sect. She had heard only rumors about the foot washing and the large meal that accompanied communion for the group known as German Baptist Brethren, or Dunkers.

What she experienced was the equivalent of a three-day slumber party.

The Love Feast was quite different than other religious practices of the day. It stemmed from the peculiar theological synthesis of the Dunkers — part Anabaptist, part Pietist, and fully determined to implement those ordinances that they found in scripture as the result of joint Bible study.

Their reading of John's version of the Last Supper mandated both a full meal and a footwashing service. John 13:14-15 indicated to the Dunkers that Jesus had commanded they wash each other's feet. Moreover, the meal, therefore, did not precede or follow worship. It was worship, and was as essential to communion as breaking the bread and drinking the cup. So Dunkers from all over the area would come together to eat good solid food, break bread, and attempt to follow Jesus as closely as they could.

However, Phebe Gibbons discovered that Lancaster Love Feast, beyond its obviously different theological underpinnings, was surprising for a number of other reasons. She thought of the Dunkers as a quiet, homogenous, Plain People.

The Love Feast was multicultural. She was astonished to discover folks named Murphy back when the Irish were nearly as reviled as blacks. It was filling. The food and coffee never stopped. It was multigenerational. Venerable patriarchs and matriarchs held court, to be sure, but children hollered during worship ("Want Pappy, want Pappy," one toddler complained while mom struggled with him), infants were breastfed, teens courted. Relatives, friends, and relative strangers mixed freely together as one family.

It was, in short, a feast based on love.

Gibbons was surprised to discover that even as an outsider she was drawn into everything — endless cups of hot coffee and plates of sweet pie, as well as hearty meals, sermons in German and English, inspiring hymn singing, good fellowship, and a giggly sleepover in the church attic with the women — the men were sleeping only a few feet away beyond a partition.

In some ways Gibbons description of a nineteenth-century Love Feast can seem just as exotic and strange to modern Christians as it did then. But there was one essential point that is easy to overlook. Easter may be a movable feast, but communion is planted firmly on holy ground. Take your shoes off.

But what sort of holy ground? How different from what the world calls holy ground. In this era of religious separatism, of fundamentalist fanatics willing to take someone's life to protect their turf, the breaking of the bread, the sharing of the cup, however you choose to perform it, is sacred yet totally safe.

The best thing of all is that we don't have to kill anybody to preserve our holy ground from infidels or interlopers. Just the opposite, this is a place where all people can come together, remove their shoes, and meet Jesus.

First-century Christians paid a great price for their separatism from the world. And around the world there are still places where Christianity is outlawed and believers pay a great price for their stand. Yet they did this willingly, risking limb and life while we who are free to worship sometimes can't even get out of our tracks on a Sunday morning to come praise the King of kings.

Why? Why would they risk all these things?

Like the credit card commercial, they can probably put a price on all the things they no longer have access to, but they've found their community to be priceless.

Priceless.

Jesus is calling us to something new, something shocking. And there's an urgency to it all. "Jesus knew that his hour had come to depart from this world and go to the Father. Having loved his own who were in the world, he loved them to the end" (John 13:1).

Jesus loved them to the end. The Greek is *eis telos*, meaning "to the finish" and "to the full extent." Jesus loved them as much as he could as long as he could. This was demonstrated in the foot washing and in giving his life.

And loving them to the end, he was about to do something new — he was going to wash their feet. This menial task was always performed either by oneself for oneself, or by a slave coerced to do this. People did not wash the feet of a social inferior. A teacher did not wash the feet of his disciples. It didn't happen.

Jesus did it, to show them that there is nothing we who are God's children will not do for each other, to demonstrate the love of God. Most of the disciples are too shocked to say anything, but

Peter is having none of it. Nevertheless Jesus warns him that unless he lets Jesus continue he will have no part of him.

Afterward, Jesus took advantage of the teaching moment.

> *Do you know what I have done to you? You call me Teacher and Lord — and you are right, for that is what I am. So if I, your Lord and Teacher, have washed your feet, you also ought to wash one another's feet. For I have set you an example, that you also should do as I have done to you.* — John 13:12-15

New ground ... holy ground. But sometimes we just can't let go of the past. The children of Israel were leaving slavery behind but they took with them a longing for what had been, a romanticized version of a past that never existed. There was nothing good about slavery, yet time and again they would lose sight of that bleak existence and make it sound like nothing short of heaven.

Jesus lived the life of service and selflessness that he wants his disciples to share — and it is in sharing it together that we enter into the priceless life. You can't buy this stuff. But you can get it.

Hospitality is at the heart of the footwashing in this story. Jesus appears as both servant and host. This hospitality is even shared with Judas who is undeserving. He will not be excused until later. He receives just as much attention from Jesus as the others. The passage tells us that Judas already has the devil in his heart. This betrayal is not only heinous, but takes place against a cosmic background. Huge forces are at play that are greater than anything we have ever experienced.

No one present, it seems, can fully understand the gravity of what is taking place. The Son of God, divinity in human form, is bending a knee in service to the created. This bending down, this girding around the waist, is uncomfortable. It shows us in miniature what it means for God to fit into a human-sized box.

It's impossible to fully understand. Jesus tells them that the Holy Spirit will give them understanding of the event later. But you don't have to understand how a dish was cooked to thank your host for what was served. Will you deny your host? Jesus wouldn't let Peter say, "No, please, no thank you." Don't turn your host down.

The biggest price we have paid to gather for this weeknight service is a little inconvenience. Perhaps we're taping a favorite show. Perhaps we have left a comfortable chair or forgone, at least for a few minutes, a bowl of ice cream. Most people are planning to go to Easter services, if they are going at all. They are considering what they will wear, how they will be seen, and what others will think. I'm sure the disciples wondered what others would think if they stumbled on the upper room and saw the great teacher Jesus washing the feet of his pupils.

We have received an invitation to intimacy with the eternal, a brand new relationship. God calls us into a new relationship and there's no telling what it means. Jesus offers himself in love on our behalf. There's no telling where this will end.

Nearly 2,000 years into the Christian experiment we seem to agree that communion remains essential. We disagree about how it is to be performed, with whom, when, and how often. We believe this is what Jesus told us to do, and that's good enough.

In a sense we're all correct. Anytime God's people come together to obey Jesus we are gathering on that holy ground.

Jesus turned the world upside down when he took on the role of a slave and washed the disciples' feet. The common meal of the early Christian church was just as revolutionary. The Roman empire was every bit as our age: rich and poor, slave and free, male and female, Jew and Gentile, Roman and Celt. The ancient church cultural, economic, ethnic, and gender lines.

An old Dunker woman named Julia Gilbert (1844-1934) put it best. A single woman crippled by a childhood disease in what was then a patriarchal church, she challenged the practice of the German Baptist Brethren of allowing men to break bread with each other while insisting sisters have the bread broken for them by an elder. Time and again she tried to get her church and district to send queries to the Dunker Annual Meeting where the elders debated practice and theology, but she went unheard for half a century. Finally, in 1910, she spoke on the floor of the annual meeting and explained why she wanted the practice changed. She said: "We want to be in touch with Jesus." She won the day.

We still want to be in touch with Jesus. We still want to be in that upper room. We want to be close to Jesus in his darkest hour. Come all ye faithful, come and adore. Amen.

You Are Here

Maybe you've seen the drawing on a T-shirt or poster. There's a picture of our Milky Way Galaxy, swirling like a pinwheel in the depths of space, with an arrow pointing to the periphery of one of the arms. Printed alongside the arrow are the words: "You Are Here."

There's perspective for you. Our earth spinning around an inconsequential sun on the edge of an average galaxy, a swirling mass so great that you cannot distinguish our star from any other. You are here.

That might seem a little depressing, or funny, or awe-inspiring, depending on your perspective, but those words can also be helpful. When we are especially confused about our location it helps to have a map that marks our position with a star or an X, and proclaims, "You are here!" Once we're oriented in this way we can begin our journey more intelligently.

Think of those occasions when you've been in a large mall, or a cavernous government office, a museum, and you're lost, confused, more than a little embarrassed, and perhaps even a little afraid — but then you see a map, pointing out exactly where you are, with those comforting words "You are here." Suddenly you're okay.

Wouldn't it be nice if there was a chart of your life with an arrow and the words, "You are here"?

There is.

It's called Good Friday. There's a cross on a hill that's suddenly not so far away anymore. There's a great drama going on, it's a nightmare, and you're in it, and there's no waking up, not just yet. Good Friday means we've got to ride this out, all the way to the end.

You are here.

You are here. Right in the middle of the crucifixion story. You are here. There's no need to ask the way to the cross. You are here — and you ought to be clear about what his journey means and what means you intend to use to get where you're going.

Now, find yourself in the story. From what angle are you seeing everything? Are you on the cross? Are you suffering? Are you one of the disciples who have deserted the cross? Are you one of the women who have stood by Jesus through the worst of it?

Or — are you in the crowd? Are you looking on, not sure what to think? Were you one of those calling for his execution?

You're probably thinking, *No I'm not. I'm not there. I'm not in the crowd. At worst I'm one of the disciples. I'm a little afraid, but I'll be back. I'll be forgiven. I would never let Jesus down. I wouldn't be shouting crucify him. I wouldn't —*

Really?

Have you never taken a look at a clothing label and wondered if it had been made in a sweat shop, here in this land or overseas, and decided there was nothing you could do about it anyway?

Have you never wondered how your food was grown and who suffered to keep your costs down?

Did you hear about the torture and mistreatment of prisoners in our midst, about the prison scandals overseas and because you were so afraid for yourself you dismissed the images and decided those people were just getting what they deserved?

Have you ever heard the statistics about the high rate of incarceration for people of one race and the low rate for those of another race for the same crimes and not been outraged?

Does it matter to you that there are people working below the minimum wage?

What did Caiaphas say?

172

You know nothing at all! You do not understand that it
is better for you to have one man die for the people
than to have the whole nation destroyed.
— John 11:49-50

That has nothing to do with Jesus. It has nothing to do with me standing there calling for his crucifixion.

Hmmm. What did Jesus say: That people would plead with him at the end of time.

"Lord, when was it that we saw you hungry or thirsty
or a stranger or naked or sick or in prison, and did not
take care of you?" Then he will answer them, "Truly I
tell you, just as you did not do it to one of the least of
these, you did not do it to me."
— Matthew 25:44-45

But there's hope. *If* you are uncomfortable — *if* you are the object of derision, you might be on the right side. *If* you think that at least you'd want to be there, even if you're not sure you would be, there's hope.

You are invited to stand next to the cross. It is difficult, painful, just plain awful. So practice. How often does one hear things like: I don't want to go to the nursing home, I hear, because it depresses me.

It was awfully depressing next to the cross as well.

There is hope. Because if we admit we are weak, then we're open to God's transforming power. As long as we think we can do it on our own we're setting ourselves up for one amazing fall.

Think of the women. Roman and Judean society discounted the place of women, who were not even allowed to be witnesses in court because they were not considered reliable. But as the fourth-century Christian orator, John Chrysostom, said: "But the women stood by the cross, and the weaker sex then appeared the manlier so entirely henceforth were all things transformed."

God uses our weakness so that his strength is revealed. The weak made strong, the strong revealed weak. We are transformed by the cross. We rise to the occasion or we don't. We stand by

173

God's suffering people — or we don't. Either way, you don't have a choice. There's no escaping the fact that —
You are here!
So you might as well throw yourself upon the Lord and beg for his strength, which is sufficient for all things, because on this day of days, we have nothing else going for us.

What keeps us going when there is no going,
When there is no knowing, when nothing is showing,
When everyone's sinking, and no one is thinking
Of anything else but themselves? And the winking
Of those who claim power means power is shrinking
For all of the rest of us. Something is stinking.

What keeps us going? There's simply no knowing,
And no one is throwing a bone to God's own,
The poor and the pained and the door that sustained
Us with thoughts of the fields of green, so serene
is simply not anywhere there. Nor now seen, it's obscene.

What keeps us riding Jerusalem's tiding that God's still
*   abiding*
And God is still siding with poor, there abiding?
Oh, there will be loss, and against us they toss the lies
*   and disguise and resize what is true with their sties*
*   but the fact still remains*
That the boss is right there in plain sight on the cross.

And that's why we just keep on going without any knowing
Despite all the pain that they send at the end where the
*   X marks the spot*
What you got is the tomb, there's a whole lot of room,
Cause it's just been vacated, the debt's been placated,
*   the collector's are sated*
The Word raised on high when the Lord was berated
In plain sight of all paid the price for the fall
And is risen

With that knowing with nothing else showing
We somehow have found the strong will to keep going.
The loss on the cross will thrill and instill in us will
To triumph, harrumph, because everything's covered
    in glory,
And that, friends, in truth, is the sum of my story.

Amen.

Another Mary, Another Martha

December 6, 2002, was my birthday, and I had no idea what a great birthday present was in the offing, if I had just waited. I'm a Lakers fan, and when I got home that evening the Lakers were down 70-46. I was disgusted. At the start of the fourth quarter they were down by 28 points. I didn't wait to see what would happen. I turned off the set.

I missed one of the greatest comebacks in basketball history, as the Lakers won 105-103. It was my own fault. I wasn't constant. I wasn't there.

In order to witness life's comebacks, in order to be a part of a miracle, sometimes you have to be there, be present, during the tough times.

A basketball match is really only fun and games. But there are some serious moments in life that we are called to be present for. I can't imagine a more serious moment than the crucifixion of Jesus.

The Bible doesn't tell us, but I sometimes wonder what some of the apostles said when questioned by new Christians about Jesus. They could tell these folks about the miracles, about the Sermon on the Mount, about the transfiguration — but they couldn't say much about the crucifixion, because they weren't there.

Those who did not wait beneath the cross — how do you think they felt later when they were asked? They were not there for the crucifixion. And they were not the first ones there when Jesus rose from the dead.

Who was? The scriptures are pretty clear. The women waited beneath the cross. The women, like Mary of Magdala, were the ones who were the first on the scene at the resurrection, because they were faithful in good times and bad.

There's a statement that's important. Only if you are willing to be as faithful as the women, who go to the tomb with no hope, to do their duty, will you be able to meet and greet the resurrected Lord.

Sometimes as we imagine the scene, we think to ourselves, look, they're about to meet Jesus. They're going to see the risen Lord.

Only they don't know it. They didn't get up that morning with heavy hearts and pack up the spices and the wrappings, then set out in the dim light before dawn to perform the funeral duties that had been neglected mere hours before when the tomb was shut before the sabbath, expecting a miracle. No, they were doing their duties.

Jesus is waiting for them. Jesus is waiting for all of those who are at their task, at their post — not the ones who are looking for a miracle, but those who are performing the miracle of obedience and service in the worst imaginable conditions.

Only if you are willing to stay faithful to your faith when there is no hope, when it makes no sense, when you see no sense in it, when the world is against you, and you stay faithful anyway, that's where you meet Jesus.

The caregiver, the one who carries the cross for others, the one willing to sacrifice a life for a friend — the message of John for you this morning is: You will see Jesus. You will behold God.

So who is the first apostle? Who is the first one to proclaim that Jesus is risen? You got John. You got James. You got Peter. You got Paul. But you don't got the right answer. You can slice it any way you want to, but there's no denying one thing — Mary of Magdala, a woman of substance and status, was the first apostle, the emissary of Jesus to proclaim the overwhelming news that Jesus is risen, Jesus is risen indeed.

Mary and the other women, the faithful disciples, the ones ignored by the church in later centuries, marginalized in the histories, are represented in the gospels as the ones who proclaimed the risen Lord.

178

The best part is their testimony wouldn't have been accepted in court. Not in their day. In the Roman world, women did not appear in court because in that male-dominated world their testimony was not considered reliable. How ironic, and appropriate, that God chose what was unacceptable to the world, to be witnesses for the truth!

We see elsewhere in the gospel of John that the transformation can begin even before the resurrection. The best example of this is the story of Martha and Mary ... the second story of Martha and Mary.

Jorge Maldonado, in his book, *Even in the Best of Families*, helps us to look at the story of Mary and Martha.[1] Most Christians know the two sisters from their appearance in the gospel of Luke, 10:38-42. Most Christians tend to like Martha. She was the homeowner who entertained Jesus and his disciples when they traveled south to Judea. It's not like there was a Holiday Inn Express waiting for them on their trips to Jerusalem, even assuming they'd have had the money to pay for one. Jesus and the disciples depended on good old-fashioned Middle Eastern hospitality to take care of their needs.

In Luke, the story is simple. While her sister Mary sat at the feet of Jesus listening to pearls of wisdom, Martha knew that someone had to plunk dinner down on the table, and that the chores weren't going to do themselves.

You may recall that Jesus told Martha that Mary was right to put the spiritual things first. What most of us don't recall is what happened to the pair in the gospel of John. John's gospel is written more from the viewpoint of Jesus' Judean ministry. We see that Martha must have paid attention to what Jesus said about spirituality being the better part, because when her brother Lazarus died she makes the most amazing statements. She says, "... I know that God will give you whatever you ask of him" (John 11:22) and "Yes, Lord, I believe that you are the Messiah, the Son of God, the one coming into the world" (11:27). She makes the spiritual statements and utters the second most important confession of faith in the New Testament. (We'll tell you what the most important confession of faith was during next week's message.)

In the gospel of John you either get it about Jesus or you don't. Martha gets it. Before this confession she scolds Jesus for having arrived so late. Isn't it amazing? Job scolds God. Habakkuk takes God to task. Martha stands before the Lord of life and gives him what for.

Take God seriously. Take God personally. Talk back and live.

In the Roman world, the purpose of biography was to show that people never changed. The great were always great, the evil were always evil, the ordinary were always ordinary. You were always what you were and you would always be that way. The fruit doesn't fall far from the tree. What can you expect?

Not Christian biography. It's all about transformation so incredible that Paul needs a Barnabas to vouch for him, and no one is beyond God's saving love. Martha's can change, an apostle like Peter who ran away and denied Jesus can change — and we can change.

Others are ready to quantify and qualify, ready to limit the depth and breadth of God's love — but we remain convinced, like the apostle Paul.

> *[I am convinced] that neither death, nor life, nor angels, nor rulers, nor things present, nor things to come, nor powers, nor height, nor depth, nor anything else in all creation, will be able to separate us from the love of God in Christ Jesus our Lord.* — Romans 8:38-39

As I said in the beginning, in order to be present at this transformation, in order to witness the resurrection, in order to take part in the great Christian drama, you have to be found at your post. You need to be doing what you need to be doing.

Live like the resurrection matters. Be ready for transformation. Don't turn the channel. Proclaim the risen Jesus. Amen.

---

1. Jorge Maldonado, *Even in the Best of Families: The Family of Jesus and other Biblical Families* (New York: World Council of Churches, 1994).

Believing Thomas

They say history is written by the victors, but I'm not always so sure. The forces of the Union roundly and rightfully defeated the forces of slavery known as the Confederacy, but 140 years later I'm not sure it's the victors who tell the whole story.

Some things are known by their Union name. The decisive battle of September 17, 1862 is known as the Battle of Antietam, not Sharpsburg, as the Confederates knew it.

Then there's the little-known Battle of Monocacy. Get off Interstate 70 at Fredericksburg, Maryland, and follow the signs and you'll learn how a raw group of Union soldiers held off crack Confederate soldiers for a single day, preventing them from getting to an undefended Washington DC before it could be refortified. But there are monuments everywhere funded by the Daughters of the Confederacy that call it a Confederate victory. Their monuments went up first. Victory?

Think about the famous charge that took place during the Battle of Gettysburg. Generals Pickett and Pettigrew led 15,000 on a doomed march, but it came to be known only as Pickett's charge. Moreover, despite the fact that it was a bad decision and a horrible waste of life, it has been commemorated for its gallantry and bravery.

A few months later, General Grant would lose 15,000 of his own troops in the Battle of St. Petersburg, but it is remembered as an example of cold-hearted butchery, not Southern gallantry.

The name given to something or someone matters. Your parents were wrong when they said, "Sticks and stones may break my bones, but words will never hurt me." Words can hurt.

I call this to mind because one of the characters in today's Bible passage is referred to by a name that is neither given to him by Jesus, nor is it used in scripture. I am referring to Doubting Thomas.

That's a defeatist name. Where is the victory of the resurrection in a name like that?

Now maybe he would prefer Doubting Thomas to the name sometimes used, Thomas the Twin. All twins are different but many prefer to be known as individuals rather than simply as part of a pair. Maybe he would have preferred to be known as a doubter instead of just a twin.

Note that the word doubt appears nowhere in the story in the Greek. Ignore the English translation. The Greek says, "Do not be unbelieving but believing." Unbelieving is different than doubting. And in John the difference is crucial.

There is no agreement either about exactly when, how, and why the gospel of John was written, but some guess that John was writing to Christians in Ephesus. The believers in that city had two radically different opinions about Jesus. There are some believers in Ephesus, evidently, who believe fully in the human Jesus and some who believe fully in the divine Jesus. John wanted these two groups to realize it's not a matter of either/or, but both/and. Both human and divine.

John is written to address the need for both the divine and human Jesus. Jesus is the example we are to follow but is also the one with the power to forgive sins. Jesus is the one in touch with both people and with God. Jesus is the bridge. He stands at the intersection of heaven and earth. But there were evidently Christians of Jewish background who thought of him as just a great teacher and the others from the Greek world who thought of him as a spiritual presence.

In John's time the first group was best exemplified by those in the community at Qumran, associated today with the Dead Sea Scrolls. They preached and practiced radical obedience to the Law of Moses in Qumran. At the other end of the spectrum were the gnostics, those who practiced a mystery religion involving secret knowledge that was gained by initiates through long study and rejection of the physical world — body and spirit — human and divine. John made it clear that these differing understandings intersected in the real world in the life and work of Jesus.

John called the church to radical obedience to the law of Love, the commandments of Jesus Christ. There is walking in light or darkness in both. John is writing with regards to both Jewish and Gentile mysticism — more obedience to the letter of the law than ever, escape from the world, and more obedience to the Spirit of the law than ever, disconnected from the world. John wants us placed firmly in the world. This is what is real. Jesus is at the intersection.

In the gospel of John, believing in Jesus means you get it. It's not just seeing, it's not just intellectual assent, it's understanding what you see to the core of your being. It means you are ready at last to change everything about your life because you get it.

When Jesus tells Thomas he must move from unbelief to belief he's hoping he'll get it.

This story takes place a week after the revelation of Easter. Jesus had appeared in the midst of the disciples and blessed them with peace — shalom — perfect wholeness in every aspect of their lives. They were all there — but Thomas. When the others enthused about the wonder of the resurrection, Thomas replies, "Unless I see the mark of the nails in his hands, and put my finger in the mark of the nails and my hand in his side, I will not believe" (v. 25).

Actually, I can't say I blame Thomas. Remember, when it came to doubting, the apostles come first, all of them. They doubted the women. They doubted Mary Magdalene. Thomas just doubted some runaways, the disciples who abandoned and denied Jesus in his hours of pain and suffering.

Do you remember the first day of summer vacation? No shoes, no shirt, no getting up until you wanted to. And the best part was that a week later it was still true!

A week later — Easter is still true, but Thomas has not received the memo — until now. Again, Jesus shares the peace that passes understanding. As Thomas, at least in my imagination, stands there dumbfounded, Jesus says, "Put your finger here and see my hands. Reach out your hand and put it in my side. Do not doubt but believe" (v. 27).

What follows is the most extraordinary confession of faith in the gospel of John or maybe anywhere, and it shows why it's wrong to refer to him as Doubting Thomas. That would be a defeat. These are not the words of a doubter. These are the words of someone who gets it. That's why I prefer to call him Believing Thomas, a name of victory. Standing face-to-face with the risen Jesus he says, "My Lord and my God!" (v. 28).

That's it in a nutshell: Lord — example for my life, teacher, guide, mentor. God — the divine on earth. John begins his gospel by stating:

> *In the beginning was the Word, and the Word was with God, and the Word was God. He was in the beginning with God. All things came into being through him, and without him not one thing came into being. What has come into being in him was life, and the life was the light of all people.*   — John 1:1-4

Later, he states, very clearly, "And the Word became flesh and lived among us ..." (1:14).

Believing Thomas can be all things — Brave Thomas, Determined Thomas, Confessing Thomas, and Converting Thomas. There is a tradition in the early church that Thomas traveled as far as India to share the wonderful Word made flesh. That does not sound like the work of a doubter.

So what name do you claim? Believer? Unbeliever? Jesus has yet another name for you. Speaking to Thomas — and to us as well — Jesus says, "Have you believed because you have seen me? Blessed are those who have not seen and yet have come to believe" (v. 29).

There's your new name — blessed. If you want it. And why wouldn't you? The world hurls all sorts of names at us for the things we do and things we have never done. Epithets are flung here and there, medical diagnoses, pop psychology, clichés. But Jesus calls us blessed because we have not seen, yet we believe. We get it.

184

We get it that Jesus is the Lord of life. In him there is light and the darkness is unable to overcome it. We see lives changed. We come to know peace.

This peace enables us to do all things. The late Clarence Jordan, a minister, a scholar, and a Civil Rights activist who founded an interracial community in the South during an era when this was not only foolhardy but downright dangerous, translated the scriptures from the Greek to the vernacular of the South. He called this the Cotton Patch Version. He translated a verse in another one of John's writings, which we call 1 John 3:18, in the following way: "My little ones, let's not *talk* about love. Let's not *sing* about love. Let's put love into *action* and make it *real*."

If we believe, if we get it, then we can take this love of Jesus and put it into action and make it real.

Hate can be transformed by love. We see this no better demonstrated than with the relationship between the United States and the German people. There were two brutal wars fought between those nations in the twentieth century resulting in the deaths of millions of people. In some ways we can trace the origins of the second war to the harsh treatment of the vanquished by the victors after the first war.

However, though these two nations have been competitors, they have not fought a war in the sixty years hence, and it seems inconceivable that such a war could ever take place. Why? First of all Christian groups were actively involved in programs of rebuilding and reconciliation work among the ruins in Europe. Hatred was repaid with kindness.

More important, it was the national policy of the United States to study the conquered enemies, even before the war ended, and through what became known as the Marshall Plan to rebuild the economic and political structure of the defeated nations, while preserving their dignity and autonomy.

That's getting it — that a war, however justified, is not a long-term solution, and that sacrifice and love, even for one's enemies, is the true work of Jesus.

This passage closes with these words:

*Now Jesus did many other signs in the presence of his
disciples, which are not written in this book. But these
are written so that you may come to believe that Jesus
is the Messiah, the Son of God, and that through believing you may have life in his name.*
— John 20:30-31

I find these some of the most frustrating words of scripture.
I'm just getting started. I want to know more. After all, I can buy a
1,000-page or larger paperback novel at my grocery store or at the
airport with no problem. If the novel is well written it'll hold my
attention until I'm finished, at which point I'll just wish there's
more. The gospels are so short, comparatively. I want more. Indeed, John must have heard that often enough because eventually
he added one more chapter.

His point is well taken. It's not the length, but the effect that
matters. John could have given me a thousand pages but if I don't
get it, if I don't believe, if I don't start living right now as an Easter
person, it doesn't matter. These words are written so that we may
come to believe that Jesus is the Messiah, the Son of God — that's
the point of this story of Believing Thomas.

These words are written so that through believing, we may all
have life, eternal life, real life, in his name.

Because, after all, and to quote once more from this very short
and very important book, "For God so loved the world that he gave
his only Son, so that everyone who believes in him may not perish
but may have eternal life" (John 3:16). Amen.

186

Low-Carb Christians

It was over thirty years ago that someone handed me a book that seemed to have the answer to the greatest problem facing people like me — how to lose weight. The book promised a miracle cure with no pain. Eat all you want and lose more than you can imagine. The best thing was that this was secret knowledge. Those who read the book were right and everyone else was wrong, wrong, wrong. There was a special delight in being one of the elite, in knowing something no one else knew.

Let me emphasize right off the top that I am not a medical doctor and this sermon contains no medical advice. However, I am an expert in weight loss and weight gain, because I've had plenty of both over the course of my life. That's because I am a fat person. As an adult I've weighed as much as 300 and as little as 180. For the last twenty years I've tended to occupy a thirty-pound swing zone between 190 and 220. Every time I let my guard down I gain weight.

Rapidly.

So back when I was in college I felt like I was handed the secret to the universe. The book told me I could eat as much as I wanted, stuff myself, gorge myself, as long as I avoided the evil that threatened the universe as we know it — carbohydrates, otherwise known as carbs.

I could eat beef, chicken, pork, eggs, bacon, and more beef, chicken, pork, eggs, and bacon. I just couldn't eat bread, tortillas, cake, and almost all vegetables, ever again.

One thing we dieters hate is deprivation. I'm one of those people who eat only on those occasions when I'm happy, depressed, relaxed, stressed, celebrating, disappointed, on special occasions, church holidays, and in ordinary time. I hate to go without. So after I devoured this book (pardon the expression) I decided to give it a try. I was attending LaVerne College (that's what we called it in those days), and a table full of us decided that our cafeteria eating would include a hefty meat course and no green stuff.

The first day was great. I never felt so full, yet so virtuous. It wasn't long before it began to work. My pants were loose. Was this great or what? No exercise, no deprivation. No pain, plenty of gain.

I lasted a week. I just couldn't do it. I felt sick all the time. And I felt deprived. Even though I thought of myself as a meat eater in those days, I soon learned that it was easier to eat less of everything than to cut out everything of something. Abundance is something more, I learned, than simply stuffing yourself silly. It's having enough of everything.

A low-carb diet works because of malnutrition. If you deny the body something essential it begins to waste away. It is not meant to be a permanent lifestyle.

Since then I've learned the true secret to weight loss — eat less and exercise more. Sorry, it's that simple.

In order for this arcane knowledge to work for me I belong to an organization that practices this as a lifestyle because I've learned I'm not a solitary dieter. I need to be present and accountable to others for this to really work.

I'm not a solitary Christian, either. I need to be present and accountable to the body of Christ in order for the faith to work.

I refuse to be a low-carb Christian.

Toward the end of the first Christian century there were those who claimed to have special "knowledge" of Jesus. They considered themselves the elite. They were called gnostics, from the Greek word *gnosis* for "knowledge." These gnostics believed that Jesus was all spirit and no flesh, that he only appeared to die on the cross, and that the resurrected Jesus was Spirit only. Our own best destiny, therefore, is to renounce the physical things of this world and embrace the spiritual, in part by acquiring strange and arcane knowledge. Spirit is good. Body is bad.

To combat this elitism, the resurrection stories of the gospels make it clear that Jesus was resurrected with a physical body. That's why he ate with his disciples, to dispel this picture of a "spiritual" Lord. The body he wears is different in some difficult to quantify way, but it's definitely Jesus and he's eating food. Body and spirit, still grounded in prayer and in practice.

In today's passage, the disciples seem to be still struggling, despite the overwhelmingly wonderful experience of the resurrection. Just as we can't get stuck in fad diets and we need to learn how to eat in the real world, so in our spiritual lives we can't stay on the mountaintop but have to learn how to cherish Jesus in our everyday lives.

The disciples have gone back to work and work isn't going well. After coming up empty all night they must be exhausted, and that's when this stranger tries to tell them how to fish.

Notice what happens when we let Jesus advise us in our everyday lives — suddenly the disciples are the victims of abundance! That's when Peter realizes: "It is the Lord!" (v. 7).

Peter swims to shore, and the others follow with a wonderful catch. That's when they discover that the thing they've been working so hard for — Jesus has had all along. Jesus has already cooked a fish breakfast for them.

They eat together — bread and fish. It was the same meal that was crucial to Christianity's spread. Look at murals of the ancient Love Feast. Jews and Gentiles had different dietary constraints, but they could both eat bread and fish. The resurrection meal found its way to their shared table.

Keep in mind that in the Greek culture of the Roman Empire and the Hebrew way of thinking the natural world was a good thing, and God's gift of the body was good.

This is not the only resurrection story that emphasizes how we meet Jesus around the table. In the story of Jesus on the road to Emmaus, the two disciples who walk with him are so distraught about his death that they don't "see" Jesus even though he's walking alongside. It is not until they insist on showing him hospitality, and Jesus broke bread, that they recognized him.

They recognized Jesus in the breaking of the bread. The language is clearly reminiscent of the Love Feast, the meal we share together in remembrance of the sacrifice of Jesus. Sorry, but there's carbs involved here. In both the gospels of Luke and John, Jesus is seen eating with the believers. And that's where is he most recognizable.

In Luke 24:42 we read, "They gave him a piece of broiled fish ..." just as in John 21:13 the gospel says, "Jesus came and took the bread and gave it to them, and did the same with the fish." A balanced diet, protein and carbohydrates, and a new life.

The life of the resurrection is meant to begin now! That life is full of abundance. God doesn't seem to want us to miss out on any of it. Worship, prayer, love of nature, joy in activities, reading, writing, sowing, gardening, reaping, cooking, eating — it's all good. These things only become idols when we put them at the center of our world. As long as we keep God in the center, there is no problem with any of these things. Nor are we to consider ourselves purely spiritual beings who would do well to transcend burgers and fries. We've just got to keep everything in the proper perspective.

The apostle Paul quotes from pagan poets on several occasions. The world of literature is not closed to Christians. Jesus sends the fishers back out into the sea. There are feasts and more feasts. Paul plied his trade of tentmaker, perhaps to support himself, but also because as a well-rounded person it was important for him to be doing it as well as preaching.

Indeed, at the center of the Christian life was a table where male and female, rich and poor, Jew and Gentile, slave and free, met to break the same bread that Jesus blessed in the presence of the disciples at Emmaus. This is what was so very threatening to the empire of Rome. Theirs was a society of separations, where people kept to their place, acknowledged Caesar as Lord, and practiced stability. The Jesus life is one where we come together at one table, proclaim Jesus as Lord, and turn the world upside down. The wisdom of this world is folly, Paul says. The last shall be first and the first shall be last, Jesus proclaims.

The low-carb Christian wants to eliminate a good deal of the goodness of life — eating, drinking, friendship, love, sex, reading, running, simply breathing the air. The unbalanced life breeds fanatics, the sort who think the death or destruction of enemies advances God's cause. They strap on blinders and see one thing and one thing only. They are malnourished, without perspective, unable to appreciate the blankets of winter, the renewal of spring, the unabashed songs of love in Song of Songs, and the tempering reminders of Ecclesiastes that to everything there is a season and a time to every purpose under heaven.

The world offers pain, alienation, despair, and hopelessness. God offers pleasures, marvels, wonders, and joys. Meat and potatoes, asparagus and bread. Putting God first means getting it all back, and then some.

The temptation is to be like the world — fearful, hopeless, suspicious. But the rewards of embracing God and life is peace, not as the world gives us, but as God intends.

How could we have failed to see it? That's what the disciples asked who walked with Jesus for seven miles and never knew it was him, until the breaking of the bread. Why does it take communion, the washing of the feet, and the sharing of the meal, the bread and the cup, to remind those who come to the table that we are one people? How can we have failed to see in our brothers and sisters the bright light of Jesus who is walking with us always, who has never left us, and who will be with us always, even until the end of the age?

One final thought — the disciples didn't know it was Jesus but they insisted on hosting him for dinner anyway. They took in this stranger and came to know the Lord. In the old days, Christians always had a guest room — for tramps, hoboes, travelers, expected guests, and surprise visitors. The peace activist, M. R. Zigler, remembers that in the home he grew up in, known now as the Tunker House of Rockingham County, Virginia, the guest room was nearly always full. Tramps did not sleep in the barn. They had a meal at the table and a bed in a room.

How are you opening your heart, your home, your table, to the work of the Lord? In what way do you practice hospitality? We are all so afraid. If folks are not for us they must be against us. When it comes to our nation it's my way or the highway.

Bread — carbohydrates — the staff of life. Drawn from many fields, ground together by Christ, baked into one loaf, to sustain us, enrich us, fulfill us. What goodness, what mercy. Break the bread of Christ. See Jesus. Live abundantly — now. Amen.

Easter 4
John 10:22-30

How Much Of An Honor?

Whether you are in school, hanging around the water cooler at work, or just talking around the table at home or at the local restaurant, sooner or later certain questions get asked. They're theoretical in nature, nothing gets settled, but it's all for fun.

Questions like: If there was a fire in your home and you are able to assume everyone is safe, what is the one thing you would grab before you left?

It's a dumb question really, because if there's a fire you shouldn't grab anything. Go, go, go! Once power is lost everything will go dark and you may never find your way out. Smoke may choke you. So don't wait.

But, what if —

Okay, just for the sake of argument, what is the one thing you would grab?

Truth be told, if we have time to think about it, we'll grab two or three items, but what do you grab. What's crucial?

What is the one thing you need?

(Let parishioners talk about this for a moment.)

What sorts of things did you grab? What was the thing you needed?

Did it ever occur to you that there is only one thing we truly need? At least that was the view of at least one Bible writer — King David. In Psalm 23, he writes: "The Lord is my shepherd. I shall not want."

In other words, as long as he has the Lord, he doesn't need anything else. There is no need to grab anything if you have to run, because with God on your side you don't need anything.

David was a king. By the time he was the king he had pretty much everything, so it might have been easy to say this. But if he wrote the psalm when he was a shepherd, and didn't own much, maybe this was a real act of faith.

Sometimes we picture David, the young man, as the shepherd, watching over the sheep. We see only a moment, and it looks pretty attractive — but it's easier to romanticize labor when you don't have to perform it. Boy, we think, would I love the simple life.

Not if you actually have to live it!

A shepherd needs endurance, because nothing happens and it happens for hours. We're used to seeing that nice little painting, but that doesn't convey the absolute duration. A shepherd needs bravery to fight off predators. A shepherd needs knowledge and practical experience of what the sheep need. And did I mention endurance? Because the job just goes on and on and on.

We are familiar with the symbol of the good shepherd as a Christian symbol, but it was a pagan symbol as well. In the Gentile world, the good shepherd was often associated with Orpheus, the god of music. This seems like an echo of David as the good shepherd, since he was known for composing music of his own.

Psalm 23, so familiar to Christians as a funeral psalm, is much more. It's about more than the peace and serenity we seek when we are feeling blue. It's not just personal. Of course the Lord is *my* shepherd, and I will dwell in the house of the Lord forever.

In the midst of the sufferings and trials, my cup overflows. It's full. We're blessed. You can't save all those blessings. You get to enjoy them now.

If you try to carry a cup that is filled to the brim then you will probably spill some. It is necessary to drink some off the top before sharing it with others, or saving it, or setting it aside for later. Indeed, God's blessings are often for the moment. We are called to be spendthrifts with God's blessings in a manner that would be irresponsible if we were dealing with any other product. Spending like there is no tomorrow — there is no tomorrow.

It's true. My cup overflows with blessings. What more do we need?

Everyone is not as well off as we are. Those who are suffering injustice have a claim to God's blessings that is stronger than the smug and satisfied. They may be like the sheep mentioned by Jesus in his address to the Pharisees, who recognize the voice of their shepherd.

At the heart of these scriptures is the recognition that Jesus is Lord and that the ideal king is a shepherd, not a ruler with an iron fist. God is all powerful, but that power is tempered with mercy and understanding. It is brimming with blessings for today, not just for tomorrow. It's not just pie in the sky when we die, but the peace that passes understanding right now.

Despite the individualistic nature of the psalm, we must not forget that sheep are part of a flock and get their identity from the flock. And without a shepherd they're toast. God keeps us alive. God is the only necessity of life, which is what we were saying at the top of this message.

David saw himself as a shepherd with a lower case "s" while God is the real shepherd. Biblical kings like David were expected to be shepherds, not despots. They were expected to put the welfare of the people ahead of their own. They were there to shepherd the people toward prosperity. Kings were expected to provide protection and tranquility. The sheep would not have to worry about anything because the shepherd was watching over them.

In David's day shepherds had respect in symbol and in fact. By the time Jesus spoke about the shepherd in the first Christian century, their reputation had plummeted. The shepherds of old had owned their flock and of course were willing to give up their lives.

Predatory lending practices during the time of Jesus had driven many farmers from their land and shepherds from their flocks. The failing economy that favored the very rich at the expense of the poor and forced people to seek loans to keep their operations afloat. When both farmers and shepherds proved unable to keep up with their loans they lost farm and flock. When Jesus spoke about day laborers it was to an audience that included many of them, people

195

forced to hire out their services on a day-to-day basis with no guarantee of future work or of fair treatment.

Shepherds were now hirelings, and as Jesus suggests in this scripture, they don't have the motivation to lay down their lives for someone else's property. They were working for wages; not for the benefit of the flock. The shepherds were no longer viewed as kings but as vagabonds.

That's why it is so crucial that at the birth of Jesus the first witnesses to the glory were shepherds. Angels did not appear to the Emperor in Rome or the religious leaders in Jerusalem. They appeared to the dispossessed, who rushed to see this thing for themselves, before rushing back to watch over the flocks.

That's why it is important that Jesus called himself the good shepherd. He was, as always, demonstrating his identification with the poor, the outcast, the dispossessed, and those who were just trying to hang on. He reminded people that these shepherds should still be seen in a royal light.

Jesus, in talking about the good shepherd, tells us he is both shepherd and gate. He is the way. He loves the sheep and has compassion for them. He wants to gather them together and keep them safe from those who would take advantage of them.

One of the things that makes Jesus the ideal shepherd is that he is portrayed as one of the sheep, the Lamb of God in the gospel of John, the Lamb bearing the marks of slaughter in Revelation. As the Word was made flesh that dwelt among us, he understands our infirmity. He is one of us.

That's why Jesus can say that his sheep know the shepherd because in this case the shepherd *is* a sheep.

This is especially hopeful when the shepherd leads the sheep beyond the still waters, the stagnant waters, filled with pollution and threatening to kill us. Instead we are led to the springs of the water of life. At the end of time we see the Lamb bearing the marks of slaughter is on the throne, that's the shepherd, and all those murdered in the name of Jesus are doing fine, thank you very much, leading us through the stagnant water.

Think of what these images meant to God's people who traveled in dry lands. It's important to know the location of the next oasis.

Jesus wants his sheep to listen to him, to make right choices now, choices based not on what seems good this instant only, but for eternity. Here is a true and worthy guide, leading to the one who is worthy to open the seals that close up history. Thanks to the Lamb, history is now an open book!

We are called to be good shepherds in imitation of Jesus, but there are those among the flock who choose to take advantage of other sheep. They see their stewardship not as a chance to imitate Jesus, but to wield power and authority. They would be wise to think of the words of Ezekiel, who wrote to the leaders of the people, comparing them to shepherds, but also stating they had abused their positions.

> *Mortal, prophesy against the shepherds of Israel: prophesy, and say to them — to the shepherds: Thus says the Lord God: Ah, you shepherds of Israel who have been feeding yourselves! Should not shepherds feed the sheep? You eat the fat, you clothe yourselves with the wool, you slaughter the fatlings; but you do not feed the sheep. You have not strengthened the weak, you have not healed the sick, you have not bound up the injured, you have not brought back the strayed, you have not sought the lost, but with force and harshness you have ruled them. So they were scattered, because there was no shepherd; and scattered, they became food for all the wild animals.* — Ezekiel 34:2-5

Leaders among God's people can prove to be just the opposite of the ideal model presented in these words from Jesus. And never forget, these are not our sheep. God refers to them as "my sheep" in this passage (Ezekiel 34:6). Because of their poor stewardship Jesus speaks to them in tones of judgment.

A final word on this subject. These images of shepherd and sheep should teach us, if nothing else, something about humility. Those who live in the cities tend to idealize sheep just like we

197

idealize all of God's creatures, instead of accepting — and loving — them for who they are.

The late and much lamented church historian, Donald F. Durnbaugh, was known throughout the world for his high level of scholarship when it came to the Radical Reformation and Anabaptist studies. He was also known for his quick wit and dry sense of humor. Back in 1978 he spoke before a graduating class who were about to receive their Master of Divinity degrees and go out into the ministry. The result was published as *Flockfood*, a sort of consumer guide to sermons. As a member of the flock Durnbaugh had to admit he wasn't flattered by the comparison to sheep.

> *As it happens I find the imagery objectionable. I have never quite forgiven Jesus for coming down so hard on the flock and sheep language. Granted that this was a natural metaphor for Palestine, I wish he would have chosen almost any other animal. I dislike sheep. It is with great difficulty that I associate myself with this imagery. One summer I helped an uncle tend a flock of sheep and ever since then I have entertained a cordial disdain for them. Sheep are stupid. They look stupid and they sound stupid; they are, in fact, stupid. I can't say that I hate sheep because they are too bland to excite hate. You know that if one sheep jumps over a cliff to destruction that the rest will follow — a clear case of the bland leading the bland. On the late-night TV westerns when there is a showdown between the ranchers and the shepherds I always root for the cowboys. I don't, in sum, enjoying likening the members of the church to sheep.*[1]

Having said all that, if we still claim the status of sheep for the good shepherd, it's good to know we are loved by God for who we are, not for who we imagine might be more lovable. This image ought to teach us humility and to accept with good humor the amazing love that called God to send his only Son to save us. Mightn't God have just ignored us in our plight, shrugging off our disaster because we deserved it?

Instead, we are not just sheep, but the inheritors of something grand and glorious that is just around the corner. Let us reflect thankfully on anyone who has shepherded us despite our sinful nature. This is the good shepherd who lays down his life for sheep. There's no one else like him. Jesus is the genuine article! Have you thanked Jesus recently? Do you realize how lucky you are? If you are asked the question, "What is the one thing you'd grab in the event of a fire?" (assuming once more that everyone else is safe and has left the building), can you now answer with authenticity, "The only thing I'm worried about keeping I've always got with me, and that is Jesus my Lord, way down in my heart"? Amen.

---

1. Donald F. Durnbaugh, *Flockfood: A Consumer's Guide to Better Sermons* (Elgin, Illinois: Brethren Press, 1980).

Simple Enough?

In the fall of 1862, the United States was reeling from one defeat after another at the hands of the Confederate Army under the leadership of General Robert E. Lee. European powers such as England and France were anxious to recognize the Confederacy, in part to discomfit the upstart United States and partly to be able to traffic in the coveted cotton needed by their textile mills.

General George McClellan of the Union, having amassed an enormous army, convinced himself over and over that Lee's forces were greater. As President Lincoln fumed, the man who was a national hero refused to attack.

Meanwhile, Lincoln struggled over when to release his Emancipation Proclamation. The European powers wanted to recognize the rebellion, but if he could declare slaves in the rebellion states free he would be able to reframe the war as a crusade against slavery. They would have no choice but to stay neutral. For that he needed a victory for political cover, and a victory with such a general wasn't forthcoming.

In the fall of 1862, General Lee began a campaign through Maryland, hoping to destabilize a southern state that had stayed with the Union. However, on September 10, Lee's plans fell into the lap of General McClelland. A soldier found three cigars on which were written Lee's orders. McClelland crowed that with these in hand he would able to defeat "Bobby Lee."

The forces met near Sharpsburg, Maryland. What followed was the Battle of Antietam, the bloodiest single day in American history. Over 23,000 died. Photographs by James Gardner of dead bodies in the Bloody Lane or in front of the Dunker Church suddenly made the war real.

It was a victory. Barely, but it was enough. Lincoln had the political cover he needed to release the Emancipation Proclamation, and England and France were unable to recognize the Confederacy. And yet — McClelland, still believing in the numerical superiority of the force he had just defeated (in reality the Confederates were always outnumbered) did not pursue the defeated Army of Northern Virginia. Many experts think he could have ended the war by following up his advantage. The Confederates were able to limp across the Potomac River to safety, infuriating the president and leading eventually to McClelland's ouster.

McClelland had the plan. He knew what forces Lee had and where he was heading. Yet he could not follow a simple plan that would have ended the war, which then dragged on for three more bloody years.

It's easy to look back in history and see what people ought to have done. We can replay key events and point out how extremely simple the solution was and criticize those on the ground with the benefit of hindsight.

How about our own celestial Civil War? Is not humanity, to one way of thinking, in open rebellion against the kingdom of heaven? How many churches, even as we profess that Jesus is Lord, put themselves first, engaging in infighting, backstabbing, and plotting?

More important, we are in possession of all the information we need to win. We know what it takes to win a great victory over the world. Will we follow through with the battle plan, or will fatigue, cowardice, or exhaustion prevent us from achieving this great thing?

Today's scripture passage is short, but there's a lot there. And it's simple. John the Evangelist knew he had an important message, and he chose to write it in the world language of his day, Koine Greek. Koine Greek was not fancy Greek. It wasn't literary Greek. It was letter writing Greek, receipt writing Greek, business Greek. Greek was everyone's second language in the first Christian century.

John's Greek is very simple and his vocabulary is limited. It seems likely that this was his second language. The result is that he tells the story very clearly so that even folks like me, who need to have very simple instructions in order to operate a television with DVR and satellite, can follow along.

This passage is an integral part of John's account of the Last Supper. The chapter begins: "Now before the festival of the Passover, Jesus knew that his hour had come to depart from this world and go to the Father. Having loved his own who were in the world, he loved them to the end" (John 13:1). Love is central to the verse. Jesus is about to demonstrate what love means — first in the upper room, and then on the cross. This love is going to be demonstrated in the face of and despite an agonizing betrayal. Judas is mentioned in the second verse, and again in today's passage when John states, "When he had gone out ..." (v. 31).

The "he" in question is Judas. Judas has left the building. Jesus knows that evil will soon have its way. One he has trusted has set out on a terrible task, and everything is about to fall apart.

Yet Jesus says,

Now the Son of Man has been glorified, and God has been glorified in him. If God has been glorified in him, God will also glorify him in himself and will glorify him at once. — John 13:31-32

Glorify is a wonderful word, but the glory will come in being raised up for all to see on the terrible cross. Surely the disciples had looked toward a worldly definition of glory, and had thought that God's entrance into history would mean driving the Romans to the sea, freeing their land of temporal enemies, and establishing the political reign of God's anointed one.

But Jesus had demonstrated at this Last Supper what love means with the foot washing. It was customary to bathe before arriving at a dinner, but people walked barefoot or in sandals; so they would arrive at the home of their host with dirty feet.

Generally there were basins for people to wash their own feet. A slave could be forced to do this menial task — and it was considered very demeaning to do this. But according to biblical scholar John Christopher Thomas, there is no record anywhere in the ancient world of a superior washing the feet of an inferior — nowhere. When Jesus girded himself with a towel and washed the feet of his disciples before the Love Feast they were shocked — scandalized. Most of them sat silent, not sure what to say. Only Peter could bring himself to protest. Jesus made it clear that if anyone wanted to be a disciple of his, they needed to be ready to do the same.

This scene shows us that there is nothing love is not willing to do for the beloved. Caregivers know this, as they share times of service and ministry in the most gut-wrenching of circumstances. Love is not just the subject of valentines and little pink cherubic angels with stubby wings. Love is for the tough times, the real times.

Having shown them what love means, Jesus wanted to say something about it as well. After addressing his good friends as "little children" (here it is worth nothing that maybe we ought to be insulted to be identified as little children, were it not for the fact that it is as children we are to accept the gospel), Jesus proceeded to explain in very simple language that he was going away. "... I am with you only a little longer. You will look for me; and as I said to the Jews so now I say to you, 'Where I am going, you cannot come' " (v. 33).

If these words puzzled them they did not say. Then Jesus continued:

> I give you a new commandment, that you love one another. Just as I have loved you, you also should love one another. By this everyone will know that you are my disciples, if you have love for one another.
> — John 13:34-35

We might ask, how is this a new commandment? Leviticus 19 is known as the holiness code. "Holy" is a word that means "separate or different." In that passage God tells the people, "You shall love your neighbor as yourself" (Leviticus 19:18), words that we know better for the fact that Jesus quoted them as part of the greatest commandment. Nor would an ancient hearer of this passage require a Pharisee to ask a clarifying question like "Who exactly is my neighbor?" Later in the chapter we read "you shall love the alien as yourself," a reminder that outsiders in our midst are part of our community.

What makes this commandment new is that now these are no longer just words that come from above. These words are being lived before us. Jesus said they are to love one another "as I have loved you." Washing the feet of his disciples was only a start. They were probably still reeling from that. But they were about to be confronted by the ultimate act of love — the cross.

That's the simple plan. That's the secret we've stumbled on. That's the message that has been decoded and dropped into our lap. We are to love one another as Jesus as loved us. That's how they'll know we belong to Jesus, "if you have love for one another."

I wish this was more difficult. I wish it was harder because we'd have an excuse. I wish there were a number of steps we'd have to go through, levels of secret knowledge we'd have to be initiated in, or training we'd have to endure under blessed masters. Not that Christian education is a bad idea. Not that workshops don't benefit us. Not that continued and regular Bible study doesn't strengthen us. But this is simple.

The world is in rebellion against the kingdom of God. The rebels have an able general who has been able to redefine bad as good, sin as attractive, atrocity as pragmatic. Their leader has won many victories. In response we have been overwhelmingly cautious.

Are we ready to live this simple plan of practicing sacrificial love for each other and for the world? Or are we just going to talk a good game.

During the early days of the World Council of Churches, one of the delegates, M. R. Zigler of Virginia, stood up and made a proposal — that the Christians of the world resolve not to kill each other. Zigler was much beloved by the other delegates and admired for the many service programs he had administered in post-war

Europe that had brought relief and healing to so many. Yet though he was given a respectful hearing, there was not a second to his motion.

This is not meant as a criticism of the WCC. It's the same everywhere. Christians are not willing to pledge that they will truly live the Sermon on the Mount, returning good for evil, turning the other cheek, and pledging not to kill in the name of Christ.

So there it is. The key to success has been thrust into our hands. We've found the key — to love one another with a sacrificial love that will stop at nothing — not at the washing of feet or other menial tasks, not even at the cross itself.

Are you ready to love the enemy to death, even if it means your own? Are you willing to answer the oft-repeated question whose answer is just as often ignored — What Would Jesus Do? Amen.

Advocate And Redeemer

Imagine the wind rushing through an open door while the roar of the propeller in an aging old Ford Trimotor airplane rattles in your ears. You can smell the smoke from a raging fire hundreds of feet below. You are dressed in thick, padded clothing, wearing an old-fashioned football helmet with a jury-rigged grille in front of your face making it hard to breathe — that is, if it weren't already impossible for you to take a breath because of what is waiting beyond that open hatch.

In a matter of minutes you will be fighting a greedy forest fire on the ground, but first there's the matter of a little jump you're about to take — in a cast-off parachute! All the good ones are being used by the armed forces overseas in World War II.

Suddenly, your squad leader gives a signal, and no matter what your thoughts or fears, you take a long step forward — into thin air.

Brethren, Mennonites, and Quakers served in Civilian Public Service Camp #103 in Missoula, Montana. By the time the war was over they had helped perfect the craft of smoke jumping: fighting remote fires by parachuting into danger. Before the war, the whole idea had been considered a pipe dream. Only crazy people jumped out of airplanes with parachutes. By the time some inside the forest service convinced others the idea was worth trying war had broken out, and the best planes, pilots, jumpers, and parachutes were rightfully going overseas.

Still there were these conscientious objectors who wanted to serve their country, but whose religious principles forbade them from killing. Many of them had not even left the rural towns they'd grown up in, much less ever taken in a ride in a plane. But the volunteers who reported for duty took the work seriously. They considered it a matter of honor to never turn down an assignment. When interviewed they described harrowing adventures, dropping between tall trees in the midst of raging forest fires, ready to combat them with shovel, axe, and grit. No one ever refused to make a jump. Their service to their country proved to be essential.

Yet for many years after the war these peacemakers were left out of the official histories of smoke jumping, in part because of prejudice against their conscientious choice. They were literally written out and ignored, as if they had never existed.

It was only years later that the wrong was corrected, when advocates among the smoke jumpers stood up for them and restored them to their place in history. Indeed, documentaries and books now pointed with pride at their courage, determination, and contribution to the cause.

In this scripture, Jesus is speaking following the Last Supper about someone he calls the advocate, one who will be there for them. Jesus said that "... the Advocate, the Holy Spirit, whom the Father will send in my name, will teach you everything, and remind you of all that I have said to you" (v. 26).

Jesus will speak of this advocate, or comforter, several times during this discourse, reminding them that though his departure may seem fearsome, this advocate will not come unless he goes, and will fill them with the spirit of truth.

We all need someone to stand up for us, especially when we are in unfamiliar territory. I'll never forget the time when I was attending seminary in the Chicago area and one of our fellow students, of Greek extraction, took us into the heart of the Greek part of town. There were no English language newspapers available, and the Greek language was spoken freely in the restaurant we visited, but thanks to Nick we had a wonderful time and felt at home. Over the years I was able to return the favor, receiving guests from around the world in my native Los Angeles and showing them around parts of the city they might never have otherwise seen. We all need an advocate sooner or later.

The concept of the advocate came from the Hebrew *goel*, the advocate or redeemer. Every family is supposed to have such an advocate or *goel*, to make things right when it all goes wrong. Boaz was the *goel* for Naomi and Ruth. Job speaks of the need for a redeemer, or *goel*, who will restore his reputation. That's why it is a tremendous act of faith when he proclaims, just as it seems that everyone abandons him, "For I know that my Redeemer lives, and that at the last he will stand upon the earth; and after my skin has been thus destroyed, then in my flesh I shall see God ..." (Job 19:25-26).

The *goel* redeemer, which in ancient times was the nearest male relative who was responsible for protecting a person's interests when that person was unable to do so, is our spiritual power of attorney.

But we also need a *goel* in our life here on earth as well. It may be the one in charge of our medical decisions when we can no longer do so. Or it may be that we are the one trusted with that duty. This is what family solidarity is all about, and God is part of that family. God is the ultimate *goel*.

For the smoke jumpers that redeemer came in the form of later historians who came to recognize the tremendous contributions these contentious objectors made to the science of fighting fire and made sure that in the official histories their exploits are celebrated today.

For Jesus, who is himself a redeemer, his redemption comes when things seem hopeless — in the form of his resurrection. This is the vindication he cried aloud for when he quoted from Psalm 22:1 from the cross, "My God, my God, why have you forsaken me? Why are you so far from helping me, from the words of my groaning?" Resurrection rewards those who are faithful even when things seem hopeless.

We who claim Jesus as our *goel*, our redeemer, must learn to put our trust in that risen Lord and count on him to be our Advocate. We must learn to trust the Spirit, too.

It means taking things on faith. The words of Jesus to Believing Thomas are especially pertinent here: "Blessed are those who have not seen and yet have come to believe" (John 20:29).

It all comes down to trust. You know where the story is heading. You get there. Do you believe?

Faith calls for a leap in the dark. It is different than knowledge. I know what part of the sky I can find the moon tonight. I know that my redeemer lives. The same word, "know," is stated with the same certainty, but one is based on scientific knowledge. The other is based on something else instead.

In both Matthew and Mark the word "afraid" is used in the stories surrounding the resurrection. Jesus tells the apostles they must not be afraid in Matthew. The women say nothing to anyone because they're afraid in Mark.

But in John's account fear is not mentioned. Why would anyone be afraid in the face of this wonderful event? What were they afraid of?

Perhaps the new life.

Most of us, even when our hearts are breaking, can handle disaster. We hunker down and absorb our losses. But there is something even more unsettling than catastrophe.

It's what writer J. R. R. Tolkien called "eucatastrophe" — the good cataclysm. In his essay, *On Fairy Stories*, he wrote, "The Birth of Christ is the eucatastrophe of Man's history. The Resurrection is the eucatastophe of the story of the Incarnation. This story begins and ends in joy."[1]

If something good might happen, it requires every ounce of our strength and courage to work to see that it does.

Living with hope can be more difficult than living without it. With the possibility of resurrection we must be ready to make changes in our lives and lifestyle. Faced with the eucatastrophe of resurrection we can no longer be satisfied with mediocrity.

This hope for the kingdom, this hope grounded in the resurrection, can easily lead to personal disaster. The Greek word for "witness" is "matryr." We who witness to Jesus stand a good chance of being ground flat.

The end of the gospel is not the end of the story. He is risen! Will we have a faith in a Christ we have not seen? Will we trust the Messiah's promise that death has been overcome, even at the

210

moment we feel most without hope? Will we live in the kingdom now, playing by kingdom rules?

Sometimes we say we want to live the resurrection. Sometimes we want to stand tall in a world that has given itself over to doom and death. That's where it is important that we allow our redeemer, our *goel*, our advocate and comforter, to stand alongside us and give us the courage we need.

Remember, even though it looks like nothing is happening, things are moving at a very swift speed toward something dark, then something very, very good.

Bulbs planted last autumn are hidden all winter, but even when things are at their darkest and coldest already the stem is pushing through the cold, hard earth toward the light of the sun. Flowers are on the way. The hills are barren, but bare trees are just about to burst into blossom. The landscape looks calm, unmoving, but the planet is spinning while careening around the sun that is flying across space around a ravenous black hole at the center of the galaxy, which is circling other galaxies in a mad dash away from everything.

When Jesus turns his face toward Jerusalem we take a deep breath. Everyone wonders why Jesus appears to be doing nothing but the die is already cast. There will be a sudden mad plunge past the foot washing in the upper room toward the cross, the grave, and beyond to an empty tomb and a risen Lord.

Our redeemer lives. It was just as true when Job said it while mired in the depths of mystery and despair. It's just as true now. Our redeemer lives. Politics change and so do policies. Empires come and go. But these three things are sure — Christ has died. Christ is risen. Christ will come again.

Our redeemer lives not only as a risen Lord, but in a risen people, living the life of a resurrected people, speaking the truth to power, living the life of the upside-down kingdom of Jesus Christ. Our redeemer lives in the faithfulness of God's people, in our shared past.

Now let us take a deep breath as well — the church needs to fill her heart with courage, because we know that our redeemer lives. The world can't see our risen Lord. It may seem like the

211

kingdom isn't happening just yet. It may not happen just yet, or anytime soon, which doesn't mean it's not going to happen. It only has to happen once. Statistics are no help here. Do we have the faith of Job, the faith of the Believing Thomas, the faith of the disciples — the faith of Jesus as he prepared, saying farewell to his disciples, to willingly go toward the cross? Can we share the faith that we shall be vindicated in the flesh or beyond the flesh? That's what Jesus is asking us to do.

There is a place where our innocence, our expectations, our hope, is vindicated. Heaven and earth will pass away, but God's word will not pass away. The grass withers, the flower fades, when the breath of the Lord blows upon it. The grass withers, the flower fades, but the word of our Lord endures forever! Amen.

---

1. J. R. R. Tolkien, *On Fairy Stories* in *The Monster and the Critics and Other Essays* (London: George Allen and Unwin, 1983), p. 156.

The Ascension Of Our Lord
Luke 24:44-53

The End Of The Beginning

Three decades ago my nephew, Nathaniel, was a toddler when he discovered the full moon for the first time. For a day or two he would talk of nothing else. Then a week later he was out on a summer evening and looked in vain for the moon. He was genuinely puzzled. "Where did the moon go?" his mother asked him.

After a moment's reflection he shrugged and said, simply, "Exploded."

That explanation covered the facts as far as he was able to observe, but it wouldn't be long before the moon again dominated the night sky.

There is nothing like the full moon if you live in the countryside. Away from city lights night is truly dark. The full moon nearly creates a second day. It's not as bright as the real day of course, but in the fall the full moon extends the time you can be out in the harvester. In winter the full moon casts wonderfully long, blue shadows on a perfect bed of snow.

The moon is the most visible and obvious object in the night sky. The sun is brighter of course, but we can't look directly at it. The downside is that the full moon obscures all but the brightest stars. Even when we can't see it, the moon still has a powerful influence through tides.

Thinking about the moon might just give us a way of looking at the ascension of Jesus, why it was necessary and why we can say in some sense that Jesus has not departed at all.

The ascension of Jesus into heaven appears in two places in the scriptures, in Luke and Acts. The accounts in the gospel of

Luke and the Acts of the apostles include a few different details. We're used to that when dealing with stories from the gospels. Different witnesses notice different things and emphasize different points for different reasons. But the same author wrote the gospel and the Acts. Why are they different?

A lot has to do with the position of the two texts. The account in Luke's gospel caps the ministry of Jesus — it's a time for blessings and farewell. But the account in Acts is the beginning of our part of the story, a book that is still being written today by every Christian who works as a missionary, volunteers in a soup kitchen, sorts clothes at a domestic violence shelter, or teaches in a Sunday school.

Far from being symptoms of some strange gospel that ignores the divinity of Jesus and his imminent return, these actions are proof that we take his words seriously and are doing exactly what we're told to do.

This day we will look at both passages, but we're going to begin with this morning's reading from the gospel of Luke. It comes right after Jesus eats with his apostles. In the face of their disbelief, standing before the risen Lord, Jesus asks the disciples for something to eat and is given a piece of broiled fish.

That fish not only confirmed that the risen Jesus was not a spirit or ghost, but a living, breathing, resurrected Lord, it also symbolized the unity of the earth church. Luke was writing some decades after the events he was describing and trying to assure the Roman authorities that the Christian faith was revolutionary in the spiritual and not political sense. It was not the intent of the first Christians to overthrow emperors. They were only temporary blips on history's radar screen. The disciples of Jesus meant to turn the world upside down in a different way. Jews and Gentiles, rich and poor, slave and free, men and women, were separated in the rigidly segregated Roman society, but fish, bread, and wine brought them all together around the table of the Lord. Whereas Jews and Gentiles could not eat the same meat, they both could eat fish — and did. Frescoes depicting meals shared by Christians usually showed bread, wine, and fish. So this fish that Jesus ate before the ascension is a sign that something great is about to happen — and God's people are the ones to do it.

Keeping in mind that the same hand wrote the ending of Luke and the beginning of Acts, it's useful to see what is written there.

Acts is the second volume of a larger work that began with the gospel of Luke. In the gospel individuals from all walks of life are introduced to the life and ministry of Jesus, who travels throughout Palestine and finally focuses on Jerusalem, where he is executed, resurrected, and ascended into heaven. The story of the good news in Acts, on the other hand, begins in Jerusalem and spreads throughout the empire, ending when Paul reaches Rome as a prisoner. The gospel of Luke brings us all to Jerusalem and Acts sends us out to the ends of the earth.

The introductions to both books are addressed to Theophilus, who is perhaps a patron lending financial support to the writing of the works. It seems clear that Acts was written by the biblical Luke who was mentioned by Paul in his letters and may well have been Paul's personal physician. In any case, Luke was writing to an influential and rich convert who is new in the faith.

In Acts, Luke begins where he left off, with the Ascension of Jesus, but in Acts 1:8 Jesus had commanded the apostles to go from Jerusalem to Judea and Samaria, and then into all the world. As former missionary Chalmer Faw put it, "Jesus directs their minds away from the matter of times and seasons and onto the task that awaits them."[1]

And then to confirm this, while the apostles are staring up into the air in awe and wonder, two individuals, who resemble the angels in the empty tomb, tell the apostles that Jesus will return in the same manner in which he left.

The story as it continues is not one in which God's people meet simply to reverence Jesus and his ministry (although praise and worship are woven throughout the story), but that they go forth to the four corners of the world to take this message to all people.

A church that is turned totally inward is not ministering. Small group Bible study, support groups, and Christian education are all essential ministries of the church — we are meant to encourage and support each other, but that must be balanced by the knowledge that not everyone has come to know the love we share as the body of Christ.

The church must be in mission — to the community as well as to the world. This activity is blessed with a deadline to make us take it seriously, for sooner or later Jesus is returning.

Christians believe that if Jesus ascended into heaven it was with the intent to return. Even as Jesus prepares to vacate the scene the disciples ask the obvious question: "Lord, is this the time when you will restore the kingdom to Israel?" (Acts 1:6). His reply is that "It is not for you to know the times or periods that the Father has set by his own authority" (Acts 1:7).

Nothing could be clearer than the fact we are not to know the day and time of Jesus' return. Despite that, a lot of time and energy is wasted trying to figure it out.

I know there are plenty of people out there who are very concerned about the exact moment that Jesus will return. They spend a lot of time calculating, speaking about arcane minutae and obtuse calculations in some sort of incomprehensible Sanskrit even though Jesus made it clear that no one knows the hour, not even Jesus himself in his human form.

The late Vernard Eller, professor and writer, in his book *The Most Revealing Book of the Bible*, makes the point that everyone who has used Revelation as a calendar is batting .000.[2] They've all been wrong. Each new crop insists they're the first ones to get it right, that they know something no one else could possibly know. But that assumes in some way God has intended everyone to get a portion of scripture wrong until the last days. I don't accept that assumption.

Sometimes it's easier to learn from the past than the present. One of the best examples of the futility of calculations comes from the nineteenth century.

On September 27, 1868, a small group of believers climbed a haystack to be closer to heaven as they waited for their Lord to descend from the clouds. Despite their fervent prayers, and their belief in the biblical calculations of William C. Thurman (c. 1830-1906), nothing happened. Eventually some local rowdies set fire to the hay, forcing the believers to come down, severely disappointed.

It wouldn't be the last time.

Thurman was a Virginia Baptist who wrote on many different subjects, including biblical nonresistance, foot washing, and baptism. But he was best known for his views on the end of the world. In *Sealed Book of Daniel Opened*, he set the date for the return of Christ on September 27, 1868. Many Christians were attracted to his ideas. Undeterred by the failure of his calculations he rescheduled the end of the world for a month later on October 28. Then on October 17, 1869. Then on April 19, 1875.

Even though his recalculations proved to be just as flawed, he attracted many followers throughout his life who left their churches and joined him. Some of these Thurmanites, as they came to be known, later rejoined their churches, but others may have been driven away from the faith through their disillusionment.

It is said that when one elder was offered one of Thurman's books he declined, wryly noting that he already had enough kindling. Thurman continued to predict the end of the world until he died, penniless, in 1906, by which time he had recalculated the end of the world for 1917.

The Christian writer, C. S. Lewis, may have said it best in his essay, *The World's Last Night*, when he wrote that the most important thing was not that we know when Jesus would return, but that we should be found at our post, doing the thing God meant us to be doing.

Let us return to the place where we began, talking about the moon. The risen Lord Jesus reminds me of the moon in that he shed light in dark places, transfigured the landscape, helped us to see the Father's kingdom that would only be truly seen with the dawn of the final day, and God's restoration of justice! And like the phases of moon, throughout his ministry and to this day Jesus seems to appear brighter and at times to disappear altogether, yet his influence, like the tides, is felt, whether we see him or not.

Most importantly, just as the full moon obliterates all but the brightest stars, so too I think that if Jesus had not ascended into heaven we might not have grasped our opportunity as disciples, at doing the work of the Father, of being the visible presence of the kingdom, the body of Christ. We might have stood, like turkeys who are said to stare up at the sky during the rain only to drown, staring with our mouths open, at the wonder of the risen Lord. There's an eternity for that. Right now the true confirmation of our belief comes from our resolve to be God's people here on the earth.

The preacher Chrysostom, whose name means "Golden Throat" in Greek, once said that "... in the resurrection (the disciples) saw the end, but not the beginning, and in the Ascension they saw the beginning, but not the end...."[3] Every day is a new beginning to proclaim Jesus as Lord through mission, ministry, service, and proclamation.

This is doable because the real celebration of the Ascension comes when we stop looking at the sky and start looking around for what God has us to do. Amen.

1. Chalmer Faw, *Acts: Believers Church Bible Commentary* (Nappanee, Indiana: Evangel Publishing House, 1993), p. 30.

2. Vernard Eller, *The Most Revealing Book of the Bible* (Grand Rapids, Michigan: Wm. B. Eerdmans Publishing Company, 1974).

3. Saint Chrysostom, "The Acts of the Apostles," Homily 2, *Nicene and Post-Nicene Fathers, XI* (Grand Rapids, Michigan: Wm. B. Eerdmans Publishing Company, 1980), p. 13.

Easter 7
John 17:20-26

That We May All Be One!

In the nineteenth century, most American denominations felt pretty smug that theirs was the real faith. Some might have grudgingly admitted that not everyone would be cast into outer darkness for the sin of worshiping in the wrong building. But overall it was a time when theological differences as well as points of practice separated people.

Having said that, some denominations had a lot in common, whether they wanted to admit it or not. Take the Mennonites and the Dunkers, otherwise known as the German Baptist Brethren. The two groups were like peas in a pod. Both wore the plain garb of the plain people. The men wore long beards without any mustache, the women wore the prayer covering and bonnet. Their worship and music styles were very similar. They spoke German in the home and in church, though they spoke English with the world at large. As the Civil War approached, both Dunkers and Mennonites who lived in the Shenandoah Valley found themselves the object of scorn and persecution because they remained staunchly against slavery.

Mennonites practiced baptism by pouring. Dunkers dunked new members three times forward in the river. To them the differences, not the similarities, were what mattered.

In 1851, a Mennonite writer named Joseph Funk translated and edited a book written by his grandfather called *A Mirror of Baptism*. It maintained that pouring or sprinkling was the proper mode of baptism. The Dunkers encouraged the Elder John Kline to reply. He published a sixteen-page pamphlet called *A Defense of Baptism*, which championed trine immersion.

Debate became heated and even bitter. Funk replied in 1857 with a work called *The Reviewer Reviewed*, which was also over 300 pages long. Kline responded with the 74 page *Strictures and Reply* the following year. Funk wrote another even longer book, dripping with acid, which thankfully was never published.

However, in his diary entry of Wednesday, October 8, 1862, Kline wrote,

> *Got to see my old friend, Joseph Funk, and succeeded in bringing about a better state of feeling on his part toward me. He became reconciled. He had been somewhat ruffled in his feelings by my* Strictures and Reply *to his published writings on baptism and feet washing. Dined with him, then home.* [1]

The timing for reconciliation was apt because within two months, the octogenarian Funk died. Indeed, some wider reconciliation was reached, because with the onset of the Civil War both Dunkers and Mennonites found themselves in common danger. Their crops and animals were stolen, they were often imprisoned together, and some were murdered. Indeed, John Kline was assassinated in 1864 by Confederate guerillas because he refused to let boundaries prevent him from going about his ministry on both sides of the Mason-Dixon Line.

It's been 149 years since the Civil War, and if nothing else has happened in the interim, Christians have begun to take seriously the prayer of Jesus that we all be one. Jesus prayed, "I ask not only on behalf of these, but also on behalf of those who will believe in me through their word, that they may all be one" (vv. 20-21), yet Christendom was anything but united.

This disunion is anything but new. When Paul wrote to the Corinthian church, he was not writing to a group of believers who gathered in one building and praised God together. He was writing to a confederation of house churches, at least four, who were divided in witness and purpose. There was the Paul church, the Peter church, the Apollos church, and the Christ church, each one claiming to be better than the others — which is why he wrote, "What I mean is that each of you says, 'I belong to Paul,' or 'I belong to Apollos,' or 'I belong to Cephas,' or 'I belong to Christ' " (1 Corinthians 1:12). And that is why he had to appeal to his brothers and sisters, "by the name of our Lord Jesus Christ, that all of you be in agreement and that there be no divisions among you, but that you be united in the same mind and the same purpose" (1 Corinthians 1:10).

When the Week of Prayer for Christian Unity was begun in 1907 by a group of Anglican friars in the United States, it was hoped that Christians would be drawn into one fellowship. Boundaries separated Christians from worshiping and serving together. Churches sent out their own groups to the mission field, duplicating each other's work, rather than working together. The same could be said of service projects.

The thing about prayer is — it works. But the other thing is, God answers prayers the way he chooses. Many who worked for Christian unity in the twentieth century argued about what form it would take. Who would write the prayers, what would the people say, what sort of worship would they all share, what would be the organizing principles, what songs would they sing, who would be in charge, where would the offerings be sent, and what name would they go under? It was assumed that churches would lose their identity in one super church.

Well, God answered the prayers of Christians to grant the wish of Jesus, that we might all be one, but God did it without tending to any of the things humans were stressing over. Unity wasn't a matter of the same practice or the same administration, the same structure, or the same style of worship. It wasn't making the people who put their hands in the air put them down by their side, nor did it mean that the ones who like to sit very still had to get up and move around. Church unity had nothing to do with whether you sang in four-part harmony, loved classical music, or sang about nothing but the blood. Church unity had nothing to do with whether you dunked three times forward or once backward, poured, sprinkled, or hosed them down. Christian unity wasn't about grape juice or wine, thin wafers of cookie-like shortbread, or a full meal. It wasn't about projecting choruses on the wall or having no bulletin at all.

The unity of Jesus Christ is simply to be found in every church among Christians who proclaim that Jesus Christ is Lord. From the largest communion to the smallest independent fellowship, from the great cathedrals to the humble house churches, we are one body.

And at the heart of it is prayer. It is prayer for each other and prayer that we may be one.

This isn't to minimize the heroes of our Christian faith who have worked for the unity of the body. But we recognize that prayer, as much as our heroes, did the trick. And if we pray to God for unity, we must take our union on God's terms. We cannot outline what we expect God to do. We must wait for wonder.

Prayer changes the world. Prayer changes life.

Now because our unity isn't structural, it means that part of it is invisible. But God doesn't have to be visible to be working. The book of Esther has absolutely no references to God, yet it is clear that God is working out his will for the people. When Mordecai tells Esther that maybe she was made queen "for just such a time as this" (Esther 4:14), he doesn't have to spell it out for us to know that God is at work.

When the churches of a community work together on a food bank rather than running three or four separate ones because they won't work together, when the churches together support the local domestic violence shelter, when they meet together to pray for the schools or worship together on Good Friday, we see that the prayer of Jesus has come true.

Not everyone is convinced. Some take pride in their solitary stance against everyone else. But Jesus willingly laid down his life to complete God's work, so that, as Jesus says, "the world may know that you have sent me and have loved them even as you have loved me" (v. 23).

This whole prayer, this long extended plea from the Son to the Father, has been about tying up all the loose ends before Jesus sets about the great task of salvation. This is not about eschatology, the study of last things. It's about taking care of first things, about setting into motion things that were set up at the beginning of time. Jesus has taken care of the power of attorney for his people, so we're taken care of. The Spirit will be with us.

Jesus tells his disciples he will no longer be in the world, but we're going to be in the world. Jesus will willingly lay down his life for his friends to complete God's work, and he is expecting us to do this for each other, to serve not only our little corner of Christianity, but all of Christendom, and beyond that the whole world, so we might also have a part in God's work.

Living as God's people puts us in tension with the world. The prayer of Jesus recognizes this. We are not to retreat from the world, even though we live in a different fashion. Though there is much mystery in his words, some things are clear. We belong to God. We do not belong to ourselves. The church is in the world. The church is the bride of Christ, and this will be made apparent in the future.

Prayer is a lifeline. It sustains us when the ship of life is sinking. Isn't the whole point of salvation to rescue us? It's time to jump into the lifeboats — and yet some are arguing about whether we're supposed to sit in the first-class section instead of the third-class. There is no first class or third class in the lifeboat. There are only all of us, dying from sin, sinking fast, and someone is throwing us a lifeline. Are you going to refuse it because it's made out of the wrong kind of rope?

Jesus closes this prayer with these words. Listen to them carefully.

> *Father, I desire that those also, whom you have given me, may be with me where I am, to see my glory, which you have given me because you loved me before the foundation of the world. Righteous Father, the world does not know you, but I know you; and these know that you have sent me. I made your name known to them, and I will make it known, so that the love with which you have loved me may be in them, and I in them.*
> — John 17:24-26

It is the prayer of Jesus that we be with him also, to see him in his glory and that we have been given to the Lord from before the foundation of the world. There's a hurting world that does not know Jesus yet, but they know about God, and if we live the love of Jesus they will see Jesus clearly. That means we must be known by one name only — that of Jesus. Everything else is just details.

There's a story that a man died and went to heaven and was given a tour by the Angel Gabriel. Everywhere songs were raised in praise and suddenly the harmony that had been hidden in life made sense. The four-part songs and cathedral organs, the guitars and drums, the rustic hymns and African chants, the Latin rhythms, the bells and the carols, the white keys and the black keys, and the tapping feet and the beating hearts all blended together in a harmony that was never heard on earth but always intended. It all worked together and it was all good.

The man couldn't help but notice that far away, on the edge of heaven, there was a little cabin. Curious, he walked toward it with the angel at his elbow, and looked inside. There, huddling quietly together, on their knees, their hands clasped in prayer, was a group that seemed oblivious to the rest of heaven.

The man turned toward the angel Gabriel with a quizzical expression. Gabriel smiled and explained softly, "They're the Exclusive Apostolic Old Order Preservationist Straightaway Cox Witnesses of the Apocalyptic Mysteries."

"Why are we whispering?" the man asked.

"Because," Gabriel replied, "they think they're the only ones here." Amen.

---

1. Benjamin Funk, *Life and Labors of Elder John Kline, the Martyr Missionary* (Elain, Illinois: Brethren Publishing House, 1990), p. 457.

224

Sermons On The Gospel Readings

For Sundays
After Pentecost
(First Third)

Veni, Spiritus
Sanctus, Veni

Arley K. Fadness

The Day Of Pentecost
John 14:8-17 (25-27)

Veni, Spiritus Sanctus, Veni

On this Pentecost Sunday, as we celebrate the birthday of the church, I want to teach you a simple and yet potentially powerful prayer. It goes like this ... *"Veni, Spiritus Sanctus, Veni,"* or as the Germans would say it, *"Komm Heiliger Geist, Herre Gott."* In English it is simply, "Come, Holy Spirit, come."

There is no prayer in German, Greek, English, Swahilli, or Latin more powerful than this — *"Veni, Spiritus Sanctus, Veni."* This prayer opens us to the Holy Spirit, who comes, fills, and leads our lives. For when the Holy Spirit appears, the miracle of new life, renewal, and *dynamis* (power) breaks loose. "Come, Holy Spirit, come!"

A ship strayed off course near San Deigo some years ago. The ship got stuck in a reef at low tide. Twelve tugboats failed in their attempts to move it. Finally, the captain instructed the tugboats to leave. He decided, "I'll just be patient and wait." He waited and waited. Then high tide appeared. All of a sudden the Pacific Ocean began to rise. The rising tide lifted the ship and placed it back into the channel. What human power could not do, the rising tide of the Pacific Ocean did![1]

Something like that happened to the early church on the Day of Pentecost! The disciples and others were all together in one place — confused, unmotivated, fearful — when suddenly the tide of God rolled in!

Jesus' promise in John's gospel was literally fulfilled on Pentecost Day.

227

I will ask the Father, and he will give you another Advocate, to be with you forever. This is the Spirit of truth ... but the Advocate, the Holy Spirit, whom the Father will send in my name, will teach you everything, and remind you of all that I have said to you.
— John 14:16-17, 26

Jesus knew the disciples would forget "all I have said to you." Jesus, knowing the tendency to get stuck or distracted by alien truths, provides a teacher who would teach and remind. This teacher/ advocate, literally, "one called to the side of," would never, ever, allow the followers of Jesus to live without help! Like an old speech professor, the Spirit of truth whispers the secret of Pentecost into the ears and hearts and minds of Jesus' followers. The secret of Pentecost is the gospel — the gospel, which is the good news — the story, the witness of Jesus Christ died and raised from the dead!

When Pilate, swimming in a swamp of half truths, myths, and political intrigue asks, "What is truth?" he unwittingly expresses to Jesus humanity's eternal yearning and longing for truth. Little did Pilate realize, standing there, right in front of Pilate, was *and is* the truth! The old speech professor, the teacher, who has been around a long time, urges all to know the truth, teach the truth, and tell the truth. "Come, Holy Spirit, come."

Today is a perfect day to give thanks to God for teachers. Many of us have been blessed with excellent teachers, mentors, and models. I attended a one-room country school for eight years learning like the characters in the *The Little House on the Praire*. There was Miss Prunty, Miss Olson, and Mrs. Watts. Later I was schooled and nurtured in a Christian high school, two colleges, and two theological seminaries. One of my favorite teachers was professor, preacher, poet, Dr. Gerhard Frost, who taught us seminarians the importance of the teaching ministry in catechetics class. Dr. Frost once said, "The art of teaching is the art of getting out of God's way. The best teacher is he who most truly transports each individual into the presence of God. God-centered, Christ-centered, Spirit-centered teaching — this is true teaching."[2]

I was never subjected to, nor crippled by, a bad teacher. History abounds with teachers who failed to teach well and who failed to teach the truth. Marcion was one bad egg. Marcion was declared a heretic by the early church, since he would have thrown away the Old Testament. Sabellis is another who taught modalism, a heresy that promoted the Trinity as expressed in three separate modes. Pelgius, an Irish monk, confused salvation by trying to mix water and oil, teaching that grace needs an act of human will to be efficacious.

The list of dubious teachers is long: Joseph Smith, Charles Taze Russell, and in our own day, Warren Jeffs, and many others.

It is refreshing that Jesus promises a teacher, an instructor, an advocate, worth listening to. This instructor/advocate, the paraclete, guides Jesus' followers into the truth.

Today when you and I pray, "Come, Holy Spirit, come" we can expect the three P's of Pentecost: *people united*, *power excited*, and *passion ignited*.

In the first place this instructor, who teaches and reminds, is worth listening to because the Spirit of truth creates *people united*. After all, they came from different countries, many different languages that first Pentecost. Galileans, Parthians, Medes, Elamites, and people from Mesopotamia, Cappadocia, Pamphylia, Phrygia, and Judea were there. People divided by national boundaries were suddenly united! All diversity was brought together. The Holy Spirit works unity through the gospel of reconciliation through Jesus Christ.

Take a quarter, dime, nickel, or penny out of your pocket. What slogan do you see besides, "In God we trust"? It's the Latin phrase, *E pluribus unum*, which means "Out of many, one."

The phrase was first cast on our coins in 1795 and has been on them ever since. Our country started out as many states but came together under one common government. The motto, *E pluribus unum*, fits our nation. It also fits the church of Jesus Christ. Out of the nations, God gives one language, one speech, one voice, one truth, one focus, one purpose, one vision, and one mission. Together we thrive, apart we disintegrate.

Beekeepers tell us that honeybees can only live in community. Individually, they cannot and will not survive. So it is the church of Jesus Christ is only vibrant and alive as the members live in community. "Come, Holy Spirit, come" create your *people united!* When you and I pray, "Come, Holy Spirit, come" expect the second P of Pentecost: power! power engaged! *power excited!* After all, Jesus promised power in Acts 1:8: "You will receive power when the Holy Spirit has come upon you ... you will be my witnesses."

Why be weak? Why be paralyzed? Why be stuck at low tide — marooned on life's sandbanks? My children sometimes gave me a farewell as I left to conduct worship at our church. They never said, "God be with you" or "preach the gospel" but "Dad, don't be boring."

A certain church signage advertised their air-conditioned sanctuary by the words: "It's cool inside." Some wit penned underneath, "Brother, you said it." Far from cool, far from boring, that first Pentecost exploded with wind, fire, and holy breath, promising a new wild freedom, an intoxicating joy ride.

When you and I are stalled, when we feel weak, disabled, and down, the Spirit of truth functions like a set of jumper cables. We have connection.

Author Robert Fulghum wrote, "Jumper cables? You want jumper cables? Sure I got jumper cables. I can hook you up to Grand Coulee Dam, buddy, or wire you into the Almighty God or whatever powers there be."[3]

God's gift to us, like jumper cables, is access to power, power from on high, *power excited!*

In the third place, pray, "Come, Holy Spirit, come" and expect *passion ignited!* What is it that you love to be and do? What is it in your life that energizes and fulfills you? Remember the old Peace Corps ad? "Join the toughest job you'll ever love." Finding your passion is more than a cliché or a fad. Finding and engaging your gifts and passion reveals God's callings for your life. Your passion is your vocation. When you discover your passion, you also discover your path.

Imagine this scene — coming into worship and the ushers giving you a helium balloon. The balloon represents your passion in life. As you hear the scripture readings, the sermon, participate in the liturgy, sing the songs, and pray the prayers, your heart is touched, your passion is stirred, a dream is kindled, a goal is inspired, and you let go of your balloon. As the balloon rises all through worship, you physically see the Holy Spirit-empowered passions ignited in the body of Christ expressed. Then in discussion groups and classes you share how God has created you and gifted you and launches you out into mission.

People united! Power excited! Passions ignited!

My dad was filling a silo one day in Day County, South Dakota, with the help of his neighbors when suddenly the WC Allis Chalmers tractor he was driving, flipped over backward on top of him and the steering wheel pinned him to the ground. In a flash, a couple of neighbors ran over, grabbed hold, and lifted that iron tractor off him in an unbelievable surge of power. Though injured, Dad's life was spared. He recovered from that accident, living until he was 96. Many have wondered, how did the neighbors do that? Where did that amazing lifting power come from in that instant of need?

Though it was unlikely that the neighbors took time to pray, "Come, Holy Spirit, come," they nonetheless suddenly became, in this crisis situation, *people united, power excited,* and *passions ignited*!

How strong, how powerful do you and I feel today on Pentecost morning? More often I feel shy, insecure, and inadequate. Too often I am forgetful and tempted to follow the latest truth or fad. Thanks be to God, through the word, the sacraments, through the Holy Spirit's teaching and reminding. I am renewed by grace, and I am able to switch the focus from myself to the work and action of the Holy Spirit. In glad response I sing the song of total grace, no act of my own will, to experience salvation full and free. Amen.

The Spirit's called me to follow Jesus,
The Spirit's called me to follow Jesus,
The Spirit's called me to follow Jesus,
God leads me still, God leads me still.

231

Called and enlightened, the Spirit gathers,
Called and enlightened, the Spirit gathers,
Called and enlightened, the Spirit gathers,
Preserving faith, preserving faith.

By my own reason, and strength I perish,
By my own reason, and strength I perish,
By my own reason, and strength I perish,
God save us all, God save us all.[4]

---

1. Bailey E. Smith, *Nothing But The Blood* (Nashville, Tennessee: Broadman Press, 1987).

2. Gerhard E. Frost, *The Law Perfect* (Minneapolis: Augsburg Publishing House, 1959), p. 1.

3. Robert Fulghum, *All I Really Need to Know I Learned in Kindergarten* (Oxford: Ivy books, 1989).

4. "The Spirit's Called Me," words by Jeffrey Callander, can be sung to the tune "I Have Decided To Follow Jesus." Used by permission.

Holy, Holy, Holy

On this festival, The Holy Trinity, we celebrate one of the great treasures and mysteries of the church — the Doctrine of The Holy Trinity.

To begin with, one must confess that it is presumptuous on anyone's part to have the audacity, the unmitigated gall, the naiveté, to presume to explain God, the Holy Trinity. No pastor, no doctor of the church, no professor of theology or philosophy, no deacon, no bishop, cardinal, or pope can describe the indescribable, explain the unexplainable, nor comprehend the incomprehensible!

When we begin to rationally approach the Trinity we can quickly become confused. Like the computer specialist, King Duncan, tells about in his pulpit dynamics sermon:

> *Well ... I was a little confused. A computer specialist in a high-tech company was required to wear a pager all the time. This beeper was to ensure that he would be available immediately for hardware or software problems. But this poor fellow got reamed out by his supervisor. "No wonder you haven't been answering my pages," said his supervisor, "you're wearing your garage door opener!"* [1]

We all know confusion in this modern world as well as in our faith and life.

The word "trinity" never made it into the Old Testament nor in the gospels. It is not in any of Paul's epistles. You'll find it nowhere in the entire New Testament. Nonetheless, the roots, the trunk, the branches, the essence of the trinity tree flowers and blooms throughout the Bible.

In the Great Commission, Jesus instructs his disciples to baptize "in the name of the Father, and of the Son, and of the Holy Spirit" (Matthew 28:19). The apostle Paul underscores the reality of the Trinity in 2 Corinthians 13:13, with a blessing to the Corinthian church, "The grace of the Lord Jesus Christ, the love of God, and the communion of the Holy Spirit be with all of you." In our gospel today, John writes, "The Spirit, sent by the Father, reveals God's truth by giving glory to the Son ... making the Son known."

The term "trinity" was first used by Theophilus of Antioch around 80 AD. Then the doctrine itself was hammered out at the Council of Nicea in 325 AD and the Council of Constantinople in 381 AD. The Trinity has had a tough go. The Trinity has been body slammed, pile driven, kicked, assaulted, maligned, and ridiculed. The cults today have no interest or patience with the "trinity." The Jehovah's Witnesses hate it. The Mormons despise it. The Unification church attacks it. So the church developed three special security guards at the Councils of Nicea and Constantinople. These three security guards are big, burly, strong, no-nonsense characters. Their job is keep out riffraff, liars, and deceivers. Every time you and I worship they stand outside the church doors without fail. One probably doesn't notice them. They stand in the shadows.

Usually one of them comes in and joins worship. They have names. Their last name is Credo (I believe) from which we get the word "creed." Their first names are Apostles', Nicene, and Athanasian. They are good friends and loyal protectors of the faith. They refuse to put up with any guff from the cults, the new agers, lazy Christians, or any distorters of orthodox Christianity.

When sincere, but misled, cult members knock on your door, shove a tract in your face, and crow foolish things like, "Jesus is brother to the devil," "Jesus was married and has children in heaven," or "Jesus was a lesser god, a created being," these burly security guards flex their muscles and shout, "No way!"

234

Because of this, on The Holy Trinity and every Sunday, Christians respond to God's grace by doing two important things. We recite the creeds and we sing our lungs out! An ancient Chinese proverb chirps, "The bird does not sing because she has an answer, she sings because she has a song."

My wife said in her childhood church in Minnesota, they always began worship with a hymn to the Trinity — "Holy, Holy, Holy." On the altar parament of a Norwegian church I served in South Dakota were the words, *Heilige, Heilege, Heilege.* Three *Holies* in Norwegian praising the Holy Trinity.

We Must Sing On This Holy Trinity Sunday Because Our Rational Concept Of God Is Too Small

We first experience God as creator. Most every morning I hike the forest near my log house. Daisy and Rascal, my two white Jack Russell terriers, happily accompany me. As we hike along the logging trail I repeat the phrase from Genesis 1, "It is good." "It is good" is the chorus in that great hymn of the creation story. I say those words, add "Lord," and it becomes a prayer. It is a mantra spoken or chanted in cadences every four steps. You can do it, too. Walk and pray in 4:4 time. I see an Aspen peeking through the granite outcroppings and I pray, "It is good, Lord." I sniff the sweet aroma of vanilla carmel floating through the air from the Ponderosa Pine and I murmur, "It is good, Lord." I see a cottontail rabbit and my tethered dogs go berserk. I whisper, "It is good, Lord." I see a midget brown bear — oh — it turns out to be a chunky marmot. He looks like he has been eating pizza all winter long and needs to go to Weight Watchers. I repeat, "It is good, Lord." I meet people — fellow hikers, neighbors, and tourists. When I hike Mount Harney, I join 80,000 climbers, walkers, and hikers, who go up every year. I say, "It is good, Lord." I see the sun, the ferns, the moss, and the blue bell flowers.

I recall the reports from astronomers who scan the stars, the planets, the galaxies and they tell us creation is still going on.

Look around you. "The heavens," the psalmist sang, "are telling the glory of God." Psalm 8 chants, "When I consider the heavens, what is man?"

How big is the universe? On February 23, 1987, an astronomer observed with his naked eye the explosion of a distant supernova. It was a blast so powerful that it released as much energy in one second as our sun will release in ten billion years. I find this absolutely mind-boggling, that this supernova exploded 170,000 years ago. It took that long for the light generated by that distant event, traveling almost six trillion miles a year to reach our watching astronomer. To top it off, the astronomers tell us that the universe is expanding.

Discoveries in 2006 and 2007 of new black holes and more exploding stars boggle our rational minds. For God, the Father creator, time and space is measured differently. Time is a convenience by which we measure things but surely not God. We would like to create God in our own image, manageable, manipulable, but God is the Divine Other. God is beyond our reason and comprehension. Rudoph Otto in, his ageless book, *The Idea of the Holy*, calls God the "mysterium tremendum." All believers cannot resist breaking out in song and singing to the rafters of the glory and majesty of God as creator. We join the psalmist in Psalm 138, "Great is the glory of the Lord."

In the presence of God our creator — the works of God the Father, I am humbled. In awe I worship and whisper, "It is good, Lord."

We Recite And We Sing On The Holy Trinity Because We Know Our God Came Near

We sing "Joy To The World" and celebrate Christmas even in June. We sing "Away In A Manger" and "O Little Town Of Bethlehem." When we celebrate not only the birth but also the life, death, and resurrection of Jesus we add to our anthems, "My Song Is Love Unknown," "Were You There When They Crucified My Lord?" and "Christ Is Risen From The Dead" along with "Holy, Holy, Holy."

Fred Gilbertson from Oregon fell in love with a lovely young lady. How was he to propose to her and tell her that he loved her? Fred decided to rent a billboard. The billboard read, "Cheri ... marry me. Fred." Cheri passed that billboard day after day but never noticed or saw the message.

Finally her friends told her about it. The next time she saw it, she read it and she said, "Yes" to Fred.

God's eternal love came down in Jesus. Easily many pass by and never "read" the message — "God so loved the world that he gave his only begotten Son...."

As a delegate to a recent church-wide assembly, I was standing outside the Elmen Center at Augustana College in Sioux Falls when I noticed a stranger standing nearby. He introduced himself and said his name was Del D. Then he said, "I'm a convict from the South Dakota Penitentiary. I'm here representing St. Dysmas, the Lutheran church behind bars. I'm a changed man, pastor, only the love of Christ can change a person."

I smiled and shook his hand and said to myself, *"You are amazing Lord Jesus."*

We believe and sing in four-part harmony of Jesus: Truly human, truly divine. Jesus, God enfleshed. Our three security guards will never allow the singing to stop, nor the truth to be compromised. Jesus only is God. Neither Shirley McLaine, nor the Mormons, will tempt us to believe that we *will be* or *are* gods in the making.

The Third Thing We Sing About On The Holy Trinity Is That Our God Is Now

God is in the present tense through the Holy Spirit. Jesus said in our gospel reading, "When the Spirit of truth comes, he will guide you into all the truth" (v. 13).

The Holy Spirit is here in this place. The Holy Spirit is as close as your heartbeat and as enlivening as your breath. The Holy Spirit is at work in and through the word of God, the sacraments, and the people of God. When we feel our faith is fainting, the Holy Spirit gets to work making *believers* out of us. When we don't feel generous with our tithes or time or resources the Holy Spirit is at work making *stewards* out of us. When we don't feel very loving, the Holy Spirit is busy creating *lovers* out of us.

A pastor who followed me in my first parish, Pastor Charles Mountain, wrote this song to the tune of St. Thomas, SM. ["I Love Thy Kingdom"]:

> *With sighs too deep for words,*
> *the Spirit in us prays;*
> *what human tongues cannot express*
> *th'indwelling Spirit says.*
>
> *With longing Ages long,*
> *the Spirit in us groans;*
> *with pangs of new creation's birth*
> *the Dove, new brooding, moans.*
>
> *With access to God's mind*
> *the Spirit intercedes;*
> *and God, who searches human hearts*
> *gives knowledge of our needs.*
>
> *O God most intimate,*
> *O Spirit, mend our minds;*
> *O help us hear the Kingdom's call:*
> *the hope that frees and binds.*[2]

The word for us today is this: *Take a hike.* Go and experience God the creator. Hike and pray in your nearby state park, the Grand Canyon, or your backyard. See marmots, moles, and mountains. *Take a hike.* See Jesus, the Savior. He who loves you and saves you by his grace. *Take a hike.* Experience the holy wind, holy breath, holy power, and peace from on high. Our God is an awesome God.

Thanks to our three security guard friends whose eyes scan the horizon while we sing our doxologies to the Holy Trinity — God the creator, redeemer, and sanctifier. Amen.

---

1. King Duncan, Collected Sermons, www.Sermons.com.

2. Charles Mountain, *Hymn-Canticles For The Church Year* (Lima, Ohio: CSS Publishing Co., 1997), p. 152.

Amazing Faith

Twice in Jesus' ministry, Jesus is flabbergasted.

Once, in Mark 6:6, after Jesus is rejected in Nazareth, his own hometown, he is dumbfounded — stunned — at their *unbelief!* Today in Luke 7, Jesus is astonished again, this time by just the opposite — he is flabbergasted at a Roman centurion's amazing *faith.* Jesus turns to the crowd following him and says, "I tell you, not even in Israel have I found such faith!" (v. 9).

Who is this man of such faith who causes Jesus to stop in his tracks and marvel? We learn he is a Roman soldier, a centurion, in charge of 100 soldiers. He is a foreigner, a Gentile, a non-Israelite. He has a slave who is ill. He approaches Jesus for healing. Despite his protestations of worthiness, his Jewish friends know he is a noble man. He is humble. He loves his slave. He respects the Jewish people and their faith so much that he builds a synagogue for them. He does not consider himself even worthy for Jesus to come and enter his home or worthy enough to approach Jesus directly.

But the centurion's insight into Jesus is even more remarkable. He perceives that Jesus, like himself, is a man under authority. Just as a centurion can command soldiers and slaves because of an authority derived from elsewhere, so Jesus has an authority derived from elsewhere. Because of this authority, Jesus can simply say a word and the centurion's slave will be healed. Such depth of insight — such faith — Jesus had not encountered even among his own people.

Walter Wangerin Jr., author, poet, columnist, and Lutheran pastor, received a letter in the mail with a single question in it. It was written with a purple felt-tipped pen and it asked this question: "Dear Walt, how can I find faith? Karen."

Have you ever wondered, how is it that some have faith and some do not? Ever struggled within yourself when you waver from faith to unbelief, from unbelief to faith? You feel like Karen, "Dear Walt, how can I find faith?"

One can go to the university and ask a professor. "Teacher, how can I find faith?"[1]

"Well Karen, sit in my classroom and I will explain faith. Faith is *notitia, assensus,* and *fiducia.*"

"Huh? I'm not sure I get it."

"Let me explain:

- *Notitia* is basic knowledge. The word "notice" comes from *notitia.* Faith assumes some basic "noticing" of objective knowledge. Faith does not begin with emotion, though emotion may color the experience. Knowledge brings to mind an awareness of sin and of grace and of forgiveness.
- *Assensus* is agreement, affirmation, ascent. We ratify, approve, and confirm the gift of faith.
- *Fiducia* suggests estates, bequests, trusts. One may have *notitia* and *assensus* but without receiving an inheritance from beyond oneself faith would be incomplete.

So Karen, faith involves *notitia, assensus,* and *fiducia.*"

Jim Henderson, in his book, *Jim and Casper Go to Church,* believes the clue to finding faith is not to simply define the faith nor to defend the faith but to "defend the space" — that is, the space for dialogue instead of engaging in debate between believers and nonbelievers. Jim Henderson, a longtime Christian, sets out on a quest to find out how non-Christian guests might interpret what they hear and see at a Christian worship service. He hires atheist Matt Casper to visit twelve prominent churches in America with him and then to talk honestly about observations, feelings, and opinions. The "space" is the relationship and time where authentic listening and frank talk may respectfully occur.

Jim discovers through the experience with his friend, Casper, that many well-meaning Christian communities come off arrogant, having all the answers, displaying dogmatic certitude, appear slick and distant from what Jesus really expects of his followers in the kingdom of God. Jim champions "defending the space" between seekers, atheists, agonistics, searchers, and authentic Christians. Jim learns that Casper, the atheist, who loves the teachings of Jesus as well as Buddha, Teddy Roosevelt, and others, functions on his own developed high moral ground with a hope and vision for the future. His ethics are based in nature and nurture and not necessarily the Bible or any Christian apologetics.[2]

In his best seller, *Blue Like Jazz: Nonreligious Thoughts on Christian Spirituality*, Donald Miller sees finding faith beginning with confession. Donald Miller, whose problem is with Christianity, at least how it's often practiced, tells about setting up a confessional on the campus of Reed College. People who enter the confession booth intending to recall and admit their sins, but before they could begin, a Christian would begin apologizing to them for all the sins the church had committed against them. This surprising action caught people completely off guard and instigated a whole new kind of relationship between a Christian and a person considered lost.

> *Telling someone, "I'm sorry for the way Christians have misrepresented Christ," always surprises non-Christians. Frankly, most non-Christians have learned to see Christians as arrogant and unconcerned about their opinions ... "defending the space" means we practice apologizing to non-Christians for the sins Christians have committed against them. We simply say something like, "I'm sorry that we've failed: that really doesn't look much like Jesus, does it?"[3]*

For some faith is perceived as a rational choice. By my will I choose to believe. I choose God. For others faith is totally unrational. Paul Scherer once said, "Faith is more like courtship than the courtroom." Faith is like falling in love. One doesn't choose faith, one is wooed by God's love. We respond back with faith and trust in our lover God.

Falling in faith, acknowledges the dead human will, for as Martin Luther taught, our wills are in bondage to sin and we cannot free ourselves apart from the work and activity of the Holy Spirit. Faith is not trying but trusting.

Finding faith is worth the hunt. There are three activities faith accomplishes: Faith heals, faith saves, and faith works.

Faith Heals

After Jesus says, "I tell you, not even in Israel have I found such faith," Luke records in verse 10, "When those who had been sent returned to the house, they found the slave in good health."

One day a young newlywed came to my office at the church. She was ill physically, emotionally, and spiritually. She shared her dilemma and after a while I introduced her to our ritual of confession and forgiveness. She confessed, we prayed, and she went home.

Her father asked me later what happened. His daughter is now well and functioning beautifully, whereas before, her parents were worried sick about her welfare and her future. Faith heals.

Faith Saves

My then 88-year-old dad wrote a sermon titled "Saved." I found the sermon, probably never delivered, in his papers after he died. He was not a preacher. He was a farmer with an eighth-grade education. Dad told in his sermon about a Native American who was lost in a blizzard in northeastern South Dakota where Dad lived. With the swirling, whirling snow and frigid weather, the traveler apparently got disoriented, because in the spring they found his body only a few feet away from safety. The man had been turned away from a white settler's cabin. For my dad, this illustrated, "almost saved but lost." Then there was another blizzard and Dad's older sister, Marmien, was at the school, and the students started out for home, but realized they could never make it. However, they found refuge in a neighbor's house, and were saved, and Dad told this story to illustrate "almost lost but saved."

242

Saved meant for Dad and his "congregation" that by the life, death, and resurrection of Jesus we are saved. Baptism is our connection in which we are grafted into that new life in Christ.

Sir James Simpson, discoverer of chloroform, was asked, "What do you regard as your greatest discovery?"

Up to that time it had been claimed that the discovery of the use of chloroform saved more people from pain than any other single medical discovery. The interviewer expected Simpson to say, "My discovery of chloroform."

Simpson answered, "My greatest discovery was when I discovered Jesus Christ is my Savior."

Faith Works

Faith is action. James 2:17 says it simply, "So faith by itself, if it has no works, is dead." Jesus perceived that the Roman centurion's faith was alive — for he loves his slave, he loves the Jewish people, he builds a synagogue, he trusts Jesus for healing, and he is humble beyond a fault. Just as a rose cannot help but bloom, and an oak tree produce acorns, so an alive faith cannot but help overflow in love, mercy, and justice.

Faith is never an arrogant dogmatic certitude. Faith is always a sure confidence in the midst of uncertainty.

Sweeping across Germany at the end of World War II, Allied forces searched farms and houses looking for snipers. At one abandoned house, almost a heap of rubble, searchers with flashlights found their way to the basement. There, on the crumbling wall, a victim of the Holocaust had scratched a Star of David. And beneath it, in rough lettering, this message:

> *I believe in the Sun — even when it does not shine.*
> *I believe in love — even when it is not shown.*
> *I believe in God — even when he does not speak.*[4]

Faith always believes in the future.

A young lady on a cruise ship kept glancing at an attractive young man. The young man could not help but notice her attention and was intrigued. Finally he mustered up the courage to approach her. "Pardon me," he said. "It may be my imagination, but I could not help but notice that you keep looking in my direction. Do I know you? Is there something?"

She blushed and said shyly, "Oh no, it's just that I can't help notice how much you resemble my first husband."

The young man looked puzzled and asked, "How many times have you been married?"

She gave a flirtatious smile and answered, "Oh, I haven't been yet."[5]

Walt's short answer to Karen's question, "How can I get faith?" is this:

> *Oh, Karen, this is how I answer you, though I tremble at the pain that goes before your peace. I say the love of God is all around you, even now. Faith is your finally falling upon that love, and your knowing who it was that caught you.*[6]

Amen.

---

1. Walt Wangerin Jr., *The Lutheran* (Augsburg Fortress, November 2, 1988), p. 5.

2. Jim Henderson and Matt Casper, *Jim and Casper Go to Church* (New York: Barna, an imprint of Tyndale House Publishers, Inc., 2007), p. 24.

3. *Rapid City Journal*, Rapid City, Iowa, Associated Press article, January 19, 2008, p. C6.

4. Source unknown.

5. Source unknown.

6. *Op cit*, Wangerin.

Sit Up And Speak!

The telephone rang in my office one day, and a mother, a member of my parish, blurted out, "Oh, pastor, they just found the body of my son, Kenneth. He drowned in the Missouri River over at Chamberlain!" I was stunned, and then I heard her sob. "It had been a hot day. Kenneth, driving gravel truck all day, decided to take a swim to cool off. And he didn't make it back to shore. Pastor, what'll I do?"

I remember swimming at that very beach with my family over the years. As I drove over to Erna's house, I thought about what she must be feeling. She was obviously totally devastated, heartbroken, stunned beyond belief. "O God, help her," I prayed.

We enter our story in the village of Nain best, when we feel a bit of what Erna felt. The mother, in Luke's gospel, from the little hamlet of Nain had only one son. And like the mother from Zarephath in Elijah's time, she had experienced death before. She was a widow. And to be a widow in the time of Jesus was devastating. When you lose your husband and *then* lose your son, you lose everything. You lose your livelihood, your status, your security, and your future. Surely this widow of Nain had dreams for her son. She fully expected her son to outlive her. But now her son lay dead. The pallbearers were carrying him out of the gate.

Just then Jesus, who had gone to Nain with his disciples and was joined by a large crowd following, appears on the scene. He sizes up the situation. Compassion overwhelms him. He consoles her, "Do not weep" (v. 13). The Greek word for "compassion" refers to the bowels as a gut-level response. Jesus reaches out, touches

245

the body of the young man, and speaks amazing life-resurrecting words: "Young man, I say to you, rise!" (v. 14). The young man sits up and begins to speak as Jesus gives him back to his mother. The large crowd accompanying Jesus and the large crowd in the funeral procession react and are struck with fear. In near panic mode, they glorify God. They believe God has visited them with this amazing prophet, Jesus.

It's a shocking and awesome thing when the dead sit up and begin to speak. I have known people who have been dead, if not physically, in some manner all their lives. They go through the motions of living, yet, are dead spiritually, or socially, or intellectually, or emotionally. Then one day by the grace of God, their lives are interrupted, and they experience a Damascus Road conversion like the apostle Paul, and they sit up and began to live and to speak. For others, the weight of deadness is lifted through clues and small insights as they grow in faith, step by step, day by day, as did Timothy under the Christian tutelage of his dear grandmother and mother, Lois and Eunice.

Jesus still speaks today, "Young man, I say to you, rise!" Some remember Mark Dayton. Mark Dayton experienced his "Dark Night of the Soul" as was reported in the *Star Tribune* Sunday magazine some years back. Mark Dayton, a young man, a rich man, politically ambitious, and a talented man, fell to the bottom. He ran for the US Senate in 1982 and lost. Soon thereafter his marriage to Alida Rockfeller collapsed, and he endured a bout with alcoholism.

One day, Mark Dayton found himself in the balcony of Westminster Church in Mineapolis. He found himself there in the balcony often struggling to find a sense of God. He bounced back and forth between the poles of desolation to consolation, and then that insightful day he found himself coming out of the "dark night," and finally, to experience the dawn. Healing came and has continued by the grace of God. Mark Dayton was eventually elected Minnesota State Auditor and later a DFL United States Senator serving from 2001 to 2006.

The psalm for today, Psalm 30, ties all three appointed texts from 1 Kings, Galatians, and Luke together in one great song. The message of the song is that God restores all. God restores health. God restores life. God restores my soul. We sing with the psalmist verse 1 (cf): "I will exalt you O Lord, because you have lifted me up — I cried out to you and you restored me to health."

Once secure, once self-confident, but then came an affliction that drove the psalmist to God. God hears the psalmist and restores. In Psalm 30:3 (cf), the psalmist sings, "You brought me up from the dead — you restored my life as I was going down to the grave." In verse 13 (cf), "Therefore my heart sings to you without ceasing, O Lord my God, I will give you thanks forever."

One of our presidents of the United States, Franklin Pierce, became angry with God when he lost his son. When Franklin Pierce had been elected, he and Mrs. Pierce and their son took a trip to Concord, New Hampshire, by train, two weeks before the inauguration. The train had not gone far out of the Concord Station when there was a lurch — a jolt — and the car the Pierces were in, tumbled off the tracks and down an embankment. Neither the president nor his wife was injured in the accident, but their son was killed. Franklin Pierce brooded over this, as most of us would. He asked the question of God that so many of us have asked. "Why would God, at this moment of triumph, permit this tragedy in their lives?" President Pierce was so upset that he refused to allow the Bible to be used at his inauguration.

Today, picture a gurney. It's a pallet with wheels. Lying on the gurney is someone waiting to be restored. Who lies there? Is it someone you know? Is it you? Is it me? Picture Jesus reaching out and touching and speaking, "Young man, young woman, young of heart, I say rise! Leave your coffin. Leave your sick bed. Leave your cynicism, your anger, your hostility with God or whatever is deadening you to the things of God and the abundant life. For after all, it is I, Jesus, who promises, 'I have come that you might have life and that you might have life abundantly.' "

The church today laments a growing gender death. Men, and especially, young men are conspicuously absent in worship, and in the life and ministry of congregations. Increasingly, we in the church are singing the folk song, "Where have all the young men gone, long time passing? Where have all the young men gone? Long

247

time ago?" The folk song echoes God's question in the Garden of Eden, "[Adam] where art thou?" (Genesis 3:9 KJV).

Dr. Curtis A. Miller, past president of the North American Conference of church men's staff, of the Presbyterian church (USA) writes,

> *The authors [*Coming of Age *by Anderson, Hill, and Martinson] show a real concern for the lost tribe of young men in the Christian community. As the Christian church has become feminized, many young men have felt lost in the shuffle and returned to the time-honored resources of sports, nature, family, friends, work and service, to nurture their spiritual journey. It is a challenge to the Christian community for change, renewal, and an increased commitment to be a transforming community, where a new partnership is developed, where a new equality between men and women is practiced, and where people are accepted where they are, as they are, and equipped for life in the real world.*[1]

In coaching twelve Midwest congregations in a visioning process, I have discovered that the majority of the congregational core values are feminine as opposed to what may be considered masculine. Typical of the 57 feminine core values, compared to 19 masculine core values, were prayer, children, kindness, acceptance, respect, nurture, caring, and compassion. Absent were what could be considered masculine core values such as influence, purpose, position, courage, fulfillment, strength, power, and duty.

David Murrow writes in *Why Men Hate Going to Church*,

> *Manly men ... have all but disappeared. Tough, earthy, working guys rarely come to church. High achievers, alpha males, risk takers and visionaries are in short supply. Fun lovers and adventurers are also underrepresented in church ... rough and tumble men don't fit in."*[2]

Today's typical church has developed a culture that drives men and especially young men away. God made men for adventure, achievement, and challenge. John Eldredge writes in *Wild at Heart* that three desires are deeply written in most men's hearts. They are a "Battle to Fight," "An Adventure to Live," and "A Beauty to Rescue." Jesus' words, "Young man, I say to you, rise!" take on a frightening contemporary relevance in the culture of congregational life today.

Thankfully, the church is beginning to sit up and speak. The Young Male Spirituality Project in the Evangelical Lutheran Church of America, invented to explore the identity and spirituality of younger men, interviewed 88 young males ages 18 to 35 and found eleven themes that impact their spirituality. Among the themes were relationships, male mentors, crises in their lives, life management issues, work, life-changing experiences, nature, sports, service, avocation, and worldly spiritual hungers.

Practical advice for Christians for action to heed the command, "arise, young man," are listed in the book, *Coming of Age*, by Hill, Anderson, and Martinson.

Young men are sitting up and speaking at a new mission church in Sioux Falls, South Dakota, under the leadership of a young visionary pastor. A men's retreat designed to meet the yearnings and thirst for vision, leadership, purpose, challenge, risk taking, hunting, and sports.

Christ speaks, "Young man, I say to you, rise!" not only to young men but to young women, to children, to Boomers, and to the elderly. All of us along with the two widows from Zarapthah and Nain, know only so well, loneliness, fear, and anxiety. Fred Buechner calls our loneliness the "truth of our existence." I call it what it is — the pits!

Nonetheless, Christ enables all to "arise" as we receive the power of his compassion, the tenderness of his touch, and the authority of his words. He is no weak Jesus. Jesus is no suggester. Jesus is the commander in the face of death. Our Easter song like Psalm 30 lifts us and releases us from our dark night of the soul. We are empowered to sit up and speak. Amen.

I know that my Redeemer lives!
What comfort this sweet sentence gives!
He lives, he lives, who once was dead;
he lives, my ever living head![3]

1. David W. Anderson, Paul G. Hill, Roland D. Martinson, *Coming of Age* (Minneapolis: Augsburg Fortress, 2006), p. 1.

2. David Murrow, *Why Men Hate Going to Church* (Nashville: Nelson Books, 2005), p. 6.

3. "I Know That My Redeemer Lives," words by Samuel Medley, 1775. In the public domain.

The Forgiven Love A Lot!

One day it became obvious that I needed to tell my two daughters, Soon Ah and Rebekah, this story — it's a story about Lulla Belle. "Lulla Belle is rich, sassy, and selfish. She prances around like a princess in her southern mansion. Lulla Belle, blond and beautiful, lets everybody know it. The boys think she is a fox. Lulla Belle expects her servants to clean her room, wait on her, feed her pizza and cream puffs, take her to the mall, and to the movies whenever she pleases. Lulla Belle is a sweet talker. She manipulates her friends. She is cranky and cross to her parents and never ever cleans her room. What do you think of Lulla Belle, my daughters?"

Soon Ah and Rebekah respond with one voice, saying emphatically, "She ought to be spanked, the little snot!" I open the door and look into their messy rooms and say, "Hmmmm" and I smile, and they roll their eyes, acknowledging the message, with an "Oh, Dad!"

In William Shakespeare's *Hamlet*, Shakespeare has Hamlet devise a method to catch the conscience of a murderer. King Claudius of Denmark, Hamlet's own uncle, has killed Hamlet's father who was the reigning king. What does Hamlet do? He recruits a few actors, writes a play, and then makes this prediction: "The play's the thing, wherein I'll catch the conscience of the king."

That is how the prophet Nathan, in 2 Samuel 11, catches the conscience of the king — King David, through an innocent but deadly little playlet. David is king of Israel. And we remember the dark days of David's life. He commits adultery with beautiful

251

Bathsheba and then to cover his crime he conspires to have Uriah, Bathsheba's husband, killed in battle.

One day God's prophet, Nathan, appears on the scene and tells David an innocent little story.

> *There were two men in a certain city, the one rich and the one poor. The rich man had very many flocks and herds; but the poor man had nothing but one little ewe lamb, which he had bought. He brought it up, and it grew up with him and with his children; it used to eat of his meager fare, and drink from his cup, and lie in his bosom, and it was like a daughter to him.*
>
> *Now there came a traveler to the rich man, and he was loath to take one of his own flock or herd to prepare for the wayfarer who had come to him, but he took the poor man's lamb, and prepared that for the guest who had come to him.* — 2 Samuel 12:1b-4

"What do you think of that King David?" Nathan asks. Nathan knows long before Hamlet, "The play's the thing wherein I'll catch the conscience of the king." David's anger is ignited and he shouts, "The man who had done this deserves to die!" Nathan withers David, "You are the man!"

In Luke 7, a Pharisee invites Jesus to his home and when a woman, a scarlet woman of disreputable character enters, she kneels before Jesus, weeps, and anoints his feet. Simon the Pharisee explodes with disgust, "If this man were a prophet, he would have known who and what kind of woman this is who is touching him — that she is a sinner!" (v. 39).

Jesus looks at Simon and says, "I have a story to tell you. A certain creditor had two debtors; one owed five million dollars and the other $5. When they could not pay, he canceled the debts for both of them. Now Simon which of them will love him more?"

Simon answered, "I suppose the one for whom he canceled the greater debt."

"You're right, Simon. You've judged rightly."

Suddenly, Simon is in the play — he, the debtor of $5 and she, the debtor of five million dollars. He loves little — she loves much.

We don't know if Simon the Pharisee, had an "Oh Dad" moment, but we do know the surprise and even shock to see oneself in an unexpected light.

I remember walking into a Sears department store when surveillance cameras were newly used and seeing this shadowy, strange figure walking down the aisle. And then, an "Oh my" moment hit me, "Why that's me!" And I now ask, "Who in Jesus' story is me?" Am I the scarlet repentant woman or Simon the Pharisee? She was a sinner. She was in deep moral debt and she knew it. However, did Simon, the Pharisee, who prided himself in following the letter of the law plus a few extra rules realize his self-righteous pomposity?

Who needs forgiveness? They both do. I do. You do. But who are we more like? Simon the Pharisee or the repentant woman?

I confess I sin by my acts. I resent people who resent people. I am judgmental over people who are judgmental. I am intolerant of people who are intolerant. I am not honest about my inner true feelings, and I feel like I'm living a lie, pretending to be and do that which I am not. I am guilty of things done and things left undone.

Like the apostle Paul, "I do not do the good I want but the evil I do not want is what I do" (Romans 7:19). But my sin is deeper than my acts. "By nature" we confess in our liturgies "we are sinful and unclean." By nature I am a sinner.

Like the lady who worked in that watch factory. She painted dials with radium paint. In the process she pointed her brush by touching it with her tongue. After working at the watch factory for a while she began to feel sick. Doctors found nothing wrong. Yet she felt sicker and sicker. One night when there was no light in the bedroom, she looked in the mirror and she let out a shriek. In the mirror she saw a shimmery, ghostly light radiating from the skin of her face and body. And her hair was luminous in the dark. Radium had migrated throughout her body and she knew she was doomed.[1]

We are not doomed. God forgives us in Jesus Christ. Jesus, turning to the woman and to Simon says,

Therefore, I tell you, her sins, which were many, have been forgiven; hence she has shown great love. But the

one to whom little is forgiven, loves little ... your sins
are forgiven ... your faith has saved you; go in peace.
— Luke 7:47-50

When Jesus speaks the word of forgiveness, the sun breaks through the clouds, angels applaud, the gloom is lifted, and Satan gets a royal shellacking.

But the struggle is always real and near. Who am I in the story? As an opponent to capital punishment I find myself conflicted when it comes to serial killers like David Berkowitz. You know what upsets me most about the infamous David Berkowitz? What upsets me most are not David Berkowitz's terrible acts, terrorizing New York City residents during the 1970s. What upsets me are not the six senseless murders and the wounding of seven others in a spree of mayhem, though that is tragic. What upsets me most are not his intimidations for years signing notes as "Son of Sam, I'll be back, I'll be back."

What upsets me most are not that when caught August 10, 1977, he enjoyed telling about the murders, smiled at the public, was cooperative and polite and pleaded the excuse, "Sam made me go out and do it." What upsets me is that in 1987 David Berkowitz, alias "Son of Sam" had a born-again experience and began calling himself the "Son of Hope."

In a letter he sent to the *New York Daily News*, now Son of Hope, he wrote, "I have nothing but deep regret and sorrow for all that had happened and for all the bad things that I have done." David Berkowitz had become an exemplary prisoner and a role model, counseling others.

My question is "Is this an act?" Does God's grace and forgiveness cover a serial killer? His sins washed, soul cleansed, and past forgiven. Is that the way it works?

Simon is repulsed at the attention and affection a sinner woman lavishes on Jesus. So the Pharisee in me questions the sincerity of convicted serial killers like David Berkowitz. Does the Son of Sam turned to Son of Hope, really pray daily, read scriptures, and work in sincerity as a chaplain's clerk? If God forgives people like him, how much more should we?

Oh, yes, "The play's the thing wherein I'll catch the co of the king." When plays, stories, and parables probe my co and prick my scruples and push my guilt buttons I may fensively at first, but ultimately I know its the truth.

Matthew 25 pictures the last judgment scene. The ragged truth is about feeding the hungry and clothing the naked and visiting the prisoners. This never fails to snare me.

Leo Tolstoy's short story, *Where Love is, God is*, hooks me and haunts me as the poor cobbler, Martin Avedieteh, waits for Christ to come to visit and discovers ultimately that three needy people appearing at his door were really the Christ. In the end, Jesus' coming is not in some great climax, but in these quiet, needy interruptions that came to the door. So when the stories, the plays, the parables convince and convict of sins, I thank God for the sweet message of the psalmist: "Happy are those whose transgression is forgiven" (Psalm 32:1).

The forgiven love a lot. And forgiveness brings reconciliation. Like the story told in Spain of a father and his teenage son whose relationship had become strained. The son ran away from home. His father, however, began a journey in search of his rebellious son. Finally, in Madrid, in a last desperate effort to find him, this father put an ad in the newspaper: "Dear Paco, meet me in front of the newspaper office at noon. All is forgiven. I love you. Your father."

The next day at noon, in front of the newspaper office, 800 "Pacos" showed up.[2]

The most powerful words spoken to anyone are: "You are accepted. I accept you as you are, my beloved. You are forgiven. Your debts are completely cancelled." No wonder she washed Jesus' feet with her tears and dried them with her hair. Jesus looks at Simon the Pharisee and says, "But the one to whom little is forgiven, loves little." The formula is simple: Little forgiveness = little love. A lot of forgiveness = a lot of love.

One can intellectualize grace. One can teach about it. One can define it as God's unearned love and favor. But when one experiences grace, one knows it. A weight is lifted. A debt is paid. A burden is gone. You feel like you've won the lottery. You feel like floating. Then one's role is to pass it on. Forgiveness and grace are like ice. Pass it on quickly or it will melt and you'll lose it.

There was a high school math teacher who had an interesting practice. Whenever he would give a test, if one person flunked, the whole class had to take the test over again. Now this seems unfair for the bright students who did well but now think of the positive peer pressure to have everyone at least pass. Suddenly it was extremely important to function as a group, as a community, and to make sure by helping one another everyone succeeded.

What if grace, forgiveness, and salvation in your community was an all or nothing proposition? Either we are all forgiven, we are all saved, everyone or none of us. With this dynamic we would be less private about our salvation in Christ. We would be much more generous and open and helpful.

Today, as you know and feel you are forgiven, pass it on, show it by the "greater" love and compassion for others. Amen.

----

1. Source unknown.

2. Illustration reprinted from *Emphasis*, CSS Publishing Co., Lima, Ohio.

Liberating The Possessed

He is a tortured man! His hair is tossed and tousled. His beard appears shaggy and matted with debris. His eyes stare saucer-like and hypnotic, betraying his clueless and clotheless dilemma. He beats and cuts himself with sharp rocks until blood flows, clots, and flows again. Blue bruises dot his skin like a leopard's spots.

He lives in the cemetery. Imagined or real zombies are his friends. Gerasene citizens try to contain him, but their shackles and chains crack and break by his strange and superior strength. How does one control craziness? How do you manage chaos?

Pilgrims avoid the area. They are clearly afraid. The local villagers know the situation is beyond their scope. Do they realize "Diablo" is at work? "What is your name?" Jesus asks. "Legion" he shouts back for he knows many, many demons entered him and possessed him (v. 30b). Since "Legion" represents 6,000 soldiers in a typical Roman army, darkness is truly in charge. Envision 6,000 bats in a dark cave and one can begin to imagine "Legion." Demons, like bats, favor darkness and despise the light.

Rational minds in modern times easily dismissed demon possession, the devil, and evil spirits. Then in 1968, a movie, *Rosemary's Baby*, based on the novel by Ira Levin, leaped from our culture and into our collective consciousness. Soon an otherworldly craziness shocked and horrified thrill seekers, the curious, the skeptics, and "the faithful." Another movie, *The Exorcist*, in 1973 portrayed a sensational, shocking horror story about devil possession and the subsequent exorcism of demon spirits from a young innocent girl of divorced parents. Earlier an exorcism true story in Mount Rainer, Maryland, performed upon a fourteen-year-old boy by Jesuit Priest Father William Boadern and Father Raymond Bishop, gained literary and Hollywood notoriety.

Some years ago, I experienced a front row seat observing the surrealness of "possession." Nine of us Church World Service staff traveled for six hours in a Service Chretian d'Haiti Land Rover through the mountains on dry river and creek beds until we reached Jacmel in southeast Haiti. We arrived in the village and met with Paul, the mayor of Jacmel, a white French Haitian. Our destination was a forty by sixty foot building with open windows all around where a Vodou ceremony was in progress. Three drummers were beating upon mahogany drums made with goat skins stretched over the top. The Mamba (priestess) welcomed us as we were ushered to front row seats. For two hours the Mamba and her two assistants led the dancing and responsive chanting. Many of the chants told stories in the Creole language. The audience appeared mesmerized.

Suddenly as the intensity of the rhythmic beat increased, six women and an eight-year-old girl who had become "possessed" the night before fell into a convulsing, trance-like state. They fell on the floor and upon one another, imitating the movements of the rhythmic drumbeat. Did this have anything to do with demon possession and spiritism like "Legion" in Luke's gospel, I wondered? More bizarre things began to happen. One of the mothers, still in a trance, left the dance area while the female chorus continued to chant louder and louder and dance more intensely. The mother returned with her small baby, holding it by its heels, carrying it on her shoulder. Abruptly, she began to swing her small baby by its heels, the baby's head narrowly missing the sharp corner of the platform. Monsieur André Poultré, our Church World Service guide, reached for the baby to save it. The mother and André struggled momentarily as we watched, stunned and helpless. The mother won the tussle and continued her reckless dance with her baby. We learned later, that the child was ill, and that the mother was going to cure it or kill it. After several other strange, weird, and scary happenings, we left the compound and returned to our lodging to engage in a vigorous discussion.

We had learned from the Mamba that to be "possessed" was to be possessed by an Iola or god and that this was induced through magic potions, the drumbeat, dance, song, and special circumstances. We wondered, was this an expression of the powers of darkness, a simple cultural oddity, or what?

In the late 1980s and 1990s adults and youth from my Mankato congregation made numerous mission/service project trips to the Pine Ridge Indian reservation in Shannon County of South Dakota, the poorest economic county in the nation. We were hosted by the Our Lady of the Sioux Catholic Church and got to know Brother René the parish director. Brother René told us of the times he was called out by Native American parishioners to exorcise evil spirits from their dwelling places and went, armed with the name of Christ, and exorcised what they sensed, perceived, and feared. Brother René saw this phenomenon as a vital part of his pastoral care ministry, was successful at it, and is still revered and remembered by many today.

M. Scott Peck wrote after much reflection and prayer, "I now know Satan is real. I have met it."[1]

The demons in "Legion" beg Jesus not to order them back to the abyss. The demons recognized Jesus as the Son of the Most High God. This Jesus who stills the storm, walks over the deep, raises the dead, heals the sick, also comes to liberate the "possessed." Jesus comes, in our text, and in our contemporary lives, to bring liberation from sin, death, and the power of Diablo. Diablo is the devil, Lucifer, the prince of darkness.

Legion has no purpose or meaning in his deranged life. God's liberating power calls him from the abyss and sets him free in a most unusual manner. Pigs or swine are nearby. Pigs are considered unclean according to Jewish teachings and tradition. Swine, in this Gerasene Gentile area, were most likely raised to feed the Roman occupying troops, who had no qualms about eating pork chops or ham. We see 2,000 swine, according to Mark 5, who are idly eating and grunting in the countryside. The demons knowing their fate with Jesus, cannot stand to be disembodied. They request to enter the swine. Request is granted. The pigs run like lemmings to the sea and are drowned.

"Legion" is no longer Legion. He is a liberated man. Christ sets him free!

What and how are dark powers manifested today? Surely they are both personal and collective. They come to us as individuals, and they come to us through the structures, processes, and policies of institutions and government as well as society as a whole.

Who can explain away the horrors of darkness? Is "Legion" among us or within us? We cringe in the face of a serial killer like Bundy, Berkowitz, or Charles Manson. We abhor the holocaust; famine in Africa; sexist, racial, and ethnic hatred; children working in sweat factories, child prostitution, sexual abuse, abuse by cults such as the Fundamental Latter Day Saints; preemptive war by our leaders; global warming; and destruction of our only home planet earth.

We struggle with personal evils within. Jesus was not deterred by the screaming. Jesus launched a direct, frontal assault on the dark and evil power that had taken control of "Legion." "What is your name?" (v. 30).

Our clue is to "name the offender." We need to name alcohol and substance abuse, not "a few too many!" We need to name lying, not "shading the truth." We need to call it cheating, not "everybody's doing it"; and stealing, not "one of the benefits of working here." One must by the grace of God look the lie in the face and name it!

"Then the people came out ... they found the man whom the demons had gone sitting at the feet of Jesus, clothed and in his right mind" (v. 35). This is what happened to Bob. His demon was his addiction to alcohol. Bob was controlled and consumed by the addiction. It colored everything he did, said, or thought. He continued on the spiral down until one day he named his demon. He was able to say in therapy, "My name is Bob. I am an alcoholic." Recovery will take the rest of his lifetime and he knows it. Bob is now an alcoholic counselor at a recovery center here in South Dakota.

It's a long way from the Gerasene region in Luke 8 to Trondjhem Lutheran Church in rural South Dakota. But I must ask the question: So what happens when a snake interrupts a wedding rehearsal? It was a hot July night. It was a beautiful full harvest moon night. Two people, Troy and Heather, in love, were standing with me, the presiding minister, touching, whispering their sweet nothings to one another at the altar. Groomsmen and bridesmaids were standing erect as they listened to their instructions. Mothers beamed from the pews. The organist shuffled her music and had just ended her processional when the bridesmaids began to scream. Coming down the aisle was an unusually large, ferocious looking bull snake, asserting himself in this new-found domain.

The snake had no intention of retreating as pandemonium erupted! One groomsmen calmly grabbed the snake by its tail, slapped it down on the church floor, stunned it, and carried it out as we all heaved a sigh of relief especially thankful that the intruder did not come the next night at the actual wedding ceremony.

Here's the application: Is Diablo not the snake? John calls him in Revelation 20:2 (cf) "that old snake who is the devil."

> One word from Christ and the demons are swimming with the swine, and the wild man is clothed in his right mind ... just one command! No se'ance needed. No hocus pocus. No chants were heard or candles lit. Hell is an anthill against heaven's steamroller. Jesus commands ... evil spirits and they obey him ... the snake in the ditch and Lucifer in the pit — both have met their match.[2]

Christ is our liberator from sin, death, and the power of Diablo. We are free to broadcast the news to all as Jesus instructed the demonless man to go and tell what Jesus had done for him.

It may be legend but the story is about Abraham Lincoln. Lincoln went down to the slave block. He saw a young slave girl. He took money from his pocket and bought her. When the purchase was made she heard the words, "Young lady, you are free."

She said, "Please, sir, what does that mean?"

Lincoln said, "It means you are free."

"Does that mean," she asked, "that I can say whatever I want to say?"

Lincoln said, "Yes, my dear, you can say whatever you want to say."

"Does that mean," she asked, "that I can be whatever I want to be?"

Lincoln said, "Yes, you can be whatever you want to be."

She asked, "Does that mean I can go wherever I want to go?"

He said, "Yes, you can go wherever you want to go."

The girl, with tears streaming down her face said, "Then I will go with you."[3]

Liberated — we are inspired to be with Christ, our freedom. We break out in joy and laughter. Like Neil who lost his wife after an illness. Neil was devastated and grieved his beloved. But one day Neil met Bobbie and the two fell in love and took a trip to the St. Martins, Dutch West Indies. Neil sent me, his pastor, a card that simply said, "Yippee, yippee, yippee! Neil and Bobbie." Amen.

---

1. M. Scott Peck, *People of the Lie: The Hope for Healing Human Evil* (New York: Simon and Schuster, 1983), p. 182.

2. Max Lucado, *Next Door Savior* (Nashville: Word Publishing Group, 2003), p. 60.

3. Original source unknown.

Keeping The Main Thing
The Main Thing

They were 5,000 feet in the air in a two-seat Cessna when suddenly the pilot slumped over. It happened not so long ago near Mount Hope, Indiana, to an 81-year-old passenger who was flying to Indianapolis for lunch. When his 52-year-old friend and pilot unexpectedly died, the elder passenger realized he knew nothing about flying and a lot less about landing! In the next twenty minutes you can bet he gave his total attention to the voices on the radio and the instructions given to him. Another pilot nearby coached him and gave him a "crash course" (pardon the pun) in flying a two-seat Cessna and most importantly in landing. He circled the airport three times and came in, bounced a few times, and landed in a soggy field. Incredibly there was no damage except a bent propeller.

If this happened to you or to me today, our number one priority would be determined very, very quickly! It would not be the time to call out for a pizza, or to scan *Field and Stream* magazine, nor to casually call a friend on one's cell to plan an outing to attend a ball game. The *main* thing and the *only* thing would be to land that Cessna and not crash!

Stephen Covey in his book, *First Things First*, a *New York Times* best seller for several years, says the issue for life is just that — first things first! So the compelling question coming out of our gospel reading from Luke 9 is this: How does one keep the "main thing" the main thing in one's life? And just what is the "main thing"?

One day, right after Jesus had been snubbed and spurned by the people in a Samaritan village, someone came up to him and promised, "I will follow you wherever you go." A bit later, Jesus says to another person, "Follow me." But the person excuses himself, "Lord, let me first go and bury my father." Jesus turns to another, "Follow me." But he answers, "Excuse me, Jesus, I will follow you, but first let me say good-bye to my family." Jesus' response is uncompromisingly direct — appearing insensitive, "Let the dead bury the dead; but as for you, go and proclaim the kingdom of God ... no one who puts a hand to the plow and looks back is fit for the kingdom of God" (vv. 60, 62). Jesus knew that a farmer who looks back when plowing his field instead of forward at the chosen guidepost, will plow a very crooked furrow.

Jesus heard many excuses in his short three-year ministry. Some excuses were lame. Many were laudable. Some were frivolous. Many excuses were admirable. It's hard to think of a better excuse than to take care of one's family. In our modern life, family is in disarray with nearly half of all marriages ending in divorce, custody battles, deadbeat fathers, abuse, incest, and neglect running rampant. What could be a better, a more admirable task than to care for one's family?

How many times have you and I said, "My family is first"? The most righteous, respectable, and acceptable statement politicians, CEOs, and others make when changing careers is, "I'm quitting so I can take more time for my family."

I wish Jesus would have contrasted "following him" with a lame excuse. But family — that's an admirable, lofty, sterling excuse. But it's not family first — it's the kingdom first! How do we keep the main thing the main thing?

The Bible is full of excusers who were called to do God's bidding. Gideon excused himself and complained that his family was poor and that he was the least in his family. Moses excused himself because he was not eloquent in speech and thus tried to disqualify himself from leading the Hebrews out of bondage from the land of the Egyptians.

Jeremiah said he was too young. My excuse when I sensed a leading into parish ministry was my lack of speech ability and how would I survive Greek? The amazing thing is that God is able to use us excusers once we get beyond our excuses. When we live in our baptismal covenant and are bathed in God's grace in Christ we can say this to one another, "Let me hear your excuses and I'll tell you mine, and we'll travel together a bit with them and eventually we'll get to the real issue."

What is the real issue? Consider the little boy playing hide and seek. He ran quickly and found a remote cabinet in the house. *This ought to be the best place of all,* he thought, as he climbed in and closed the door. He remained absolutely quiet. But his sister saw his shoelace sticking out under the closed cabinet door, followed it, and found her brother. Excuses like shoelaces are to be followed and eventually they will take you to the real source and issue.

A man I knew did not worship. He was a member of my parish and he always had excuses. I followed his "shoelace" and found out one day that he had been hurt by someone in the church and that festering wound was the source of his excuses. Often the "shoelace" trail leads to fear or grief or guilt or a hurt. If someone followed your "shoelace" or mine where would it lead? Our excuses hiding behind our heart's cabinet doors are cover-ups and need to be exposed.

Dive into the gospels most anywhere and you will find Jesus asking someone to follow. The Greek verb is *akoloutheo.* I was raised in a Christian tradition "to believe" and not necessarily "to follow." Dr. Ernest Campbell, who once served as pastor of Riverside Church in New York City made this statement:

> *It began innocently enough — a friend recommended a book by Jon Sobrino. The Salvadorian Jesuit blew most of my ducks out of the water. He threw a hat down on my scrabble board and messed up many of my combinations. He forced me to contend for the ground that I had claimed. The question Jon Sobrino put to me I must share with you: "Are you following Jesus, or believing in Christ?"*[1]

Harry Wendt of Crossways International asks:

> *If* akoloutheo *represents a dominant motif ... why, then, do we hear so little about following Jesus in the church today? I've been in, with, and around the church for more than fifty years. Not when I was in communicants class; not when I joined the church: not when I became a candidate for the ministry; not when I was ordained; and never in any of my services of installation. Always the questions have dealt with* belief. *"Do you believe in God-Father, Son, and Holy Spirit? Do you believe in the veracity of the Scriptures and the Westminster Confession? Do you believe in the unity and purity of the church? Do you believe in Christ?" It isn't hard to answer that ... but when someone asks, "Are you following Jesus?" — this can get to be expensive. This question has to do with my lifestyle, my attitudes, my values, my surrender.*[2]

For me it is easy, painless, and comfortable to confess I believe in God, Father, Son, and Holy Spirit as I do constantly in the three creeds, in relational sharing of my faith, and in my preaching and teaching. But hold it. I live in a beautiful log home in the lovely Black Hills. I own three automobiles, have closets stuffed full of clothes, have a good pension, and all the amenities of life one might want or think one needs. Am I following Jesus in a world of hunger and deprivation? Am I following Jesus when I deplete the earth's resources? Am I following Jesus if I am not washing my neighbors' feet in love, compassion, and generosity?

I was taught in my confirmation instruction Ephesians 2:8-9: "For by grace are you saved through faith...." But what about Ephesians 2:10? "For we are what God has made us, created in Christ Jesus for good works, which God prepared beforehand to be our way of life!"

Of course we are never saved by works, we are saved for works. It seems that those works are that we follow Jesus, our crucified and forgiving Savior. If the question, "Are you following Jesus or believing in Christ?" seems unfair or artificial because the two are inseparable. Theoretically, yes, they are inseparable but pragmatically, no. We separate them all the time. I suggest if we must separate them let us err on the side of following. Harry Wendt says, "One can believe without following, but one cannot follow without believing."

"Come follow me," Jesus says over and over in the gospels. "Let the dead bury the dead; but as for you go and proclaim the kingdom of God...."

In 1 Kings 19, Elijah not only anoints Elisha as his successor but also allows Elisha's request to "Let me kiss my father and my mother and then I will follow you." Jesus is less tolerant and insists on first things first. He keeps the main thing the main thing.

One practical way to put first things first is to begin to live by the compass and not the clock. The clock represents our appointments, our commitments, schedules, goals, and activities — what we do and how we manage our time. Often we are overscheduled and time that originally was a gift has become a tyranny. The compass on the other hand represents our direction, vision, values, principles, conscience, purpose, and mission — what we feel is truly important as God leads our lives. What is the main thing? But to earnestly seek to follow Jesus and proclaim the kingdom to all in word and deed.

John Wesley, the great founder of the Methodist church wrote in his diary:

> *Sunday a.m. May 5 — Preached in St. Anne's. Was asked not to come back anymore.*
> *Sunday p.m. May 5 — Preached in St. John's. Deacons said get out and stay out.*
> *Sunday a.m. May 12 — Preached in St. Jude's. Can't go back there either.*
> *Sunday a.m. May 19 — Preached in St. Somebody Elses. Deacons called a special meeting and said I couldn't return.*
> *Sunday p.m. — Preached on street. Kicked off the street.*
> *Sunday a.m. — Preached in meadow. Chased out of the meadow as bull was turned loose during service.*

Sunday a.m. — Preached out at the edge of town. Kicked
  off highway.
Sunday p.m. — June afternoon, preached in a pasture.
  Ten thousand people came out to hear me.[3]

Jesus says, "No one who puts his hand to the plow and looks back is fit for service in the kingdom of God." It's about first things first. Amen.

---

1. George S. Johnson, *Beyond Guilt* (Minneapolis: Augsburg/Fortress, 2000), pp. 19-20.

2. Harry Wendt, *2008-2009 Workshop and Resource Catalogue* (Washington, DC: Crossroads International), p. 3, president's message, "Believing Vs. Following."

3. Source unknown.

Appointed And Sent!

The wheat harvest was glorious that year on our farm in South Dakota. Our pastor even came out from town and shocked grain for us. The two men from Arkansas that my dad hired were less ambitious. When Mom brought lunch out to them she often found them resting in the shade of a shock of grain. Nonetheless, the golden sheaves of wheat were so full and heavy they seemed to bow down to us as we passed by on the road. Soon the threshing machine and crew would arrive to separate wheat from straw. It was an amazing time — harvest time!

After Jesus had appointed "the seventy" and sent them ahead of him in pairs, he said, "The harvest is plentiful, but the laborers are few; therefore ask the Lord of the harvest to send out laborers into his harvest" (v. 2).

It is a great honor to be so trusted to be sent! Gerhard Frost, my poet professor and seminary teacher, recited this one day in catechetics class:

> *The Sent One*
> *I remember being sent;*
> *it made me ten feet tall.*
> *How dignifying*
> *to walk in borrowed presence*
> *down that winding road*
> *to the country store.*
> *I carried a note,*
> *not in my handwriting, of course,*

269

because I couldn't write;
but I could scribble.

I never scribbled on that note.

And I was careful,
so careful lest it fall in the dirt.
I was content just to carry it.

To be sent is
an exercise in being third.
First, there's the sender;
second, the one to whom you're sent;
and then, you, the sent one.
Any two without the other won't do.

"He called to him the twelve,"
the scriptures say,
"and began to send them two by two ...
and he charged them...."
He called them, he sent them, he charged them.
What an honor to be carriers of his love![1]

The "sent ones," the twelve and the seventy, back then, and we, the called, baptized, authorized, equipped, and commissioned, now today, face many opportunities: The first opportunity and challenge is that "the harvest is plentiful, but the laborers are few!" The harvest is vast. In chapter 10 of Genesis, the Hebrew text enumerates all the nations of the world. How many? Seventy! The number suggests that the harvest, the mission is to the entire world. The Acts of the Apostles records Jesus' final words to his "sent ones," "You will be my witnesses in Jerusalem, in all Judea and Samaria, and to the ends of the earth" (Acts 1:8).

A place to start is in "Jerusalem" or our own contemporary hometown culture. The "sent ones" are most effective in sharing the word when there is understanding of the expectations, values, norms, and perspective of each of the five different generations in our society. For example, a baby boomer lives in a far different world than a Millennial or Generation Y. The implications for the gospel and church life are immense.

So who are the "laborers"?

It is interesting and significant that in Numbers 11:16-17, Moses gathers seventy elders and places upon them the Spirit so that they might help bear the burdens of the people of Israel. Who are the seventy today? Surely the laborers are missionaries, pastors, deacons, and bishops. These, and oh yes, more!

All the laity who are called by virtue of their baptism into the life, death, and resurrection of Jesus Christ are the laborers. So why "so few"? Because in part most of the laity have not been instructed in how God has made them, gifted them, and empowered them. The role of church leadership is to help the laity identify their gifts and integrate them into ministries that match their gifts. When one lives according to one's spiritual giftedness, one no longer works in one's own strength, but the Holy Spirit, is at work within.

Our Lord envisioned that as the harvest is plentiful, the labor force under the tutelage of the Holy Spirit, would become more and greater. "After the Holy Spirit has come upon you, you shall be my witnesses...."

The second opportunity and challenge is that "the harvest is plentiful but the *leaders* are few!" Jesus saw the multitudes like sheep who wandered aimlessly, and leaderless, who needed a shepherd who knows how to not only feed, nurture, and protect, but especially to lead!

The major crisis in the church today is the crisis of leadership. Most of us pastors were not trained to be leaders. We were trained to be chaplains of the faithful. Many of us pastors should be arrested. Our crimes are not about boundary violations, nor poor preaching nor extravagant lifestyles, but about leadership that is inadequate, misdirected, and mismatched with the needs and challenges of our current environment. We were trained in "expressive leadership" that is, to preach, teach, announce, talk, exhort, lead liturgy, counsel, and chaplaincy care. We were not taught "instrumental leadership," that is, using instruments, processes, structures, administration, and visioning.

One leader in the Old Testament who possessed both expressive and instrumental leadership abilities was Josiah (2 Kings 22-23). King Josiah was a great leader. When he came to the throne of Judah at age eight, the nation was essentially pagan. Heathen altars stood on the high hills, and the people offered incense to false gods. Jehovah God was forgotten. The law was lost. The temple was closed and the Passover was only a distant memory.

When King Josiah died 31 years later, the nation had completely changed! The pagan altars were only a pile of rubble. The covenant with God had been renewed. The law once again was read and revered. The temple doors opened up and the priests functioned faithfully. The Passover was recovered and the Lord God Yahweh was worshiped. Josiah was a leader who knew how to lead God's people Israel.

Ken Blanchard and Mark Miller in their book, *The Secret*, dedicate their work to "the next generation of serving leaders." Blanchard and Miller suggest the acronym SERVE as benchmarks of great leadership. **S** stands for *See*. See the future. Leaders create and empower compelling visions.

> *When Disney World opened in 1971, Walt Disney was not present to witness the grand opening of his greatest dream come true — he had died five years earlier. During the spectacular opening ceremonies, the host of the festivities introduced Walt's widow, Lillian Disney, who would say a few words on stage for the occasion. "Mrs. Disney," the host beamed with reverence, "I wish Walt could have seen this." Lillian stood up, walked over to the podium, adjusted the microphone, and said, "He did." And then she sat down. That simple statement said it all.*[2]

E stands for *Engage* and develop others. Blanchard and Miller illustrate E.

> *One of my favorite historical examples of this is the story of Spartacus. Spartacus was a slave who led an uprising against the Roman government ... but the slaves*

are all captured by the Romans. The Roman general tells them if they reveal Spartacus to him, he will spare their lives. At that moment, Spartacus stands and says, "I am Spartacus." Unexpectedly, the slave next to him stands and says, "I am Spartacus." And the next and the next until the entire Legion is standing.

This inspiring scene illustrates the role of a leader to create levels of engagement such that when we, as leaders, stand on an issue, our people will stand with us.[3]

R stands for *Reinvent* continuously. Reinvent continuously applies to systems and processes asking how can we do better. Reinvent continuously applies to structures and organization.

V represents *Value* results and relationships. Great leaders appreciate both results and relationships. The two are equal and one must not be raised above the other. John Maxwell said, "People will not give you their hand until they can see your heart."

E suggests *Embody* values. Trust is built when values are clarified and followed diligently. Great leaders establish, articulate, model, and enforce core values.

Serving leaders makes a powerful difference in society and church. Like leaven, light, and salt, great serving leaders are examples like Josiah, and also Nelson Mandela, who after 28 years in jail came out, not angry. In fact, he invited his jailers to his inauguration. Jimmy Carter is perhaps the greatest ex-president winning the Nobel Peace Prize, championing Habitat for Humanity, and various peace initiatives. There's Martin Luther King Jr. and, of course, our Lord Jesus of Nazareth who served with a servant heart all the way to the cross.

Two leaders who have inspired me are Ed Yost, visionary, adventurer, and inventor of the modern hot air balloon. I personally drafted blueprints for him. Hot air balloons inspire awe as they appear like floating flowers around the planet. The second is Korzak Ziolkowski who began sculpting Crazy Horse, the largest monument in the world. After sixty years, long after his death, his vision is still alive as Korzak's family blasts away the Crazy Horse mountain in order to honor Native American heroes of North America.

Randy Pausch of *The Last Lecture* fame was asked who inspired him as a leader and he identified Captain James T. Kirk, commander of the starship *Enterprise.*

> *Kirk was not the smartest guy on the ship ... so why did he get to climb on board the* Enterprise *and run it? The answer: There is this skill set called leadership. Kirk was the distilled essence of the dynamic manager, a guy who knew how to delegate, had the passion to inspire, and looked good in what he wore to work. He never professed to have skills greater than his subordinates ... he established the vision, the tone. He was in charge of morale.*[4]

The third opportunity and challenge is: "The harvest is plentiful but the lovers are few!" Wherever Jesus went, he had compassion for the people. "Then Jesus called his disciples to him and said, 'I have compassion for the crowd' " (Matthew 15:32) and "When the Lord saw her he had compassion for her ..." (Luke 7:13). When the people of the harvest know and feel that they are loved, they will respond to the gospel message. Paul encourages the "ones sent" to "bear one another's burdens, and in this way you will fulfill the law of Christ" (Galatians 6:2).

My friend, Pastor John, since he came to Christ the King Lutheran Church in Newcastle, Wyoming, has expressed incredible love and affection for his small flock. The members have so responded that he now consistently has ninety to 100 adults in Bible study weekly. Pastor John's acceptance, compassion, and love seeps through every crack in the congregation and they respond.

Finally, "Therefore ask the Lord of the harvest to send out laborers [leaders and lovers] into his harvest." To ask is to pray. To pray is to ask. It is the Lord's role to do the sending. There's the sender, the one to whom you're sent, and then you and I the "sent ones." Amen.

> *A young man approached the foreman of a logging crew and asked for a job. "That depends," replied the foreman. "Let's see you fell this tree." The young man stepped forward, and skillfully felled a great tree. Im-*

pressed, the foreman exclaimed, "You can start Monday."

Monday, Tuesday, Wednesday, Thursday rolled by — and Thursday afternoon the foreman approached the young man and said, "You can pick up your paycheck on the way out today."

Startled, the young man replied, "I thought you paid on Friday."

"Normally we do," said the foreman. "But we're letting you go today because you've fallen behind. Our daily felling charts show that you've dropped from first place on Monday to last place today."

"But I'm a hard worker," the young man objected. "I arrive first, leave last, and even have worked through my coffee breaks!"

The foreman, sensing the young man's integrity, thought for a minute and then asked, '"Have you been sharpening your ax?"

The young man replied, "No, sir. I've been working too hard to take time for that!"[5]

1. Gerhard Frost, "The Sent One," recited in class, Luther Seminary, St. Paul, Minnesota, 1964.

2. Pat Croce, *Lead or Get Off the Pot!* (New York: Simon and Schuster, 2004), p. 9.

3. Ken Blanchard and Mark Miller, *The Secret* (San Francisco: Berrett-Koehler Publishers, Inc., 2004), p. 53.

4. Randy Pausch, *The Last Lecture* (New York: Hyperion, 2008), pp. 43-44.

5. Wayne Rice, *More Hot Illustrations for Youth Talks* (Grand Rapids: Zondervan Publishing, 1995), p. 155.

Checked The Ditch Lately?

We were driving west on Highway 16 from Custer to Newcastle, Wyoming, when Pam and I spotted this magnificent bird along the road. It was feeding on a deer carcass, and as we approached, it sprang into the air and soared off to the south alighting on the branch of a ponderosa pine. It watched us. It waited for us to pass. Yes, it was a golden eagle with a wing span of at least six feet.

The next day, we were surprised and disappointed to see on the front page of our local *Custer Chronicle* paper a photo of a golden eagle that was found in a ditch along Highway 16 with a bleeding head and broken wing. It had apparently been hit by a passing vehicle. Then we realized, it was the same golden eagle we had seen, because they found it in exactly the same spot.

In Jesus' parable, it is a man that is found beaten and bleeding, lying in a ditch by the side of the road. A sharp lawyer had just asked Jesus in a series of questions, "Who then is my neighbor?" Jesus responds by telling this story: "A man was going down from Jerusalem to Jericho and fell into the hands of robbers" (v. 30).

Jerusalem and Jericho are only seventeen miles apart. Jerusalem is the city set on a hill nearly 3,000 feet above sea level, whereas Jericho, at 840 feet below sea level, is the lowest city on planet earth. Both cities are safe places: Jerusalem, the Holy City, and Jericho, a desert oasis. To get from one city to the other is to travel a crooked and dangerous road. As this certain man travels, robbers leap out from the rocks and attack him. The robbers strip him, beat him, and leave him half dead in the ditch.

Some of us have had robbers invade and mess up our lives. When thieves break in we feel violated, vulnerable, insecure, and angry. We become less trusting and fearful.

One summer Monday morning, I got up to go to work at the engineering firm where I drafted blueprints in downtown St. Paul. I walked out of our apartment door and was shocked to see my car was gone. It was stolen. I had just paid for that beautiful 1955 black Chevy, and as a seminary student, I could hardly afford to buy another.

Car thieves and carjackers do that. Robbers and thieves live by the rule, "what's yours is mine."[1] Pick-pockets, embezzlers, shop-lifters, abusers, and rapists also live by "what's yours is mine!" Your freedom, your person, your possession, your body is mine. So we live our lives afraid, cautious, and mistrusting.

This Jericho-bound traveler loses his possessions, his security, and almost his life. But help is coming. Along comes a priest and later a Levite. They know Deuteronomy 30.

> *For the Lord will again take delight in prospering you, just as he delighted in prospering your ancestors, when you obey the Lord your God by observing his command-ments and decrees that are written in this book of the law, because you turn to the Lord your God with all your heart and with all your soul.*
> — Deuteronomy 30:9b-10

They know the law, "Love the Lord your God with all your heart and soul and mind and your neighbor as yourself." They teach it. They lecture on it. They expound on it. They represent the reli-gious community of the time — the Pharisees. But they pass by on the other side. They leave the bloodied creature in the ditch. They offer no help. Why? Perhaps they are afraid of lurking bandits or because they have appointments to make and because of their fear or busy schedules practice, "what's mine is mine!" My time is mine. My resources are mine. My money is mine. My work for God is mine. "What's mine is mine!"

The priest and the Levite are like the wealthy man driving his BMW who sees a poor, hungry family along a country road are eating grass. The rich CEO stops. "Get in, I will help you." The hungry family gets into the BMW. The rich man drives them to his own estate and says to them, "Here, the grass is taller for you to eat." No real help. *What's mine is mine!*

How long that golden eagle lay in the ditch, we do not know. How long the man lay in the ditch, we do not know, either. Presently, along comes a Samaritan, in Jesus' parable, a Samaritan despised by the Jews, but when he sees the man in the ditch, he is moved with compassion. He stops, goes to him, bandages up his wounds, puts him on his own animal, and takes him to an inn with the instructions, "Take care of him and when I come back, I will repay you whatever more you spend."

Conservation officer Ben Chambers found the injured golden eagle we had seen and rescued it. Ben took the eagle to Gillette, Wyoming, where Diane Morse operates N.E.W. Bird Rescue and Rehab center. The bird was given electrolytes to stabilize her condition. Next a steel pin was inserted to fix her broken wing. After a recuperation time, the plan was to release the bird in the same area where she was found.

The Samaritan, we traditionally call "good," lived not by "what's yours is mine" nor "what's mine is mine" but the higher moral ground of "what's mine is yours."

Edgar Guest, the poet and writer, wrote this when his first child had died.

> *There came a tragic night when our first baby was taken from us. I was lonely and defeated. There didn't seem to be anything in life ahead of me that mattered very much. I had to go to my neighbor's drugstore the next morning for something and he motioned for me to step behind the counter with him. I followed him into his little office in the back at the rear of the store. He put both hands on my shoulders and said, "Eddie, I can't really express what I want to say, the sympathy I have in my heart for you. All I can say is, that I'm sorry, and I want you to know that if you need anything at all, come to me. What is mine is yours."*

Years later, Edgar Guest thought about this experience.

> *Jim Potter, a neighbor across the way, the druggist, may long since have forgotten that moment when he gave his hand and his sympathy, but I shall never forget it — never in my life. To me it stands out like the silhouette of a lonely tree against a crimson sunset.* [2]

My friend, Charles, and I were driving home from Chicago, when we ran out of gas somewhere in Wisconsin. It was on the interstate, and I was not going to wait around for help to come with our raised hood, so I leaped over the barrier fence and looked for assistance. A man in the nearby community came up to me and said, "I'll help you. I'm a Mormon and I'll help you get gas." There is no religious group that I disagree with more doctrinally. The Church of Latter Day Saints claim to be Christian but fail to hold even one orthodox Christian teaching. Nonetheless, it was this kindly Mormon who helped my friend and I get enough gas to get to the next station. He said and acted out essentially, *"What's mine is yours."*

Who is my neighbor? Who is your neighbor? Helmut Thielecke said, "The road to hell is paved, not merely with good intentions, but with good reasons."

"Sin" reflected the priest in Shusaku Endo's book, *Silence*, "is not usually what people think it to be. It is not to steal and tell lies. Sin, is for one man to walk brutally over the life of another and to be quite oblivious of the wounds he has left behind."[3]

We talk so glibly about loving our neighbor. If I love you and do not know anything about you, my statement about loving you is nothing else but hypocrisy. One of the neighbors that we have the greatest encounter of fear with right now is Islam. And unless we know who they are, we can't love them. We really are in a crisis. We don't know how to deal with Islam. Islam is not going to go away, and we can't continue to maintain hostilities and war. It just doesn't work. We need to transform our relationships so that we are no longer hostile with each other.

Who is my neighbor? "Of course," the lawyer says to Jesus, "the one who showed mercy!" The good news is that, in Christ Jesus we have received mercy and in turn get to show mercy to others.

I see good Samaritans all the time. I see Jim working and directing our Habitat for Humanity here in my hometown. I see Kim and Allen picking up Alice from the assisted living home and bringing her to worship every Sunday. I see soldiers in Afghanistan building schools and various projects in the presence of sniper fire and threats of IED (Improvised Explosive Devices) bombs along the roadways. I see my pastors offer listening ears to grieving and desperate folks.

I received mercy when my dear brother, Marlowe, died. He was my playmate and lifelong friend. I shall never forget the hugs, the stories, and kind words that helped heal my loss and utter grief.

Even though the parable did the trick and helped the lawyer see who his neighbor is, I have often wondered about the rest of Jesus' untold story. I would guess two possible endings. The wounded man got healed and went about healing others practicing, *What's mine is yours*, or the wounded man got healed and sunk back into the norm, *What's mine is mine* or worse, became a robber practicing, *What's yours is mine!* I would rather believe the wounded man, now healed, became himself, a healer and a helper.

The Monday I was robbed of my '55 Chevy, my roommate offered, that same evening, to take me for a drive in South Minneapolis in order to console me. Driving hundreds of blocks from our apartment in North Minneapolis, I looked down an alley and there was my car! I couldn't believe it. Nor could my friend. When we reported this miracle to the police they could not believe it either. One simply does not find one's stolen car in a metropolitan area like St. Paul and Minneapolis, by chance.

I began watching for that golden eagle west of town. I traveled to Newcastle for six months every week as an itinerant interim pastor. One day, sure enough, there she was, soaring again. Same place, same old bird, alive, healthy, and free. Like that eagle, you and I, healed, get to show mercy and compassion, too. Amen.

1. Frank Lyman, "Like Everest Without Oxygen," *Pulpit Dynamics.*

2. Jack R. Van Ens. Arvada, Colorado, *Leadership*, Vol. 8, #4.

3. Shusaku Endo, *Silence* (Tokyo: Monumenta Nipponica, 1969).

Sister Act(s)

Today's gospel from Luke 10 follows the parable of the good Samaritan. Luke positions the good Samaritan and the Mary-Martha story back to back for good reason. The parable and the story are examples of the Great Commandment "to love the Lord your God with all your heart and your neighbor as yourself." The good Samaritan parable illustrates "love to neighbor," whereas the Mary-Martha story illustrates "love to God."

Meet the two M & M sisters — Mary and Martha. They are two peas in the same pod and yet so different. Martha and Mary live in the same town — Bethany in Judea. They live in the same house. They have the same brother — Lazarus. How can two sisters, so alike, be so different?

We are told by Luke, that Jesus comes to Bethany and to the two sisters' home for a visit. This is one of many happy times they spend together. Rest, conversation, and friendship, no doubt, occupy their time. Mary sits at Jesus' feet as a disciple would sit at the feet of a rabbi master, listening, observing, and learning. Martha is busy with her many tasks in the household and rather crossly asks, "Lord, do you not care that my sister has left me to do all the work by myself? Tell her then to help me" (v. 40). What would Jesus' answer be? Jesus surely loved and valued both sisters equally — Mary, the sitter and Martha, the worker. How can two peas in the same pod function so differently?

Every church needs a Martha. Change that. Every church needs a hundred Marthas. Sleeves rolled up and

283

ready. Because of Marthas — the church budgets get
balanced — church buildings get repaired and cleaned
— babies get bounced on loving knees in the nursery.
You don't appreciate Marthas until a Martha is missing
— and all the Marys of the church start scrambling to
find the keys to lock doors, turn off the lights and turn
off the fans. Yes, Marthas are the Energizer Bunnies of
the church. They keep going and going and going.[1]

However, Jesus rebukes Martha by saying, "Martha, Martha, you are worried and distracted by many things; there is need of only one thing. Mary has chosen the better part, which will not be taken away from her" (v. 41).

Mary, sitting at the feet of Jesus, looks into the eyes of the Master. Mary listens to his words, his teachings. Mary feels loved, special, affirmed, and graced by Jesus. "Mary has chosen the thing needful ..." whereas Martha hurries and scurries about.

Three flies get into Martha's soup!

The first fly is *worry*. Martha is worried, anxious, and stressed! We, too, in modern life, know only so well about worry, anxiety, and stress. We are plagued with stress overload. Our internal emotional wiring network blazes hot and shorts out.

This is the age of the half-read page.
And the quick hash and the mad dash.
The bright night with the nerves tight.
The plane hop and the brief stop.
The lamp tan in a short span.
The Big Shot in a good spot.
The brain strain and the heart pain.
And the cap naps 'til the spring snaps —
And the fun is done.

In the next twelve months, we will consume over 20,000
tons of aspirin in some form ... that totals 225 tablets
per person per year, or 2/3 of a tablet per person per
day. It appears that most everyone in the US has a head-
ache most of the time.[2]

We are worried, anxious, and stressed. In Martin Luther's day the populace asked the question, "How can I find a gracious God?" Years ago they asked, "How can I get to heaven?" Now today, people are asking, "How can I get through the day?" "Martha, Martha, you are worried...."

We are like that couple who had their home broken into. The husband heard a noise in the middle of the night. He went downstairs to investigate and found a burglar emptying the silver chest. He said to burglar, "Stay where you are. I want to get my wife. She has been expecting you for twenty years."

We are anxious and troubled about not only our "silver chests" but about many things. Jesus speaks the word of grace: "One thing is needful. Only one. Mary has chosen it."

Sit with the scriptures by a quiet lake and you know of that which Mary chose. Or kneel at holy communion ... light a candle in the dim darkness on Christmas Eve and let the candlelight glow touch you and move you. Discover the one thing needful.

The second fly in Martha's soup is *distraction*. "Martha you are worried and distracted by many things." To be distracted is to be unfocused. Our thoughts, our plans, and our lives feel like we are out of control and pulled in every direction. To be focused, on the other hand, is to have a plan, a purpose, a meaning that directs and enhances one's life.

What are those things that keep us from sitting and drinking from the fountain of life? What keeps us from looking and listening and loving? What are the events that distract us from worship? What are the plethora of ideas and thoughts and impulses that obscure the awesomeness of Christ and Christ's mercy and love? A thousand distractions leap into our lap and demand, "Follow me, buy me, go here, go there, do this, do that!"

Besides being worried and distracted, the third fly in Martha's soup is *resentment*. "Lord do you not care that my sister has left me to do all the work by myself?" To be resentful is to be indignantly aggrieved at someone. Resentment can rust a relationship. Resentment can freeze out a friendship. Resentment can alienate your allies and associates.

When I was a child, I resented my siblings when I was assigned chores to do, and especially was I resentful when my only younger sister appeared to be getting preferential treatment. As an adult, I resented unfair treatment by my colleagues. I carried anger too long after being passed over for a desirable position or when I was falsely accused. But I am learning slowly that resentment is an energy drain and is unhealthy. It is sin. I'd like to shed it like one would recover from a bad virus.

Even though we see three flies in Martha's soup — *worry, distraction,* and *resentment,* the gospel does not call us to irresponsible behaviors. It's not to say, forget the kitchen, the garage, and the work; play and then go to five Bible studies a week. Rather, it's to see a balance. Work and worship teeter back and forth in our lives. When the busyness is dominant, then Jesus says, "there is need of only one thing...." Always in response to grace we seek ways of being intentional about our life with God. Prayer, times of solitude and meditation, and aligning our wills to God's will becomes the priority. My favorite song from the musical *Godspell* is, "Day By Day." Look the lyrics up online and read them carefully.

In Ecclesiastes chapter 3, we hear the rhythmic cadence of the wisdom writer who portrays time and timing. There is a time ... "for everything there is a season and a time for every matter under heaven ... a time to be born and a time to die ... a time to break down and a time to build up ... a time to cry and a time to laugh ... a time to keep silence and a time to speak ... there's a time for everything."

There is a time for every matter under heaven. There is a time to labor and a time to love. There is a time to work and a time to worship. There is a time to be Martha and a time to be Mary. It is all about timeliness and balance.

Social activists soon burn out if they do not center themselves and replenish their souls in prayer, worship, and meditation. On the other hand, to focus on only learning, worshiping, and omit the practical application of the gospel, can lead to a self-absorbed life.

A perfect example of a Mary-Martha balance is in the ministry of the Marymusicians from Edison Lutheran Church of Bow, Washington. These Marymusicians are not Christmas carolers though they have that look about them. They are parishioners who pile into cars like Julie Wilkinson Rousseau's '66 Mustang convertible, at sundown, Wednesday evenings in the summer, to drive through the countryside sixty miles north of Seattle and make their way onto the porches of the ill and grieving to sing them to sleep. With Gretchen Johanson on guitar, they sing songs like: "Seek Ye First The Kingdom Of God," "Dona Nobis Pacem," and "Day By Day" from *Godspell*. It's a very simple ministry, two to ten, singing to people with special needs on their porches or outside their bedroom windows.

> *Marymusic is the "sister" to Marthameals, the name coined when Rousseau was scheduling three groups to provide dinners for a cancer patient. On one food delivery, Rousseau says she realized, "The meal nourished the patient's family but her need was food for the soul." So Rousseau gathered singers from church and told them not to bring food but music ... they sang to Dorothy Anderson after her husband, Gus, died. And to four-year-old Thor Knutzen, who's on the heart transplant waiting list. A widower, Fred, who's not a member of this 400-member congregation still talks about the parishioners who sang for his wife, Kai, who was then dying from cancer. She requested "Somewhere Over The Rainbow" and later said, "I just had a real sense of peace sitting there."[3]*

Two sisters representing two aspects of the Christian life alert us to the task of balance as we remember "the one thing needful." Amen.

---

1. Original source unknown.

2. Virginia Brasier, "Time Of The Mad Atom," www.crosswalk.com/devotionals/Day_by_Day/115.

3. Julie Sevig, *The Lutheran* magazine, "Porch Lullabies," September 2003, p. 24.

Sermons On The Gospel Readings

For Sundays
After Pentecost
(Middle Third)

Where Would You Go
To Meet Jesus?

Rick McCracken-Bennett

Forgive Us

I'm ashamed to say that too often I behave like the guy laying in bed with his family refusing to get up to give loaves of bread to his friend. I wish it were otherwise, but the truth is the truth. And where better to tell the truth but in church?

My life, much of the time, is all tucked in nice and warm. My doors are bolted shut. My children are sound asleep. The worries and cares of the day are well behind me. Each of my children has already been up for the obligatory glass of water and trip to the bathroom and now, finally, all is calm and I just want to drift off for a few hours of peace and quiet before it all starts again. Then comes the knocking at the door. And even though he is a friend, I do not want to get up, put my bare feet on the cold floor, wrap my robe around me, and lend him the three loaves he says he needs.

"Go away," I want to cry. "Come back in the morning. What in the world do you need bread for in the middle of the night anyway?"

The more he persists, the more annoyed I become until, grudgingly, I rise, calm my children who are now wide awake, and get the bread and try ... try, at least, to be civil and kind. This is just barely a metaphor.

For instance, I am in my nice, warm office working on the sermon of the century that is certain to bring rave reviews from my congregation, when the phone rings. I let the machine answer it but through the wall of the office I overhear the message. It's an interruption. Someone once said that interruptions *are* our work but I often don't act like I believe it. What could be more important than a well-crafted sermon that will inspire people for weeks to come?

Still, oblivious to the fact that I've got other things to do, the phone rings, people come to the door, my email program "beeps" to alert me to either an urgent message or to the announcement that someone I've never heard of from a country I could hardly find on a map wants to give me $83.6 million dollars. Well, he isn't going to give me all of it, but enough that I'll never have to work in this job where I get interrupted all the time.

Eventually I give in. I respond, not out of the goodness of my heart, but because they keep persisting. Yes, eventually I come to my senses and reach out to those who have come to me in need. I'm ashamed to admit this shortcoming but someone once said that confession is good for the soul.

There is a woman from somewhere in the county who calls me every day. Honestly — every day she calls. Sometimes she only rings me up once, but often she calls two or three times.

Each time there is a new crisis; her electric needs to be turned back on, the phone reconnected, or a truck is needed to move the family to yet another house. Once, she even called to ask for Easter candy because she didn't realize that Easter was coming so early that year and hadn't planned the baskets for her children!

Our church has been extremely generous with this family and so I rationalize my resistance for days and sometimes weeks or even months because I know that as soon as I give in, even with a few dollars, the ante will be upped and I'll be answering her calls twice as often as before.

It's not that she doesn't need the help. It's that there are others who are in need as well and if I give in to her ... well, you get the idea.

Still, I give up and buy oil for her car, turn her phone back on, or buy some food for her. (I drew the line at Easter candy.) Somehow her persistent calling gets through to me. This is a family in need, not like the woman who wanted me to make a payment on her flat screen television. But then, that's a story for another day.

Jesus says that God answers persistent prayer. When we pray that God would give us today the bread that we need, God answers that prayer. But when we pray for things we want, like Easter candy, and not for things we need ... I suppose, those prayers are less likely to get through. Prayers for things we need are one thing. Prayers for stuff we *want* are something else indeed.

When I was approaching my twelfth birthday I wanted a go-cart more than anything in the world. I loved the look of them, the smell of them, the speed, and especially the noise. My uncle raced go-carts and in the summer we would visit him and run around his little town, tearing through neighbors' yards, and screaming up and down the street for hours. I can't tell you how much I wanted one of those. In my eleven-year-old mind I thought that I *needed* a go-cart. We lived in the country and there was a seldom-used road in front of our house that would be perfect. It would be safe since people could see us for miles. Oh, how I wanted a go-cart!

As my birthday drew closer I finally got up the nerve to ask my dad if I was getting a go-cart. At first he would just stand there and grin at me. I convinced myself that the grin meant *yes*. After a while he told me I would just have to wait and see. I was all the more certain that this meant that I was getting a go-cart because certainly he would have told me *no* to such a direct question.

Finally my birthday came. My little party would not take place until after my dad got home from the shop. It was the longest day of my life. After lunch I walked down the road to my grandpa's farm and looked everywhere I could think of to get a glimpse of my go-cart. I looked in the barns, the granary, and the sheds that held the tractors, combines, and plows. I gained new respect for my dad that day as I realized just how good he was at hiding things.

At last he came home and took a quick shower while my mother called my grandparents to come down for cake, ice cream, and the opening of presents. All I saw was a box under the picture window. Certainly it wasn't big enough for a go-cart. It was not even close. It had to be a trick gift. I would open it only to find a picture of my brand-spanking new go-cart.

"Aren't you going to open your present?" my mother asked, nodding at the solitary box. I moved slowly toward it, pulled off the birthday card, pretended to read it, and ripped the paper off the box that held my brand-spanking new ... telescope.

I could see through my tears that my parents were beaming.

"Here, I'll help you set it up," my father said. But I could barely hear him. Maybe it was a joke. For a few moments I thought that we would set up the telescope, take it in the front yard, and then my dad would point it down to the farm where my real present was.

No, this *was* my real present. There was no go-cart that year or any other year.

I have to admit that once I got over my disappointment, the telescope took me places that I could never have gone otherwise. Living in the country I would take it outside on pitch-dark nights and gaze at clusters and nebulae and planets and their moons. My imagination soared as my world became bigger and bigger.

That birthday was 47 years ago, and I still have that telescope and on dark nights in the country where I now live I take it out on the deck and gaze at the wonders above. You know and I know that I wouldn't still have the go-cart.

I think this is what Jesus was thinking when he said, "Is there anyone among you who, if your child asks for a fish, will give a snake instead of a fish? Or if the child asks for an egg, will give a scorpion?" (Luke 11:11-12). We might make a twist of his proverb, *Is there anyone among you who, if your child asks for a go-cart, would not, if you were able, give them instead a telescope?* You might argue that I didn't need a telescope any more than I needed a go-cart but you'd never convince me of that.

I want to address the context in which these sayings were placed.

Jesus' disciples have asked him to teach them to pray and he first gives them what we have come to know as the Lord's Prayer. He then reminds them and us to be persistent, even pestering in our prayer, knowing that our Father in heaven would never give us anything that would be bad for us, even if we asked him for it.

The phrase in the Lord's Prayer that always brings me up short is when we pray "and forgive us our sins, for we ourselves forgive everyone indebted to us" (Luke 11:4b). The problem I have with this is that while I'm pretty good at asking for forgiveness, I can be stingy about handing it out. How about you? "Oh, God, I'm sorry," we cry. "Please forgive me." But let someone do us wrong and then ask for forgiveness and we're not always so quick to forgive.

Jesus says, "*For* we ourselves forgive *everyone* indebted to us." If I take this to its logical conclusion I think that this means that we forgive even those who don't ask us for it. And that *everyone* means *everyone* and not just those I choose to forgive.

A few years ago I was sitting in a large, white tent in Jonesborough, Tennessee, listening to the folk singer John McCutcheon. Somewhere in the middle of his set he sang a new song based on his own experiences with the Lord's Prayer. The song was called, "Forgive Us."[1] He sang about his early memories of the prayer he grew up with in church. Then he came to the bridge of the song and sang about an event that had shocked us all a year before. He told about the Amish girls ages six to thirteen in Pennsylvania who were taken hostage and then gunned down. Almost as shocking his song reminded us of the unbelievable response of the children's parents, families, and friends and how they even went so far as to set up a scholarship fund for the gunman's children and in so many ways obviously forgave the person who had caused them so much harm and heartache. John then sang the chorus, which repeated the words over and over, "Forgive us, as we forgive."

Since then, every time I feel I have been wronged and want to get even, or at least, want to hold onto a righteous grudge, I begin to sing the chorus of that song in my mind and heart. And, if I am open to the God who forgives me no matter what I do or don't do, I become, at least, a bit more open to forgiving this person first even if they don't ask for it.

Only then can I ask, as I pray the Lord's Prayer, for the forgiveness of my sins. Only when I have *first* forgiven those who have sinned against me may I stand before my God and pray: forgive me my sins for I have forgiven those who have sinned against me.

---

1. John McCutcheon, "Forgive Us," *This Fire: Politics, Love, and Other Small Miracles* (Framingham, Massachusetts: Appalsongs, 2007).

Stuff!

It's everywhere you look.

Stuff! From garage sales, to trunk sales and flea markets, to dumpsters, to folks riffling through your trash to find something of value ... and if they're lucky, something with your social security number on it. Stuff is everywhere.

Don't get me wrong. I love stuff. By most measures I have too much of it. When Nancy and I were first married the only reason she could drag me to garage sales was the fact that I wanted to be with her all of the time. But standing there, looking at other people's stuff that, by the pure fact of it lying there on a dew-soaked blanket in someone's front yard showed that it was stuff they didn't want anymore, just wasn't my idea of a fun way to spend a Saturday morning.

In the interest of full disclosure, there were times when Nancy dragged me along and I wound up enjoying myself and almost always bought some stuff that I just couldn't live without.

Honestly, there is no way around it ... I've got too much stuff.

I'd love to de-clutter my house, garage, and basement, but that would mean getting rid of stuff. Wouldn't it be simpler to build a barn in the backyard and move some of it there? I thought of that but barns cost more than I imagined. Still, it might be worth it. I would just have to prioritize what stuff needed to be close by in case I needed it and what other things I could put in the barn marked with the name of one of my children so they won't fight over it when I'm gone.

Or how about renting one of those storage garages that dot the boundaries of our communities? Obviously I'm not the only one with too much stuff. Using one of these would have the added benefit of allowing me visitation rights 24 hours a day without having the stuff underfoot every day.

That feels better. Just fessing up to my hoarding feels better. And you know what else it does? It makes me go just a little bit easier on the rich man who finds himself with a bountiful harvest and wants to keep every last kernel of grain. But let's be clear ... just because I can identify with him doesn't mean that I think he and I have the right idea. As you can probably tell, I feel guilty about keeping all my stuff and not sharing it with those in need.

There is an old story about two brothers who inherited the family farm. They also inherited the core value that, within the family, everyone must be treated with absolute equality. One brother was single and the other was married with three children.

As the story goes, there were two houses on the farm, so each brother got one. There were two large barns and two smaller barns and the brothers got one of each. The animals were divided equally and when there was an odd number they had a cookout in which they, of course, equally shared down to the last bratwurst. The land was divided equally as well, acre by acre, pasture by pasture.

Some thought these brothers were taking this fairness thing to extremes because every evening they would make certain that the animals were back to whichever brother they belonged and any grain left over was divided into sacks and taken to each one's granary. Absolutely everything was divided equally, just as their father had wanted it.

This worked just fine until one day when the younger brother began to think about this arrangement. "This is not fair ... not fair at all. We must change this arrangement. My brother has a wife and three children while I am single. He has more mouths to feed than I. Ah! I know what I will do." And that evening, under cover of darkness, the younger brother took a sack of grain from his own granary and took it to his brother's granary and left it there. He continued to do this every night thereafter.

298

That same day the older brother thought to himself, "This is not fair ... not fair at all. We must change this arrangement. My brother is single while I have a wife and three children. They will take care of me when I am old and can no longer work on the farm while my brother will have no one to care for him. Ah! I know what I will do." And that evening, under cover of darkness, the older brother took a sack of grain from his granary and took it to his brother's. He continued to do this night after night.

One very, very dark night, as the story goes, when each of them was moving grain from their granary to the other's they smacked into each other. When they recovered and realized what the other had been doing, they embraced in a brotherly embrace and, I'm told, they continued their practice until the day when they were too old to carry the sacks of grain anymore. To this day, their children and their children's children, and even *their* children carry sacks of grain each day to help them remember and honor the unselfishness of their ancestors.

As the legend goes, the spot where they met, where they collided with each other that dark, dark night, was the very spot that God declared that his temple would be built. For nowhere, on the entire earth was there a place where a better example of unselfish, brotherly love could be found than there.[1]

How different from the parable of Jesus! It is so different that, at first, it is tough to get our minds around it. We've all known unselfish people, but the degree to which these two brothers loved each other and only wanted what was best for each other goes far beyond simple unselfishness. It's much easier to imagine the rich man stuffing his new barns full of excess grain than someone freely giving it away to another.

Greed, on the other hand, is something we understand pretty well. All one has to do is turn on the television when the Power Ball jackpot reaches some obscene amount of money and listen to the interviews of people saying what they will do if they hit the big one. We've heard plenty of these and I won't say that it's *never* happened, but I don't remember anyone saying that they were going to tithe their winnings to their church or some charity. You can

299

almost hear them thinking, *I want it all and I want it now.* Now *that* ... greed of that magnitude, I understand.

Of course it doesn't *always* happen, but I've heard enough stories about people who win the lottery and end up within a few years in what my parents would have called the "poor house." Most, it seems, take trips, buy motor homes or motorcycles, quit their jobs, build bigger barns for their stuff, and hide from long-lost distant relatives scheming for a slice of the pie until there are no more slices for anyone.

There are the stories about groups of factory workers who together buy a number of tickets each week and one day hit the big one. I've never seen it fail that there was at least one person who bought into the pool every single week except *that* one. Friends who once dreamed their water cooler dreams become, the day of the big drawing, bitter enemies as one of their own threatens to sue because the group should have known that they would have paid their share of the ticket. Those fights aren't pretty. Yes, greed like that I understand, sadly, because I've seen more examples of it than ones like the two brothers in the first story.

Those who want it all and want it now are like the rich man in Jesus' parable who receives a more abundant crop than normal and instead of finding a way to give a portion of it away, pulls down his barns, builds larger ones, and stores the grain and everything he owns there. Then he sits back to relax, eat, drink, and be merry not knowing that tomorrow he will die. If I were the person making the billboards from God that dot the highways these days I would put one up that said, "What part of *you can't take it with you* don't you understand? — God."

Before we get too high and mighty and smug about how we would behave if we received a more than abundant crop, let's be honest with ourselves. Would you or I, regardless of what we might say to a television reporter while in the line at the 7-Eleven, really, in our heart of hearts, give our abundant harvest away?

Take the so-called economic stimulus package some of us received a couple of years ago. Despite cries from the Hunger Network to consider tithing our windfall, how many of us actually did that? The most often used excuse I heard was that the government told us that we were to spend the money, not save it or invest it. How convenient that our government didn't tell us that we ought use this money to lend a helping hand to the most needy in our world so that they might also benefit from the program!

Sarcasm aside, and that was sarcastic I'll have to admit, are we really so different from the rich man in today's parable? Is *more* ever enough? Are we ever satisfied with what we have, or do we constantly strive for more and more? It doesn't help that a recent news item told us that we would need at least a quarter of a million dollars if we want to retire comfortably. I wonder what message that sends to the poorest of the poor in our country.

It reminds me of a folktale from England about a poor woodcutter who went out to cut some wood so that he could make enough money to feed himself and his wife for the day. He found a tree that would bring an adequate price but as he raised his ax a forest fairy stopped him. The tree was much older than he and so he was asked to spare its life. The man countered that without the money that the tree would bring him, he and his wife would starve. "Then," the fairy said, "if you spare the tree I'll give you three wishes." Three wishes! He thought, dreaming of the wealth he could acquire with those wishes. The man agreed and promised to never cut down the old trees in the forest and the three wishes were granted.

The poor woodcutter ran to his wife screaming that they were now rich. His wife, as you can guess, was skeptical. But the woodcutter explained about the forest fairy and how he promised never to cut down old trees and was then granted the three wishes.

The woodcutter and his wife began to argue about what to wish for. "A house," he said.

"No, a palace," she replied.

"A bag of gold then, to pay for the servants we'll need," he said.

"Why wish for only a bag when we could have a wagon full of gold?" she countered. On and on through the evening they argued.

Finally, worn out from arguing, they stopped and the woodcutter said, "I'm hungry. I wish we had some sausage." You know what happened. His wife began to tear into him since he so foolishly wasted a wish. "Oh," the woodcutter said, "I wish those sausages were attached to your nose." And so they were!

Sobbing, the wife sat on the floor and her husband said, "I suppose there's only one thing to do now." And so he wished that the sausages were off of his wife's nose. And they sat down for dinner and a fine dinner it was![2]

Our parable today asks us to think about our stuff in two ways: How much stuff do we really need and when we have excess stuff why not give it away? I ask you, after asking myself first, how much stuff do you really need and what do you intend to do with the stuff you don't? When you have a more abundant "crop" than you expected; a good year, a bonus, do you first rearrange your portfolio and build new barns with CDs, mutual funds, and stocks, or do you thank God from whom all good things come and give, if even just a little bit, to those whose crops have failed while yours flourished? Amen.

---

1. A version of a story by Anthony de Mello, S.J., *Taking Flight* (New York: Image Books, 1990), pp. 60-61.

2. There are many versions of this English folktale. A more complete version can be found in: Heather Forest, *Wisdom Tales* (Little Rock, Arkansas: August House, 1996), pp. 111-113.

Proper 14
Pentecost 12
Ordinary Time 19
Luke 12:32-40

Don't Be Afraid

"Don't be afraid." How many times have we heard those words in our lifetime? Our parents whispered them: Don't be afraid of: thunder, darkness, branches scraping against the window. Don't be afraid of: striking out on the ball field, flunking your physics exam, or your driver's test. When those words are spoken with love and sincerity they can be some of the most soothing words we could ever hope to hear. "Don't be afraid, I'm here with you. You're going to be all right. I love you. Stop worrying. Don't be anxious." They are wonderful words when spoken by a loved one. I'm here ... "Don't be afraid."

Jesus says to his disciples "Do not be afraid." Besides our parents' voices, where have we heard those words before? In the Bible alone we hear them over fifty times from the Lord speaking to Abram in Genesis (15:1) to the book of Revelation (1:17) we hear them over and over. It seems to be one of God's favorite things to say to us: "Do not be afraid." In the verses right before our gospel passage this morning Jesus instructed his disciples not to worry about food or clothes; that they should consider how well God takes care of birds and flowers and grass and he tells them not to be anxious about such things but to "set [their] minds on [God's] kingdom and the rest will come to [them] as well" (12:31). If the disciples are going to continue to follow him they have no reason to worry about the things that they need. They are not to fret about their lives, their food, or their clothes. "Think," he says to them, "about how well God cares for the birds and the flowers and stop your worrying. Quit spending so much of your time fussing about

303

these things. Instead," he says, "set your hearts on the kingdom and these other things will come along just fine."

Then, in the gospel for today, Jesus steps it up a notch. He repeats that they don't need to be afraid since it gives their Father great pleasure to hand over the kingdom to them. He goes on to say, "Sell what you have, give to those who need it more than you, and focus your lives on things that do not rot or wear out and can't be stolen. That's where you will find your treasure."

Deep down inside of me, in my less than stellar spiritual moments, I hear a voice that says if I give what I have to those in need then I might become one of those people in need. What then? What then, Jesus ... who's going to take care of me then?

Can't you just hear Jesus now? "Haven't you been listening? I told you that God will take care of your needs. And since you won't have to be fussing around worrying about such things, you can attend to the work of the kingdom, which, in case you've forgotten, is breaking in as we speak."

Honestly, isn't this getting a bit monotonous? Last week, right here in church, we heard Jesus telling us the parable of the rich man who tore down his old, inadequate barns and built new ones to house his abundant crop. We get it Jesus. Don't hoard our goods, sell what we have, give to the poor; let our Father in heaven take care of us. We get it already. We really do. We understand what you're trying to tell us. But, honestly, we aren't too sure if we're ready to take that step. It's a big step, Jesus. You understand, don't you?

There is a folktale about a king whose son was always sad no matter what his father did for him and no matter what good things happened to him. The king loved his son deeply and became so despondent that he vowed to do whatever was necessary to make his son happy and appreciative of all that he had. He called a meeting of his advisors and after much discussion and consultation (which got them nowhere), one of them, a very wise man, took the king aside and told him that the solution was to dress his son in the shirt of a man who was happy. If he found a truly happy man and gave this man's shirt to his son to wear, the son would be happy forever.

The king set out on a journey to find a man who was truly happy so that he might obtain his shirt and pass alone this happiness to his son.

He entered a village and was told of a priest who was thought to be quite happy and content. The king found the priest and asked him if he would accept the position of bishop if it were given him. The priest quickly said, "Yes." The king thanked the priest but left at once, knowing that if the priest were truly happy and content with his life, he would not have wanted for more.

He traveled to a foreign country where he met another king and asked him what made him so happy. "Why," he said, "I have everything I could possibly want. But to tell you the truth," he went on, "I worry all the time that someone might come and take what I've worked so hard for." Again, the king saw that this was not a truly happy and content man.

Finally he came upon a poor farmer working in a modest vineyard. He was singing and had the most beautiful smile. The king greeted him and asked what made him so happy. The man replied, spreading his arms out to display the vineyard, that he had everything he could possibly want. Then the king asked if he would come to the castle where he would never want for anything the rest of his life. The man refused, saying that there was nothing in the whole world that could make him happier nor take him away from his beloved farm.

The king was thrilled for at last he had found a truly happy man, and his son would be saved. He asked the man for a favor and was told that he would give the king anything he wanted. The king then asked him for his shirt to give his son. The man opened up his jacket and the king saw that the truly happy, content man was not wearing a shirt.[1]

This is not unlike the story of the businessman visiting a beautiful tropical island and upon seeing a fisherman unloading a modest catch of fish asked him what he was going to do the rest of the day. "I will sit with my family, talk with my children, spend time with my wife, and cook supper."

The businessman told him that he ought to hire some men to help him.

"Why?" the fisherman asked.

"You could catch more fish," he replied.

"But why would I want to catch more fish?"

"So that you could make more money and buy more boats."

"But why do I need more boats?"

"So that you can have other people do your fishing for you."

"And why would I want to have other people do my fishing for me?"

"So that you could take time off, go to some exotic place for vacation, spend time with your wife and children ... oh!" and the businessman walked away reevaluating his own life while the fisherman took his catch to market and spent the rest of his day with his family.

Jesus said that where our treasure is there our hearts will be also. I believe he was talking about the fundamental orientation of our lives. What is most important to us? I used to repeat this saying backward. It made more sense to me: where your *heart* is there your *treasure* will be also. I thought he was saying that our money would follow our heart's desires. Put your money where your heart is. I suppose that, too, is true. But it's not what Jesus said. He was saying to us that the money goes toward something first and then our heart will follow.

These words had special significance to the early church I think. Get your life in order, rely on God for the things that you need, give yourself an attitude adjustment because Jesus is coming again and you darn well better be ready. We just don't know when. It has a lot more weight than the bumper sticker I saw a few years ago, "Jesus is coming back ... look busy." A longer bumper sticker could read, "Jesus is coming, don't be afraid, sell what you have, give to the poor, put your wealth where you want your heart to be." That's closer to the point but it's a bit too long to be read at 65 miles an hour.

Let us pray: Lord Jesus, you have told us to not be afraid, to give away what we have, and rely on the Father for everything. You had to know that this would be a difficult commandment for us, especially those of us who have trusted mainly in ourselves and the money and possessions we've acquired through our own hard work. We sometimes find it difficult to say, "All things come of thee, O Lord, and of thine own have we given thee." Help us not to dismiss your words as naive or as a message meant for others but instead help us to see where it is that we put our treasure and where our heart follows. May we choose wisely where we put our money and our talents and our time and may these be used more and more for the sake of your kingdom where you live with the Father and the Holy Spirit, world without end. Amen.

---

1. For a more complete version of this story see: Heather Forest, *Wisdom Tales* (Little Rock, Arkansas: August House, 1996), pp. 117-119.

The Great Divide

I have to admit, this is not the Jesus I'm comfortable with. All this talk about bringing fire to the earth and that he can't wait until it's set ablaze. What kind of talk is that? Then there is the part about how households will become divided because of him. For goodness' sake, that's exactly opposite from the kind of community we're trying to build here.

Can you imagine if I announced an adult education program that promised to teach you how to divide your families in five easy sessions? You wouldn't come. And I have no doubt but that the number one item on the vestry's agenda at their next meeting would be to ask the question as to whether or not I've lost my ever-loving mind. Nope, I don't like this passage one bit. Perhaps it's because I can hear an echo of church member against church member, minister against people, and people against the minister.

And fire? Talk about incendiary speech!

No, I don't like this passage one little bit. But such is the luck of the preacher. This is our text for the day. I didn't pick it. I wouldn't have picked it. But I am stuck with it and consequently since you chose to be here rather than working the *New York Times* crossword puzzle over a coffee or two, you are stuck with it, too. So let's make the best of it, shall we? Let's see what Jesus is telling us about his mission.

Peace wasn't part of the deal. John was a trained interim pastor and a good one at that. Work for him was never done. As soon as he completed his assignment with one congregation and they called their new pastor, he was asked to move on to another place.

309

Some of these churches were pretty healthy while others were not well at all. It didn't matter to John. In either case, though his tactics might differ, he came not to bring peace, but division and fire. Sometimes, even though he knew in his heart that this was what he was called to do, it was enough to tear him apart.

The most difficult situations for John were when the church thought they were in good shape. On the surface things looked smooth, with everyone getting along with everyone, or so it seemed. What he always seemed to find was that the peace that looked so good was only there because the congregation wasn't being honest with each other. Peace at any cost seemed to be their motto. Never were the sticky and sometimes embarrassing denominational or congregational issues mentioned in polite company lest someone get offended. Controllers, and there were always controllers, were tolerated and even elevated to board or elder status in hopes that they would see what reasonable and thoughtful people the other leaders were and then would stop their contrary ways. If the controllers held their ground and didn't budge, well then the rest of the leadership would cave in. Don't trouble the waters. Don't stir things up. Let's keep everyone happy. What a sad, sad mission statement for any church!

Then there were the controllers who specialized in gatekeeping. They were usually longtime members who joined the church before God. And they knew better than anyone who fit in and who didn't. They were usually beloved by the rest of the congregation, or perhaps they were just scared to death of them. They took their role very seriously. Whenever someone who was deemed "unworthy" because of their age, their race, their clothes, or their sexual orientation showed up on Sunday morning, they would make certain that person learned in subtle but no uncertain terms the church down the pike would meet their needs far better than this one. They performed this "duty" so well that the visitor almost never knew that they were getting the "bum's rush."

As I said, these were the situations where John did his best work. But it wasn't easy work. It wasn't easy at all.

If you asked him, he would tell you that his job was to be a truth-teller, no matter what the cost. It was up to him to point out where the congregation was being dishonest or avoiding the deeper issues of their common life. Even if John wouldn't say that he came to bring fire, at least not out loud, he would admit he came to bring light. While he would readily tell you that he didn't come to bring peace, he did plan to show them where the dividing lines were, but not discussed, as I said, in polite company.

Most congregations didn't like John very much. His reputation always preceded him and often the congregational leaders would balk at the suggestion that they needed him as their interim. Why not bring someone in who could help keep things on an even keel? Why not someone who could be a placeholder until the next pastor was called? No, churches didn't like John very much. At least they didn't at first. But in time, if they didn't throw him out under the guise of not having enough money to pay him, they sometimes came to see the wisdom of his ways. They saw that his way was much more the way of peace than it first seemed.

Divisions in churches or in families are never pleasant. And they aren't usually sought. Yet before true peace can be obtained, congregational members need to recognize that the divisions exist and then go about the business of seeking understanding between those who are divided.

For instance, as long as the issue of ordaining openly homosexual men or women is kept out of discussions with polite company, some might think that everyone holds the same opinion that they do. Or take the so-called, pro-choice or pro-life positions. If we really discussed what seems to divide us so sharply, we just might come to see how close we are to those that we so often vilify.

What is often missing, when we avoid those troublesome conversations, is that we don't learn how to respectfully disagree with each other. We don't learn how to sit still and make sure we understand what the other's position is. That was how John saw his role. He would point out the hot-button issues and then make sure people had a safe place to talk about them in a respectful way. He kept their feet to the fire until all positions were heard and understood. While some of the divisions were more than even John could overcome, most of the time people found that they were closer together than they had ever thought and despite their differences, they could find aspects of mission and ministry in the church that they could work on together.

We have all experienced examples over the years of respectful disagreement that would make the angels sing as well as nasty, over-the-top hostility that would make a professional wrestler blush. We have seen churches and dioceses that have found ways to live together and work for the kingdom together despite some rather sharp differences. We have also seen churches and dioceses where one or often both sides dug in their heels and never gave an inch nor acknowledged that the other side had anything worthwhile to offer.

I am reminded of a folktale about a heron and an oyster. One day, as the story goes, an oyster was lying on the beach sunning herself. Along came a heron looking for breakfast. When the heron dove down to the oyster and was just about ready to take a bite, the oyster closed its shell.

The heron cried, "If you don't let go there will be one dead oyster by the end of the day."

The oyster replied, "If you don't let go, there will soon be one dead heron."

Along came a fisherman who said, "Well, you're both right!" And he picked them up and stuck them in his bag and went off down the beach to prepare his own breakfast.

In contrast to this, I recently attended two different but equally moving events. At the first, over 3,000 people from every Christian faith imaginable met to recommit ourselves and our churches to the work of justice. In that room over the three days of this "revival" I know that if we cared to we could have found huge differences in theology as well as differences in moral issues like abortion, same-sex marriage, and so on. We all knew that these differences were there, but for the time being at least, we put them aside so that we could be about the work of doing justice together instead of the sometimes piecemeal efforts our relatively small congregations attempt on our own. We never said that these differences weren't there or that they didn't matter, but we did say that the only difference that mattered was the difference we could make if we didn't sweat the "small stuff."

A week later, I went to yet another rally and joined a reported 2,300 people of faith communities from all over the county. Once again this group was extremely diverse in theology and moral beliefs but that night we were united around the justice issues of payday lending, preparing children for kindergarten, and expanding our county's drug court. It is amazing to me what we can accomplish if we set aside our differences and work together.

One day I asked a rabbi friend of mine why Jews didn't believe that Jesus was the Messiah. Without going into a long explanation that the question undoubtedly required he replied, "Where is the peace? The Messiah is supposed to usher in peace and we didn't and still don't see evidence of that." Good answer, I thought. How do we reconcile that expectation with the reality we face? And while we're at it, how do we reconcile it with Jesus proclaiming that he came as a fire starter, a division bringer?

Part of the answer for me is not found in contentious church board meetings, or wars in the Middle East, or starving children all over the world, but in the potential I see at meetings like the ones I shared. There we experienced a time of peace when what divided us didn't matter as much as the work that God had given us to do. We learned how, for now at least, to bash our swords into plowshares, to put down our weapons of words, to hold hands together, and to walk toward those parts of our world that have known nothing but devastating war and hunger and poverty and division.

When we do that, we are people of peace and justice. When we stop our bickering and begin attending to the root causes of hunger, poverty, and war, we are people of peace and justice. When we stop looking for what divides us and instead strive toward what unites us in Christ, we are people of peace and justice. If we are, as followers of Jesus, also to bring division and fire — let us set fire to the underbrush of hatred, mistrust, and prejudice and let us be people of peace and justice in Jesus' name. Amen.

Proper 16
Pentecost 14
Ordinary Time 21
Luke 13:10-17

What If The Disciples Had Email And One Of The Disciples Was A Woman?

From: Priscilla@galilee.net
To: Mom&Dad@jerusalem.org

Dear Mom and Dad,

I just wanted to write and let you know that I'm doing just fine. I know you don't approve of me traveling from place to place with this fellow, Jesus, and his companions, but I need you to know that things are going amazingly well. Before you get to worrying more than you already are, none of the "boys" as you called them, are giving me any trouble at all. Not a single one of them has hit on me, if that's what you're worried about. Jesus wouldn't stand for it. Besides, all of us are on a pretty steep learning curve about the kingdom of God and we don't have time for any fooling around.

First, I want to clear up something I said in my last email, about Jesus saying that he came to bring division, not peace. That bothered me for a while, too, until I realized that you and I are living this out in some way. Here I am following this man, being his disciple (though I would *never* tell the men I consider myself to be a disciple), and you are so against this, so angry with him and even with me, that his words and my actions are bringing division to our own family. I would love to have peace between us and have things back to the way they were before I started on this journey, but I know in my heart that this is the right thing to do. I'm just sorry that I'm hurting you. I never meant for that to happen.

Anyway, we're getting ready to take off now — it seems like we're always going somewhere — and I wanted to get this emailed

315

before we leave. If I don't write for a while it's because the cyber cafés in this part of the world are pretty scarce. Never forget, I love you, Mom and Dad.

Your daughter,
Priscilla

To: Priscilla@galilee.net
From: Mom&Dad@jerusalem.org

Dear Priscilla,

Well, I really don't know what to say. You know that your mother and I disapprove of your escapades with this charlatan or magician or sorcerer or whatever he is. More than anything, we just don't want you to get hurt. We're hearing every day from people who think that he is bad for us, that he is simply getting the Romans in an uproar and that he might have to be dealt with, if you know what I mean. Please come home. All will be forgiven.

Your father,
Jacob

From: Priscilla@galilee.net
To: Mom&Dad@jerusalem.org

Dear Mom and Dad,

Thanks for your email, Father. I know that neither you nor Mother think much of Jesus, but then again you really don't know him. All you know are the lies that the powers that be are saying about him. It's disgraceful. It's like those political ads we used to see on Jerusalem TV. I've heard that some of the Pharisees have been "swift-boating" him something terrible. They even show up when the master is teaching and try to trick him or shout him down. It's awful the way some of them treat him. Even so, I've never seen him back down or not have a clever way of putting them in their place.

Take what happened last Friday evening. We were in one of the synagogues and Jesus was teaching. Oh, how I love to hear him teach and I can tell that the others do, too. I especially love watching those who are hearing him for the first time. Oh my! The looks on their faces are priceless whether they like him or hate him!

So anyway, we were in this synagogue listening to Jesus (it was like a town hall meeting) when a crippled woman came in. She was so bad that she couldn't even stand up straight. I heard later that she had been like this for eighteen years! Can you imagine? Well, Jesus looked up from the scroll he was reading, called her over, and told her that she was free from what ailed her. He put his hands on her and right away, just like that, she stood up straight like a young woman and began to shout praises to God. Isn't there something in our scriptures about the lame walking ... that it's a sign of the Messiah?

The leader of the synagogue got all hot and bothered and he kept saying to the crowd that Jesus had broken sabbath laws; that there were six days in the week when healing the sick was lawful, and what earthly reason did he have for doing this on the sabbath? Technically he was right, Jesus did break sabbath laws, and I couldn't imagine how he was going to respond because the rest of his disciples and I knew in our hearts that he had done the right thing.

Jesus turned it right back on them and called them hypocrites. He said that there was not a single one of us who would not water our livestock on the sabbath and technically speaking that was breaking the sabbath law. I could tell by the look in their eyes that he had them right then and there. He went on to point out that this daughter of Abraham was more important to God than any ox or donkey and that her being set free from her bondage on the sabbath was not a sin any more than watering their animals. I think he was asking us all to consider which was worse, a broken rule or a broken person?

He was right, of course, a broken person is much worse and those who opposed him were sure put in their place. But the rest of us, the ones that had in the past been put in *our* place by the overly

317

rigid use of the law rejoiced in what he said and what he did. We could hardly contain ourselves.

I hope this will help you better understand why I'm going to continue to follow Jesus and why I believe he is the Messiah, the one who was to come into the world to set us free.

Your loving daughter,
Priscilla

From: Mom&Dad@jerusalem.org
To: Priscilla@galilee.net

Dear Priscilla,

Your father doesn't know I'm sending this email so please don't mention it in anything you write back to us.

I just wanted you to know that I fully approve of what you're doing. I'm nervous and a little scared for you, of course, because there are some very powerful men out there who are threatening some awful things against your teacher. Still, I think that if I were younger I would be right there with you. But, Priscilla, please, please be careful. Your father is right that there are so many different ways to get hurt or at the least get your heart broken. I pray for your safety every day.

Love,
Your mother

From: Mom&Dad@jerusalem.org
To: Priscilla@galilee.net

Dear Priscilla,

Your mother doesn't know I'm writing this email so please don't mention it in anything you write back to us.

I just read an account in the *Jerusalem Sun-Times* of the scene Jesus made at the synagogue. I know you know this, but I want to remind you that there are many magicians out there who can do the same sorts of so-called miracles that this Jesus claims to do.

We've had to put up with these so-called Messiahs for quite some time now. Our ancestors even warned us in the story about Moses and Pharaoh, how the court magicians could do *almost* everything that Moses could do by the power of God.

Yet, Priscilla, I also know that you are a bright girl and that you are a good judge of character and that you will know whether or not he is the real deal *not* by his works but by the *fruit* of his works.

If I had my way, you would be home with us safe and sound, but you are of age and I trust your judgment. I just want you to be careful.

Love,
Your father

From: Priscilla@galilee.net
To: Mom&Dad@jerusalem.org

Dear Mom and Dad,

Well, we're off and running again. It sounds like we're going to be traveling from town to village for the next few weeks. I can't wait to hear more of his stories and see the miracles he'll perform in those places. More and more people are joining our group but I have to admit, there are others who are not at all pleased with him. Some are actively working against him while others just turn and go back home.

It makes you think, just as you have warned me, whether or not he is the real deal. My heart tells me he is and even though you have your reservations about all this, I choose to follow him wherever he goes and whatever happens. I hope you understand. In so many ways I feel like that woman who can now stand up straight because of Jesus or the man who can now see. I am free at last from the bondages of sin and society and free to follow Jesus as one of his disciples.

Love,
Priscilla

From: Mom&Dad@jerusalem.org
To: Priscilla@galilee.net

Dear Priscilla,

Disciples! Our daughter thinks that women can become disciples! Now we've heard everything. You're on your own now, kiddo.

But of course, we still love you and will always love you no matter what.

Your mom and dad

But I Really Like The
Best Seat In The House!

Years ago I was a director of alcohol and drug programs in a neighboring county. Sadly, I developed a new addiction. I'll put it as honestly as I can ... I became hooked on self-help books, tapes, and videos, especially those that promised if I followed their ten simple steps I would rise to the top of my field. I practiced *thinking and growing rich* and I studied *the magic of thinking big.* You name it, and sadly, I probably read it and treated it with close to the respect I gave the Bible at that time. I read sales books (because you never knew when you would have to "close the sale" with a client), goal setting books (the sky's the limit they told me), and testimonials, which inspired and convinced me that no matter what I thought was holding me back, if I wanted something bad enough, I could achieve it. I attended every workshop I could and always had an outrageously expensive tape series playing in the car. I dreamt my dreams, set my goals, became more assertive, and at times, even aggressive, in order to climb to the top of the heap. I dreamed of being at the pinnacle of my field. I was on my way ... but on my way to where?

I began working with a national consultant in the hopes of becoming one myself and even though that didn't work out, I learned from him what I needed to do in order to make the leap. Or so I thought. I attended the right conferences, talked to the right people, wore the right clothes, and schmoozed with the movers and shakers. All the while I was attending a church where I heard a very disturbing message Sunday after Sunday that I had, of course, heard all my life but now began to get under my skin and bother the daylights out of me. "The first will be last," the minister would read, and "the last will be first," he went on to proclaim. "If you want to be at the top you had to serve those at the bottom. If you exalt yourself you will be humbled. If you humble yourself you will be exalted." The dissonance was so intense I could feel it in my bones.

"Well, that wouldn't work in my business," I would smugly say to myself as the readers read and the preachers preached. "You must become like a little child to enter the kingdom," I would hear. I decided that this was only a metaphor and not to be taken literally or seriously. "Give away all that you have and follow Jesus," and I would inwardly shake my head in disbelief. Jesus sure didn't grasp the ways of the world. He certainly didn't understand the twentieth century. Nor did he understand how in business the ones who were last stayed last and the ones that were first had to scrape their way to the top and keep scraping to stay there. "Give away all that you have and follow ... anyone who wants to be first must be last of all and servant of all," Jesus cried. And I wanted to cry as well, because I wasn't about to be last of all. I wanted to be at the top and Jesus wasn't buying it. I struggled with this for many years and those of you who know me well are probably aware that from time to time I struggle with it to this day. Exactly how I became so cynical about this part of the gospel is the topic for another sermon with far more self-disclosure than I am comfortable with, but for now it will suffice to say that I had no interest in being *last of all* and of *taking the lowest place* at the banquet table. Nope, I wasn't interested at all. But in time I began to come around.

Consider this story: Once there was a king who threw a large banquet for his son and his son's bride. Invitations were sent out far and wide and when the day arrived the banquet hall was nearly full. A man dressed in rags, looking as poor as poor can be, made his way past the guards and was almost seated at the banquet table when the king spotted him and had this disgraceful excuse for a human being thrown out into the street. The "poor" man then went to a tailor and paid to have fine garments made. He then returned to the banquet dressed like royalty himself. At once he was seated at a place of honor very near the king. And the banquet began.

The soup was served first. The man stared at the soup for a moment, then picked up the bowl, pulled out the collar of his shirt and poured the soup down his chest. The eyes of the guests around him grew large as he set the bowl down and patiently waited for the next course. When the salad arrived he picked it up and stuffed it into the pockets of his coat. And when the main course was served he smeared the meat all over his pants and put the potatoes in his shoes. The king had had enough. "How dare you come in here and insult me and my guests! What is the meaning of this behavior?"

The "poor/rich man" looked at the king for a moment and then replied, "Your highness, when I came to your banquet dressed as a common beggar you threw me out into the street and told me never to return again. But when I came dressed as a rich man, and mind you, nothing else had changed except my clothes, I was treated with great respect even to the point of being seated in this place of honor. I can only surmise that it was my clothes that made the difference and allowed me this courtesy. Therefore it only seemed right that I should feed my clothes first."[1]

This story and Jesus' parable call me up short regarding my drive to be at the top of the heap. "When you are invited somewhere," he says, "don't rush to get the best seat in the house. Be humble and take a lower place because you don't want your host to tell you that those good seats weren't for you but for someone more important than you."

How different this is from what we see all too often in some of our churches. If you don't think so then just wait until a visitor, especially a less than perfectly dressed stranger, sits in a matriarch's pew! They won't get tossed out into the street — we're far too polite for that — but if looks could kill! I have seen this happen often enough to know that I'm not the only one who has had a problem with the last being first and the first being last.

I remember reading about a new church a while back where their rule of thumb was that when someone expressed a desire to serve, the pastor would thank them profusely, hand them a broom, and ask them to sweep up after coffee hour. And this might go on for months! "If you want to be somebody in this congregation," he was showing them, "then you have to be willing to be a servant of all." Of course, the pastor and all the lay leadership never hesitated to sweep floors, or clean out the refrigerator, or pull weeds around the building either.

Many years ago I was talking with the storyteller, Ed Stivender, and I asked him what the first step was to becoming a professional storyteller. He told me that I should join my local storytelling guild and set up the chairs for the meetings. I waited for more "wisdom" and he didn't say anything. So I asked, "And then what?" He said, "Oh ... then when the meeting is over you put the chairs back." I had always thought that Ed was a little strange and now I was sure of it. But in time I figured out what he was trying to teach me: If you want to move to the top in the field of storytelling (or any other field for that matter), you had better be willing to serve others, even if it means setting up the chairs. I saw Ed at the National Storytelling Festival a couple of years later and the first thing he asked me was how my storytelling was going. I said, "Well, Ed, I'm still setting up the chairs." And he grinned and said, "Keep it up." Albert Schweitzer once said, "The only ones among you who will be really happy are those who will have sought and found how to serve." I'm only just beginning to understand that. But then I've always been a slow learner when it comes to some of this discipleship stuff. How about you?

So Jesus says to us, when you throw a party don't be so quick to invite family and friends and relatives and your rich neighbors because they might return the favor and repay you. Actually, forgive me; I've softened what Jesus said. What Jesus *really* said was, "*Don't* invite your family, friends, relatives and rich neighbors. Invite instead, the poor, the crippled, the lame, and the blind. Invite," he is saying to us, "the broken ones of this world." Now that would be an exercise in humility!

Many years ago I was preaching on this text and as I got to the part where I said, "Into the kingdom they came: the poor, the crippled, the lame, and the blind" the backdoor burst open and in walked one of our more colorful couples oblivious to the fact that we had already started. But no one laughed at the coincidence, nor frowned at their interruption, for we all knew that it was to such as these that the kingdom belongs.

When I get off my high horse and leave my "I want to be at the top" attitude behind; when I disregard those symbols of importance that I cling to in order to show myself and you that I've got it all together; when I recognize that you and I are as broken as any poor, crippled, lame, or blind person out there, then I realize that Jesus is inviting me and all of you as well to the banquet.

If I humbly invite you to my party, not because of what you can do for me, but because we share a common, broken humanity, a whole different thing begins to happen. Perhaps my guest list changes, or my motives for having a get-together change. Maybe I invite folks, not for what they can do for me or my career or my image, but in order that I might have an opportunity to serve them; to serve people who are just as broken as I am.

Over the years I have talked with many people who, like myself, have felt like imposters in our jobs, our community, wherever. The higher I rose at the hospital where I worked, for example, the more I was haunted by the fear that someday I would be found out. In time I was certain that I would be exposed by someone who knew that I had absolutely no clue about what I was doing and then I would be fired on the spot, ushered to my office by security to clean out my desk, and be told never to return. Oh, the diplomas on my wall and the credentials I carried as a Certified Alcoholism Counselor were real. It was the lack of internal diplomas and credentials that I was having trouble with and that made me feel like an imposter. No wonder I tried to be something I wasn't instead of humbling myself to be exactly who I was. If I tried hard enough perhaps I could convince my boss that I belonged in my job. And if I really worked at it, maybe I could convince myself!

Sometimes, though, I wonder if this attitude is such a bad thing. Maybe it's just that we take it the wrong way. Perhaps it is a small, inner voice that is reminding us to be humble and modest; reminding us that we don't know it all, that we're not God's gift to humanity, and that if we really want to be first we must be willing to be last of all and servants of all. Maybe it is saying that all this striving to get to the top could be better spent striving to get to the bottom where we might better serve others.

I know what some of you might be thinking: that if you do all this humbling stuff you'll be humbled right out of a job. But don't be so sure. Some of the most influential executives are ones who are clearly servants. It's how they choose to lead. Still not convinced? Then perhaps you might use Jesus' statement as a sort of mantra in your prayers this week and see what happens. "For all who exalt themselves will be humbled, and those who humble themselves will be exalted" (v. 11). Chew on these words for a few days or weeks and then let them bother you for a while. I know that they bothered me. And I know that they still aren't finished doing their work on me. May they never be finished. Amen.

---

1. I have heard several versions of this story. One written source is: Heather Forest, *Wisdom Tales* (Little Rock, Arkansas: August House, 1996), pp. 60-61.

Finish What You Start

I remember as I was growing up, before gas became more precious than gold, that our family would go on buggy rides, as we called them, on Sunday afternoons after church and dinner. It was a great time for the entire family to be together, to wander back roads aimlessly, and to talk about just about anything you could imagine.

Most of the time my dad would surprise us but sometimes he would ask us where we wanted to go. One place I always asked my dad to drive to was the park in town. One reason was that I loved it when we would drive through the creek where there wasn't a bridge (I'm sure that it's gone by now) and listen to the water slosh under the car and get little chills imagining that a huge wall of water would come along and wash us downstream. The other reason I wanted to go to the park was that we would drive past one of the strangest houses any of us had ever seen. When we would see it my brother and I would get the giggles. It was, I suppose you could say, a house in progress, built by someone who had not sat down to estimate the cost, to see whether he had enough money to complete it (Luke 14:28).

Here's what I mean. Just when the house was nearly complete, the owner who was also the builder, decided to leave that portion unfinished and start on an addition. And, you guessed it, before that wing was done he would knock out a wall, pour footers, and stretch out in yet another direction. Now I don't know how the building and zoning inspectors treated him but I know how his neighbors and passersby did. He was treated with ridicule. It was a corner lot and so this house began to sprawl out first one way and then the other. On the outside it looked strange but somewhat finished except for the siding on whatever happened to be the latest addition. But on the inside it was something else altogether. Inside it was a disaster!

Even though I saw the inside of the house only once I still remember my jaw nearly hitting the floor (where, of course, there was a floor!). We walked on boards to get from one room to another. Dry wall was stacked in piles; the uncovered floors were bare plywood. And where there weren't floors, you could see the unfinished basement below.

I'll never forget our drive home that day. My father was his typical quiet self but finally he spoke. "Always finish what you start," he simply said. "Don't let that ever happen to you." Now I couldn't imagine at my tender age of ever building my own house but still I got the message and could think of other projects I might not finish. Even now, every time it doesn't look like I'm going to finish something I think of my dad and I think of that house, and I get back on the ball and complete my latest undertaking.

Jesus said the same thing but in even more blunt terms. Discipleship, he said, is more important than your family; your cross must be willingly picked up; and if you are going to start following Jesus you had better understand this because if you get surprised by the price you will have to pay and miscalculate what discipleship is going to cost you, you just might not be able to finish what you began.

When I was ordained years ago, I helped pick the music and was asked to choose the first reading for the ceremony. I chose a reading from the apocryphal book of Sirach that began, "My child, when you come to serve the Lord, prepare yourself for testing" (2:1). I liked that reading. It made me feel rather noble and just a little bit smug, though I would never have admitted it. Here I was, sitting there with eleven others, and we were ready for anything that came our way. We knew that we had signed up for a life of service that would likely, from time to time, result in some amount of suffering, of hardship, and of testing.

Little did I know how true those words would be. In my naïveté, I would soon be able to relate quite well to the person in Jesus' parable who failed to estimate the cost of building a tower. I was no different than the king who decided to wage war but never sat down to ascertain if he had enough soldiers to finish the job. In short, I was shocked, though I shouldn't have been, when the hardships began. I would sit in amazement when difficulties came my way. It didn't help, I suppose, that they began with an early morning phone call on my first day in the parish. But I was warned and shouldn't have been at all surprised.

In case you think I'm only talking (or am I whining?) about what happens to ordained clergy I am not. Each one of us, parent, teacher, social worker, bus driver, attorney ... you name it, each one of us, when we decide to follow the Lord, if we are to be true to our call, must willingly pick up our cross and put discipleship above even our own family. It's not much fun to think of, but we must prepare ourselves for hardships.

For instance, I have rarely been in an earnest discussion with parents about their children and not heard one of them say, "Do you ever stop worrying about your children?" I've thought of that question myself when I haven't heard from my children for a day or two or when I know they're going through a tough time at work or at school. Not long ago I asked my mother when she finally stopped worrying about her children. I expected her to say that finally, now that we were all grown up and have families of our own, that she has, at last, stopped worrying about her children. But no, even my mother answered, "Never. You never stop worrying about your children." And then she looked at me and shook her head sadly. I'm not sure what she meant by that and I didn't ask. The point is that no matter what our particular path in life, if we are walking with the Lord, there will be hardships. You should count on it.

I don't remember who said this but I've never forgotten it, "If you read the Bible and are comforted, then you've missed the point." I can't imagine how often I've looked for comforting words in the Bible during difficult times. And if you find yourself comforted with *this* gospel passage then I don't know what to tell you. Still, with the risk of taking away the sting of it, we should make sure we understand what Jesus is asking of his disciples and us, and it's not about joining some kind of cult.

The word "hate" in the Old Testament didn't have the emotional baggage that it does when we use the word today. It means something a bit closer to a *lesser love*. Certainly Jesus who commanded us to love our neighbors and strangers and even our enemies, would not ask us to turn around and hate our fathers and mothers, wives and children, and brothers and even life itself. He would never say that. What he is saying is that discipleship and love of God must come first and foremost. Nothing, not even our closest relatives should keep us from living out our discipleship.

What about this, carrying your cross, stuff? I know what it doesn't mean. It doesn't mean how we usually use it; something like, "Oh, my husband left his dirty underwear on the floor again. I guess this is just my cross to bear." Instead, when Jesus talks about us carrying our cross he means that, being fully aware of what the cost of discipleship might be, we willingly pick up this cross when it comes our way. It is our choice, not something that is flung upon us that we have no other option but to bear it. It is the cross, the sacrifice, and the hardship that we freely embrace knowing full well the price we will pay.

What if we paraphrased this passage a little and Jesus said, "Whoever comes to me and does not hate Sunday morning soccer games or ballet recitals cannot be my disciple"? Or what if he said, "Whoever comes to me and does not hate their country club membership cannot be my disciple"? Or, "Whoever comes to me and does not hate gas-guzzling SUVs cannot be my disciple"? Or "Whoever comes to me and does not hate late night parties and sleeping in on Sunday morning, cannot be my disciple"?

If Jesus said these things we might be tempted to say back to him, "You'd better stop it, Jesus. Now you've gone from preaching the gospel to meddling in our personal lives." And since I've said them, maybe some of you are thinking that I've gone from preaching to meddling.

Early on in our church plans many of you remember that we got anxious for a building. Oh, the synagogue was nice and later the school cafeteria where we worshiped was fancier than any cafeteria I'd ever eaten in. But we wanted our own place. Barely a day passed that someone didn't whisper at me, "If you build it they will come."

"Perhaps," I often replied, "but will they stay?"

So we put together a building committee, hired an architect, and launched our building program. We dreamed about how we would use our first building. We set priorities for the space and estimated the attendance in five and ten years. Then we put our architect to work by first asking him to show us what we could do on our property if the sky was the limit. The result was a beautiful design with a cost of over twelve million dollars! If you had looked up the word "crestfallen" in the dictionary you would have found our picture.

"Oh," we said once we caught our breath. "Well then, tell us what it would cost to build part of it. Maybe the sanctuary or maybe a multi-purpose building." Even so the cost was so high over our heads that we couldn't even conceive, at that time, of making it work. Still there were some who pushed us and chanted, "If we build it...."

Lucky for us we had a little bit of sense and set the building of the building aside while we went about building the church of people. Had we not slowed ourselves down, looking back it is clear to see that we would have found ourselves unable to finish what we started. We would have gone, as too often happens, from being a new start to being a false start.

Let's try to sum all this up. It's simple really: The cost of discipleship, or at least, *a* cost of discipleship is that we are asked to put nothing in the way of following Jesus. If we decide we are going to follow Jesus then we must prepare ourselves for hardships. And, if we think of ourselves as disciples of him and we haven't experienced hardship, haven't had to ask tough questions about our priorities, then maybe we're lucky or perhaps we need to take a good hard look at what we think it really means to follow Jesus. Don't forget, if you decide to follow the Lord, prepare yourself for testing. Truer words have never been spoken. Amen.

Proper 19
Pentecost 17
Ordinary Time 24
Luke 15:1-10

Where Would You Go
To Meet Jesus?

I remember reading in a church development book some time ago of the experiences of a church planter who spent a whole lot of his time in bars. Don't get me wrong. He didn't even drink! What this church planter decided right off the bat was that he would not seek out ready-made Christians (although they were welcome) but that he would go after the lost. He would go after the people that most churches avoided. This man, despite the grumbling of the Pharisees and scribes, welcomed sinners and ate with them.

As a result of spending time outside the church (in coffee shops, libraries, and malls, not just bars!) rather than inside the church, he grew the congregation very fast. A side benefit was that he found some great musicians in the house bands that were willing to play at church on Sunday morning.

This church planter, now a consultant, pleads with other developers to get out of their offices and seek out people who normally wouldn't be caught dead in church. All this reminds me of the old story of the man who lost a coin and was out on the sidewalk on his hands and knees looking for it under the street lamp. A friend came along and offered to help, got down on his knees as well and asked him, "So where exactly did you lose this coin?"

The man with his nose still to the ground replied, "In the house."

"Then why in the world are we looking for it out here?"

"That's a silly question. The light is better out here."

Isn't this what happens too often in the church? We build and adore our nice buildings, we pastors stock our libraries with all the books we could ever need to prepare our sermons, and we create

333

work for ourselves that keeps us coming back to our buildings where the light is better. All the while, the ones who are lost are outside and we never see them unless they rudely interrupt us with a request for food or utility assistance or for advice while going through a life-changing event. We too often expect the lost to be attracted by our buildings and our manicured grounds, by our flashy websites, or our latest direct mail piece promising a splendid preaching series for the summer, but we don't spend enough time with them to see if this is what they are looking for or what they in fact need. They may be looking for Jesus only to have us offer them a potluck dinner. So they stay lost. Or, and I must say this, perhaps it is we ourselves who are lost.

What would happen to our church if we focused on those outside these walls rather than on making sure that each of us received exactly what *we* wanted from the church? What would happen if the church stopped being about us? What would happen if we focused our attention on the lost and neglected of the world instead of on what color carpet we should put in the guild room?

Our bishop recently encouraged us to imagine the church and the world switching places. He wanted us to picture our churches being in the world and the world being in our churches. I found that notion intriguing even if I don't exactly know how far to stretch the image. But then it's not unlike how we understand the ministry of the deacon as a person who stands at the door of the church and, turning toward us shows us the world, and turning toward the world, shows the world the church. It is, as someone said about his comments, a paradigm shift. It is indeed.

A friend of mine, and former member of this church, writes reflections on the gospels for the outreach committee and, of course, for the members of her new church. She sends them to me every month to use as I see fit and when they arrived this week I saw one that I'd like to share. It struck me since the main character is a priest she calls Father Don. Father Don was the person who kept after me during college to come back to church, to make a weekend retreat and eventually, when I mentioned to him that I thought I might be called to the ministry, counseled me and took me on seminary visits. I was, before this, one of those "lost sheep" or "lost coins." I had not been inside a church for years except for visits home or, when Don would pay me to play the upright bass, in folk masses. He never gave up on any of my friends or me. Up until his untimely death he kept pursuing the lost, the ones, he would say, Jesus would have gone after.

Here's what my friend wrote about him:

> Father Don would consistently divert folks driving him home from teaching Tuesday morning Bible study to what appeared to be the absolutely worst bar in one of the worst sections of the city. "Best burgers and coldest beer in town," he would say as he shouted, "two hot and two cold" at the surly waitress behind the bar as he guided his driver toward a table in the back. Everyone who drove Don to that bar described their own uneasiness and even fear as Don engaged others in the bar (in the middle of the morning) in conversation. Each driver asked the same question, "Why are we here?" And the consistent answer from Father Don was, "Because this is where we will meet Jesus." Don was always clear about the gratitude with which he accepted the gift of love and mercy that was the sacrifice of Jesus in his own life. He acted on that gratitude every day of the rest of his life by acting with love and mercy, by living in just relationships with everyone around him, by "seeking and serving Christ in all persons." It's not comfortable seeking out and choosing to engage all of those "others in our midst," but Don would tell you that that is exactly where you will meet Jesus.[1]

What she knew but didn't share with her new congregation is that Father Don continued to do all this for years following a debilitating stroke. Nothing kept him from seeking out the lost and sharing with them the good news of God in Christ. Nothing kept him from meeting Jesus in the stranger. Nothing should stop us, either.

Over the past couple of decades it has become fashionable to survey neighborhoods to find out the needs and wants of the people who live there before actually developing a new church. The church would then be designed around what the majority of the people in that area wanted. One such church plant took that method a bit far in my opinion when they offered a class to parents on how to potty train their toddler. I am not kidding. As they say, you can't make this stuff up.

How different this is from the approaches I've already mentioned. When we design churches around what people think they need we may never get to the mission of Christ. Instead, we'll be putting on potty training seminars instead of ones on how to reach the unchurched in our families and neighborhoods. We will be focused so much on the needs of the dwindling number of people already in the building that we will not have energy left to open our doors to the world and go out to the highways and byways, the coffee shops and the shopping malls, and engage those outside our church walls.

A friend of mine built a wonderful church from the ground up by going door-to-door and building relationships with literally thousands of people around the area where their new church was being planted. As a result the church grew very fast and became, if you'll pardon the expression, a "successful" church in just a few years. Yet within eleven years the grumbling became so loud that the vestry asked him to consider leaving since he wasn't spending enough time with the established members of the church but was out in the streets still bringing new people to Christ. I wonder what they expect from their new pastor.

Now I realize that this might not be exactly the kind of message you came looking for this morning. I understand that, I really do. I have a hard time going to places where I might need to step out of my comfort zone like I'm suggesting we do. I, too, wish there was a church where my every need was anticipated and met. But to be honest, a church like that would give me the willies. I would have a difficult time even calling an organization like that a "church."

So instead, let's step out together. Let's stand alongside our deacon who week after week stands figuratively and sometimes literally at our church door and welcomes the world in and welcomes us out into the world as disciples of Christ. Let us stand with and walk with those who leave this comfortable setting and seek out those whom the world has forgotten. Let us do what Father Don did up until the time of his death, what Jesus did up until and after the time of his death on the cross, and despite the grumbling of the Pharisees and scribes among us, welcome sinners and eat with them.

---

1. Leanne Puglielli, "Outreach Reflections on the Gospels" June 2008. Used with permission.

How Do You Know The Good Guys From The Bad Guys?

I'm going to dispense with the niceties and cut to the chase. Everywhere I turned this week commentators on this gospel told me that it is the most difficult of all the parables of Jesus. They told me how it has caused incredible problems for the church for 2,000 years now. Some said that the problems were caused because folks didn't understand what he was trying to say. I read so many of these that I got a class-A case of writer's block. I became stuck worrying that I'd come in here this morning with a dull, sad look on my face apologizing all over the place, happy that my wife is in Pennsylvania with her mother so that she wouldn't be embarrassed by my ineptness. I finally decided to cut to the chase as I said, get to the point and clear up as much of the confusion as I am able. If it ends up that I don't really cut to the chase or get to the point or clear up all the confusion please don't tell me. Just smile and say, "Nice message, Father" and I'll never know the difference. Oh, and when my wife returns next Sunday, tell her that she missed a great sermon. Then make sure you confess your sin, of course.

The problem, I think, is that often when we listen to these parables our first reaction is to assign parts. I noticed this recently when I told a folktale in which the king was the main character. Many of you tried to understand the story by equating the king with God and right away you got stuck in your interpretation. Doing that was no better than equating the snake in the story of Adam and Eve with the devil. The snake is not the devil. The snake is a snake. And by the way, until it messes with God, it is a snake with legs! But I digress. I trust you'll look it up when you get home. The point is, in the folktale I told, the king was just a king. Not God, not us, just a king.

When we try to interpret the parables by assigning parts, we usually pick for ourselves the role of one of the good people and from that, we hope to learn something about how we might better live our lives. So we know who the good guys are in the story (us, of course) and who the bad guys are (always someone else). But Jesus' parables are never that simple. They are meant to cause dissonance; to make us think on deeper and deeper levels. If we simply say, in the case of this story, that the rich man is God and we are the manager and the debtors are those who got in too deep with payday lenders, we immediately get in trouble.

Still, let's see how this would play out in the story we're faced with this morning, which begins with a rich man bringing charges against his manager. Most of us are not going to identify with the rich man. Someone once said that no matter how much money we have, being rich means having more money than our neighbor.

So we're not the rich guy. And who would want to be with all the recent corporate scandals. Imagine if Jesus had begun his story, "There once was an executive who worked for Enron." So, no ... we're not going to identify with the rich man. He probably did something dishonest to get where he is anyway.

Perhaps we'll have more luck with the manager. Most of us grew up with the stories of Robin Hood. He was always stealing from the rich and giving to the poor. We love stories where the rich and powerful go down in a blaze of glory and the little guy winds up on top. Remember how a few years ago the tabloid television shows were having a ball with Donald Trump's casino losses. We love those stories.

Well, we love them until *we're* the rich guy. We don't mind kicking them when they're down unless the foot is smacking *us* on our behind. So it's decided, we'll identify with the manager.

But immediately another problem arises: the manager is lazy — not even strong enough to dig ditches, and he's proud — he's ashamed to beg. However, he *is* clever and before he's dismissed, he discovers that he's not too lazy to cook the books. He calls in the people who owe his master money — lots of money; one owes

900 gallons of olive oil and another somewhere in the vicinity of 1,000 bushels of wheat. He discounts the bill for olive oil by 50% and the wheat by 20% thus insuring that they will treat him well when he's kicked out into the street. There's no question that he's dishonest. Oh well, so much for rooting for and identifying with the little guy. We like him and all, and we're all for the boss getting his comeuppance, but this is just plain wrong. So ... if we can't use the rich guy as a role model and the manager falls far short, what are we to do?

And wait! This story gets more complicated by the commendation of the rich man. He praises the manager because he acted shrewdly. Now if the story was just sitting in a book somewhere we might not have so much trouble with this. But Jesus told this story. Somewhere in here there's got to be good news. Somewhere in this strange story is a glimpse of how we're to act in the kingdom of God. But where is it? What in the world, or better, what in God's kingdom does he mean?

One place we might focus our attention is on the last half of verse 8: "for the children of this age are more shrewd in dealing with their own generation than are the children of light." This may not be a parable so much about rich and poor people as it is a story that should wake us up to the realities of a post-Christian world, that is of course, a world very much like the pre-Christian world of Jesus' time. A Christian talk-show host I quote once in a while sometimes talks about how gullible some Christians are. Sometimes he's talking about the internet schemes aimed at Christians. Other times he's talking about conspiracy theories. Still other times he's just talking about how quick Christians can be to believe anything and everything that comes over Christian radio or from the pulpit. He urges his listeners to think and discern. Good advice, I think. Sometimes the children of light are not very shrewd in dealing with the rest of the world, with the children of this age.

I have often thought about how Christians are so gullible at times. Now, if I'm not already, I'm going to get in trouble, but here goes: I have a problem with the word "Christian" being attached to everything. It's not unlike the controversy a couple of years ago about whether a particular presidential candidate wore a flag lapel pin. The assumption was that if he wore one, he was patriotic; if he didn't wear a flag lapel pin, then he was unpatriotic. In the same way it seems like tacking the word "Christian" onto something makes it better, more reliable, less likely for the consumer to have a bad experience dealing with that business. The other day my wife brought home a copy of the *Christian Blue Pages*. She said she had never seen them before and asked me what they were. I said it was simple. If you want a Christian plumber or insurance agent or auto mechanic you simply had to look here. She thought I was making this up. But I wasn't.

Here's my problem, if I believe that just because a person puts a fish symbol in his ad or calls himself a Christian attorney, that they will be good or better or more honest than someone else, I might find myself sadly surprised someday. Likewise, if I believe everything I hear on some of the so-called Christian cable television shows I might begin to think that the fact that I'm not rich means I'm not as faithful as I should be, or at the least, I haven't "sowed a seed" into some particular televangelist's Mercedes ... oh, I'm sorry, I meant ministry.

Perhaps it would be a good idea if we prayed about this: Dear heavenly Father, sometimes the parables that Jesus told are too much for us. It would seem that he is teaching us to be shrewd and crafty when dealing with the people of the world. That doesn't sound very Christian to us. Yet it is so easy to be taken in by some people who profess one thing and do something quite to the contrary. Help us to keep our eyes open, our minds alert, and to use all of our smarts when dealing with those who perhaps have values that differ from ours. We ask this of you who with Jesus and the Holy Spirit live and reign, one God forever and ever. Amen.

Proper 21
Pentecost 19
Ordinary Time 26
Luke 16:19-31

The Great Divide

Some of us are old enough to remember the old Cat Stevens' tune, "Father And Son." That song, as you might recall, is in the form of a dialogue. The father speaks first and tries to share with his son some of the wisdom he's gained from his years of living. He says that it's not yet time to make a change, relax, and take it easy. Perhaps the son ought to look for a wife.

The son, in the next verse, responds that his father is more interested in talking than listening. Dad then replies with his same message: don't make changes, take life more slowly, get married, settle down, blah, blah, blah.

In the last verse, they both sing — *at* each other. Neither is listening to the other. There is a great chasm between the two of them. A great emotional distance had developed between the father and the son in the song.

This father and son had grown far apart and even though each of them had much to teach the other, neither one could really hear the other because they were too busy trying to make their point. That song gets me to thinking of all the relationships where we experience such distances. There is often distance between parents and kids to be sure; but also there is sometimes a divide between us and our neighbors, other church members, or people of different political parties or religions. Lately, the distance between people who differ in one way or another has grown to such a degree that in some cases we are no longer able to hear each other and are no longer are able to learn from each other, and sometimes, we no longer treat each other as a brother or a sister.

During a presidential campaign a few years back I was late for an appointment in part because the interstate was filled with police both in cars and on overpasses. I mentioned this when I arrived twenty minutes late and said I thought it was because a certain candidate's motorcade was using that route. When I said that there were police with rifles on some of the overpasses my acquaintance clapped his hands and asked gleefully, "Did they get him?" I could not speak. I was astonished at what this man thought passed as a joke. I wondered if the distance fostered by the nature of the political discourse in this country had brought us to a point where this was supposed to be funny. My friends, the distance between us has grown too great.

That, I think, is the point of the parable of the rich man and Lazarus at least for me today. It is, among other things, a story about distance. The rich man lived the good life while Lazarus lay at his gate, covered with sores, fending off the wild dogs, and starving because he didn't even get the crumbs that fell from the rich man's table. When the two die the poor man is swept away by the angels to the bosom of Abraham while the rich man is tormented in Hades. The rich man begs Lazarus to dip his finger in water and come over to quench his thirst. But this cannot be done since there is now a great distance between them, a chasm, not unlike the abyss that existed between them while they were living.

So the rich man begs Abraham to send Lazarus to his brothers and warn them to change their ways — to not treat their fellow human beings the way he did; to stop putting distance between themselves and those in need. But Abraham refuses. They had their chance (just like the rich man) since they had the teachings of Moses and the prophets. Heck, they wouldn't even be convinced if they were to be told by someone who rose from the dead!

Stories like this often show a reversal of fortunes; rich in this life — poor in the next; poor in this life — rich in the next. But if we focus only on this we'll miss a major point. The problem for the rich man is not that he is rich. Most of you would agree that there's nothing inherently wrong with being rich. The problem is that even though he cannot leave his own gate without tripping over the suffering Lazarus, he does nothing to help him — he ignores him. He is blind to his misery.

The chasm, the great distance between the rich man and Lazarus began in this life by the rich man's indifference to the suffering of Lazarus. That is his sin. Moses and the prophets, time and time again, speak about our responsibility for the poor, the orphaned, and widowed. This particular rich man, while not creating a physical distance between himself and Lazarus (although he may have wanted to) created an emotional one. He simply appeared not to care about what happened to the man who was lying at his gate. He stepped over him and went on about his business. That is the rich man's sin. He created the distance, the chasm that followed him even into the afterlife.

What is remarkable to me is not that we see such examples of inhumanity — it is that we find places, like many of our churches, where we work so hard to see that it does not happen. We're not perfect — we fall short from time to time — but we get up and try again and again. We strive to keep our eyes open to those who are struggling and to see that the distance between people inside the church and outside the church, for instance, are not made greater but are made less and less.

There are so many needs; so many Lazarus' laying at our gates that it would be easy to have compassion fatigue. Hurricane victims, flood victims, devastating earthquakes, school children in Liberia, or that neighbor of ours living in the shadow of the shopping mall with not even the money needed to buy decent clothes for his boys. Yet, we seem to say, even though there is physical distance between us that we might not be able to lessen, there is not going to be emotional distance — not on our watch. We will not stop caring even if we feel that the help we are able to give seems like too little, too late.

While none of us can help each and every cause that presents itself at our gate, we can and do help as many as we are able. When one member stood in the back of church a few weeks ago and held up a plastic glass asking for help for a good cause, she actually had to turn away contributions. Tertullian, one of the early church fathers once wrote, "He who lives only to benefit himself confers on the world a benefit when he dies." Now that's right to the point, isn't it?

We know better than to live a life that only benefits our families and ourselves. We realize that part of the reason we are here is to benefit the larger world, to change the world, to help those in need by seeing them as our brothers and sisters and not just sore-covered annoyances lying at our gates.

Likewise, unlike some other places in the world, we work to be civil in our discussions of issues that have divided other houses. People on all sides of the issue have talked calmly and thoughtfully about the ordination of openly homosexual men and women, and even over issues in unbelievably contentious presidential elections. While strong feelings are present on all sides, we have found ways to stay connected with each other, to not think or act in terms of them and us.

This parable, then, is not simply a story about how we are to care for those in need, it is a story that reminds us we are all connected, and we should do all in our power to stay that way and not step over the other and pretend they don't exist or don't matter. For there are consequences when we aren't connected. Not just at the end of our days as this parable illustrates, but now, right here there can be severe consequences when we distance ourselves from our brothers and sisters. Still, by opening our eyes, and coming face-to-face with those we might have avoided in the past, we can change at least ourselves.

A few weeks ago, our congregation took our turn cooking and serving a meal for about 125 folks downtown. A dozen people arrived early to help prepare barbequed chicken and other fixings, set the tables, and otherwise get things ready so that we could feed people who would no doubt be hungry as it was the end of the month.

Sure enough, this week's meal was no different. Some of our congregation arrived early and attended a prayer service upstairs and when they finished and the doors opened, our guests streamed in. Our youth worked hard and when it came time to serve the family-style meals they jumped right in, served the food, filled their glasses, talked with the neighborhood children, and enthusiastically handed

346

out dessert at the end of the meal. We were nervous that we hadn't prepared enough, but somehow, some way, no one went home hungry, and those with small children took with them some milk and a few meals of leftovers.

We always feel like we've done something that has a real, if brief, impact on that neighborhood, and I'm always interested in watching your reactions and especially those of the children, who serve for the first time.

That evening as the meal came to an end I walked outside to talk with three of the people who had just eaten. I asked if they got enough. "Best meal I've had in weeks," one said.

"My wife cooked it," I said proudly, patting my belly and immediately feeling embarrassed since not one of the three was anything but skin and bones.

"You're a lucky man!" he replied and I thought, he's right, I really am a lucky man.

We talked for a little longer and then I asked, "So ... where do you guys live?" They stared at me and then looked back and forth at each other with little grins on their faces. I suddenly got it, "Oh my ... you're ... you're homeless!" They just nodded. I tried to recover from my *faux pas* and asked them how they did it ... how did they live on the streets? Where did they eat? How did they stay safe?

"You have to have at least *some* money. Where do you get it?" I asked.

"At the exit ramps around town. We hold up signs."

"Do people really give you money?"

"Some do. Some act like they don't see us." They began to laugh and one pointed to the woman and said, "When she's on my exit ramp holding her sign that says, 'Homeless' I stand on the other side of the ramp with a sign that says, 'She ain't homeless but I am.' "

It was getting late and the pastor came out and said she would be giving them a ride. "Where? Where are you going?" I asked, hoping it was to a shelter somewhere nearby.

"You've never been there. Down by the river if the cops haven't moved the camp."

347

They thanked me again for the meal and for talking with them and then left with the pastor. I went back downstairs to finish with cleanup and then drove home. All the way I thought about our conversation and how the one guy looked so familiar. I was almost home when it dawned on me where I had seen him before. He had been at the exit ramp I took on my way there, holding a cardboard sign that said he was homeless. Only a few hours earlier, he had been an anonymous homeless person holding a ratty-looking brown cardboard sign that I only caught out of the corner of my eye as I tried to make my way through the light before he could rap on my window and ask for money.

I wonder what I'll do the next time I see someone with his or her cardboard sign. Will I help to satisfy his hunger with what falls from my table? I wonder.

I still don't know this man's name but in my prayers each night I call him Lazarus.

I find that I have tried to make two points; that's never a good idea in a sermon but that's the way it goes sometimes. One point is to remind us to care for the Lazarus' of the world and the other point is that the same distance that sometimes keeps us separate from a Lazarus can separate us from each other, and we must not let that happen. In the kingdom we are to nurture our relationship with Lazarus and with each other. I pray that I will always have the courage to narrow the chasm that exists between you and me and Lazarus. And I pray that you will as well. Amen.

Proper 22
Pentecost 20
Ordinary Time 27
Luke 17:5-10

When The Going Gets Tough ...
The Tough Start Praying!

Ever since the sign went up on our property that our church was coming I've gotten phone calls from people asking when we'll have a church. I can be a smart aleck as some of you will attest and so I'm often quick to respond that we already have a church, we just don't have a building. "Well," they usually say, "give me a call when you get the building done; I'm not going to worship in a high school cafeteria." Before I can give my canned speech about the difference between a church and the building I realize I'm talking to a dead phone. A friend of mine, who planted a church fifteen years ago told me not to be surprised if at our first service in our new building that some of these people will show up and say either, "I'm sure glad you finally got the church built" or "When are you going to build the *real* church building?" I'll bet he's telling the truth and I know that it won't be easy to keep a civil tongue. At least, it won't be for me. But, of course, we must.

I understand that way of thinking, I really do. Like most of you I have worshiped in buildings that looked, felt, and smelled like a church. I love that experience. I never imagined, as has been the case for us, that we would worship in so many unique settings, but what rich experiences those have been for us, even though the high school cafeteria with humming pop machines and sticky floors and the acoustics of a ball-bearing factory was difficult for many of us. Some guests never returned and when we asked them why we found that they just couldn't get their souls around worshiping in such settings. Oh, dear ... what's a church to do without a building?

And now, as I say to people who ask, we're in the middle of our first building program. Finally we're off and running. In some ways, that's true. But every time I say it, I feel like I'm lying. It seems most times that we're right at the very beginning of the project and since there have been so darn many stumbling blocks I often wonder whether we'll ever get on with the actual work of building the building. Every time we turn around there are red flags and roadblocks. I know that you and I don't have anything close to the patience of Job ... but here we are, trying to build a building while building the church. Or as I've often said, it's like trying to build a plane while flying it. Wherever it is that we are, it just feels lousy most of the time and our supply of hope and faith is sometimes running low.

It's probably a folktale, but I heard about a little church in Tennessee that went through something like we're going through. It seems that a wealthy friend of the congregation willed them a chunk of land and they proceeded to build their worship facility. They didn't find out until very close to the planned opening that the parking lot was too small and until they greatly increased the capacity of it, they wouldn't be allowed to use their new building. Unfortunately, they had used up every square inch of their land except, of course, for the hill behind the building site. If they were going to build a larger parking lot they would literally have to move a small mountain.

Undaunted, the pastor announced on the Sunday morning two weeks before the long-anticipated opening that he would meet that evening with all members who had "mountain-moving faith." They would ask God to move the mountain as well as provide the money to have the land paved and striped before the scheduled opening dedication service in two weeks.

Only a handful of the 300 members assembled for prayer. But, boy did they pray! For almost three hours they lifted their voices to God pleading with him to intercede. At last, huddled in the dark, cold and sore from standing in the cool evening air for so long, the pastor gave a hearty "Amen" and then, "We'll open in two weeks as scheduled." This pastor felt that God hadn't let them down before and that he wouldn't start now.

350

The next morning (and here comes the part that's hard to believe) there came a loud knock at his study door. Standing there was a construction superintendent who got right to the point. They were building a strip mall nearby and needed a "mountain's worth of fill dirt" before they could do anything else and wondered if the congregation had ever thought of leveling that hill behind them to give the church a little breathing room. If they would let him take the dirt, and it had to be right away, the construction company would level the land, tamp it down, and pave and stripe it. "How does that sound?" he asked. You know what happened, of course. The church opened as planned, in two weeks.

In our gospel passage today, Jesus is asked by the apostles to increase their faith. He replies that if they had faith even as little as the size of a mustard seed they could uproot a mulberry tree and plant it in the sea just by saying so. Well folks, it's time for those of us with mountain-moving faith or mulberry tree-tossing faith to start praying and not stop until we've moved a mountain or two, or a mulberry tree or two ourselves. This building is not going to be built on time until we get God involved in all this.

I was at a meeting with other church planters recently and came back to the office to the message that we had to file two more easements (in addition to the two we filed earlier in the week) because someone had forgotten to tell so and so that it needed to be done. "Great!" I shouted to no one at all. "Another delay in an already long-delayed building project." I flipped. "Lord, how many more stumbling blocks would there be? How much more delay? Why is this happening?" I was ranting and raving until I suddenly realized that I was praying. Not the nice sedate prayers of my childhood or seminary days, and certainly not the kind of prayers that were expected of me on Sunday mornings, but I was praying nonetheless. I was praying as best I could with faith the size of a mustard seed hoping it was enough faith to move mountains.

I didn't know how I would tell the congregation that we were delayed yet again, that this building was really going to be built, honest it was. I knew your patience was stretched, so was mine, so was that of everyone working on the project. I finally settled down enough to realize that I needed to do something productive and that's when I read today's gospel again. It was clear as can be. Jesus was saying that we already have enough faith, that it was time to start praying, fasting, and pleading. It was time to start putting this faith (small as it might seem to us) into action. We had a mountain to move and prayer is what we needed to get it done. We needed to meet, strategize, and figure out a way through this mess, but the prayers of everyone needed to go with us so that we'd act with wisdom and grace. As we so often say in the prayers of the people, "pray for the church." Yes, please, pray for the church.

I once heard the story about a drought that threatened the crops in a small village. The priest told his flock to go home and to fast and pray and return to the church the following week for a special prayer service in which they would ask God for rain. The villagers went home and prayed and fasted and returned just as the good father had asked them but as soon as the priest saw them, he was furious. He yelled at them, "Go away, we will not do our prayers. You do not believe."

"But, father," they protested, "we fasted and we prayed and we believe."

"Believe? You believe? Then tell me, where are your umbrellas?"

I am asking you to pray and bring your umbrellas. Pray with whatever faith you have that obstacles will be removed, that whatever is working against us will be cast aside, and that we'll be able to proceed quickly. Drive out to the property and stand on the spot and dream of the ministry that we'll be able to do in and through this building. Come and walk on the lot and ask God how we can use the time we have to prepare for the work that lies ahead in ministry and to prepare for those who have yet to come through our doors. Don't wait to start new ministries but rather get creative and ask God to give you an idea of how they might be started now. Ask our Lord to give us wisdom and courage in dealing with the powers that be. If you feel so moved, fast from a meal or two, or from your favorite television show, and offer that as prayer. We all must pray. You never know how God is going to work.

There is a story from an unknown source that I heard long ago about an old man named Sam who had three sons: Danny, Johnny, and Samuel. No one in the family ever set foot inside a church as far as anyone could remember. The pastor and the others in the church tried for years to interest the family in coming to church but to no avail. Then one day, as the story goes, a rattlesnake bit Sam. The doctor was called and he did everything he could to help him, but it looked certain that Sam would die from the bite. So, to the astonishment of everyone gathered at his bedside, Sam asked that the pastor be called.

The somewhat surprised pastor arrived, and after greeting everyone began to pray as follows: "O wise and gracious Father, we give you thanks that in your wisdom you sent this rattlesnake to bite Sam. He has never darkened the door of our church and we have no reason to believe that he has, in all his time on earth, ever prayed or even acknowledged that you exist. So now we pray that this experience will be a valuable lesson to him and will lead to his genuine repentance and his acceptance of your Son as his Savior.

"And now, O Father, we pray that you will send yet another rattlesnake to bite Danny, and still another to bite Johnny, and a third really nasty one to bite Samuel. For years we have done everything we knew to get them to turn to you, but it was all in vain. It seems, therefore, that what all our work could not do, this lowly rattlesnake has done. Therefore it seems to us that the only thing that will accomplish your will for this family is rattlesnakes; so, Lord, send us bigger and better rattlesnakes. Amen."

By now you may be confused. I've asked you to pray and bring your umbrellas. I'm a little afraid that some of you might pray for rattlesnakes. I'm actually afraid that I might pray for rattlesnakes! But most of all ... most of all I'm asking all of us to please pray that we will remain in communion with each other.

We're going to be all right. We're going to move mountains and we're going to continue to learn what it means to be a part of the body of Christ — to learn what God wants us to do and be — and how to wisely use this extra time that's been given to us.

Pray this week, my brothers and sisters in Christ. Pray without ceasing. Pray for your leaders and for those working for us. And next week bring your umbrellas — and be sure to watch out for rattlesnakes! Amen.

Sermons On The Gospel Readings

For Sundays
After Pentecost
(Last Third)

Knowing Who's
In Charge

Scott Bryte

Proper 23
Pentecost 21
Ordinary Time 28
Luke 17:11-19

Can't Stay Away

On the way to Jerusalem Jesus was going through the region between Samaria and Galilee. As he entered a village, ten lepers approached him. Keeping their distance, they called out, saying, "Jesus, Master, have mercy on us!" When he saw them, he said to them, "Go and show yourselves to the priests." And as they went, they were made clean. Then one of them, when he saw that he was healed, turned back, praising God with a loud voice. He prostrated himself at Jesus' feet and thanked him. And he was a Samaritan. Then Jesus asked, "Were not ten made clean? But the other nine, where are they? Was none of them found to return and give praise to God except this foreigner?" Then he said to him, "Get up and go on your way; your faith has made you well." — Luke 17:11-19

What a bunch of ingrates, those guys — all nine of them! It's not like a little "Thank you" would have killed them. It wouldn't even have taken up all that much of their precious time. All they had to do was turn around, make a quick jog back to Jesus (maybe not even all the way back), and give a little wave from the distance; a shout of, "Thanks for the healing" and they'd have been back on their merry way, the requirements of polite society all nicely filled. What would have been the big deal?

When we think of leprosy, we think disfigurement; the loss of fingers and toes. We think of what is now called Hansen's disease. Hansen's disease causes numbness and weakness in the limbs and

357

deterioration of the extremities and the face, the nose in particular. It is a horrible thing. You can catch it from other people, but not easily. The problem is that you can have it for a long time, and pass it around, before you know there's anything wrong at all. It is on the rise, worldwide, mostly in places where the sanitary conditions are poor. It is highly treatable and almost always curable. Mycobacterium leprae, the bacterium from which Hansen's disease develops, succumbs easily to antibiotics.

In the ancient world, on the other hand, it was quite a different story. They didn't know about bacteria, antibiotics, rates of infection, or any of that. What they knew was this: Sometimes what starts out as a simple rash on the skin, can lead to some very bad things, and what starts with one person can end up affecting many more. So what did they do with that knowledge? They kept those "lepers" away is what they did. They separated them from other people, and didn't let them live with anyone or eat with anyone, or even talk with anyone, except for other lepers. A scaly patch on the back of your hand; a sudden discoloration on the end of your nose, could cost you your job. It could cost you your family and friends. A little shiny white spot on the thick of your thumb, and life as you know it is gone. Unclean — outcast — away — off you go, with the other "lepers." There were rules to make that happen, laws about how far away lepers had to stand from other people, about how they had to wear worn-out clothes and warn people in a loud voice whenever they were walking down the street. There were even commandments from God.

What if what you had wasn't anything nearly as devastating as Hansen's disease, but simply a rash that would clear up on its own? Well, there were laws about that, too.

Jesus is just walking into a little, unnamed town outside of Galilee when ten lepers see him, apparently recognize him, and head in his direction. They don't get too close, though, because the law says they can't. Instead, they yell to him from a distance, "Jesus, Master, have mercy on us" (v. 13). "Go and show yourselves to the priests" (v. 14), Jesus answers, so they turn back around and start to do precisely that. No sooner do they start walking, going where

Jesus told them to go, than they are healed. One of them, a Samaritan whom none of the priests would have given the time of day to anyhow, turned again to face Jesus.

Of course, he did. How could he not? He had his health back. He had his life back. How could he not, at the very least, take a minute or two to turn around and say, "Thank you"? But the others didn't — not a word. What a bunch of ingrates, those guys. Or maybe not. Of course they were thankful. Jesus gave them their health back. Jesus gave them their lives back. So they obeyed him. They did exactly what he told them to do; they went and showed themselves to the priest. But Jesus was disappointed. Something was wrong. The nine obedient lepers had somehow missed the mark and the Samaritan, the one who was bound to be an outcast healed or not, had somehow gotten it right. Jesus said to him "get up and go on your way, your faith has made you well" (v. 19), whatever that means.

The other nine lepers had faith. They called out to Jesus, believing that he could heal them. They made tracks to go and show themselves to the priests even though they didn't look or feel any different when they started walking. They trusted. They acted on faith. And they were healed. The medical problems of the other nine, Hansen's disease or who knows what else, were cleared away as they walked. So what was it they did that was so wrong? What made them really different from the one who remembered to say, "Thank you"?

Here's the difference. All ten lepers were healed as they were walking away from Jesus. Nine of them kept walking. But one of them found that he couldn't leave. His life had changed. Jesus gave him his life back. Jesus restored his skin and probably also his job, his family, and his place in the world. He had to go back to Jesus. He had to return and give thanks. He just had to. He couldn't keep away. That's what faith is. Faith is being unable to stay away from Jesus. To have faith in Jesus is to be in love with Jesus.

Jesus loves you no matter what. Jesus heals you, he puts your life back together, makes you whole again with a whole life again, no matter what. Jesus died and rose. That's the plain and simple truth. Jesus calls us to be his people, his children, by baptism into his death and into his resurrection. That's the way it works. Faithful life does not ignore those truths. But Christianity is not just a bored nod of the head blandly acknowledging what Jesus has done for us.

To be made well, to live well, is to always stay by Jesus. Christian life is a constant returning in praise and in thanks, in humility and in service, in gentleness and in mercy, to the Lord who has saved you, has healed you, and has made you whole. Healing and forgiveness always take us back to Jesus. Hope always takes us back to Jesus. Faith always takes us back to Jesus. It's not because it's polite to go back and say, "Thank you." It's because you're in love and you can't stay away. Amen.

Proper 24
Pentecost 22
Ordinary Time 29
Luke 18:1-8

Will He Find Faith?

Then Jesus told them a parable about their need to pray always and not to lose heart. He said, "In a certain city there was a judge who neither feared God nor had respect for people. In that city there was a widow who kept coming to him and saying, 'Grant me justice against my opponent.' For a while he refused; but later he said to himself, 'Though I have no fear of God and no respect for anyone, yet because this widow keeps bothering me, I will grant her justice, so that she may not wear me out by continually coming.' " And the Lord said, "Listen to what the unjust judge says. And will not God grant justice to his chosen ones who cry to him day and night? Will he delay long in helping them? I tell you, he will quickly grant justice to them. And yet, when the Son of Man comes, will he find faith on earth?"
— Luke 18:1-8

It's that last line that's the hard part. The story Jesus tells at the beginning of Luke 18, known popularly as the "parable of the un-just judge" has a reputation for being a tough story to deal with. And in fairness, you'd have to say that the "parable of the unjust judge" deserves that reputation. If the point of a parable is to make a deep truth easier to understand, then this parable doesn't quite work. What makes it so tough to deal with is that the main charac-ter is not a nice person. He's a man who became a judge, but not for any of the right reasons.

361

We learn that he doesn't fear God. Here he was, in a position to say what was right and what was just. But he didn't feel accountable to any universal ideas of good and bad, of right and wrong. It was his job to lay down the law. It was his job to judge the actions of other people. All well and good, but he didn't think there was anyone judging him. He felt no accountability to a larger sense of justice. It's not that you have to be all religious and whistle hymn tunes on your way to work and teach Sunday school in order to hold public office. That's not the problem. The problem is that this man, this judge, had no belief, or at least no interest, in the higher good. And that's not all. We are told, of this judge, that "[he] neither feared God, nor had respect for people" (v. 2). He didn't judge in response to God's law, nor did he act out of a simple sense of fairness.

A woman came to him and begged for his help, but apparently he didn't become a judge in order to help people. She pled with him for justice, but he didn't have any interest in justice. She pleaded and she begged and she nagged and she persisted. Finally the judge gave in to the woman and helped her. After all this time, did she convince the judge of the rightness of her cause? Did the judge suddenly realize the selfishness of his ways and resolve to turn his life around and do good with his power? No, it was nothing like that at all. At long last, the judge assisted the woman because she was annoying him, and he wanted her to go away.

It's easy to see why this is not one of the stories that gets told in vacation Bible school. What's it supposed to mean? The whole thing is introduced with these words: "Jesus told them a parable about their need to pray always and not to lose heart" (v. 1). If this is a story about prayer, is the poor woman supposed to be us? More to the point, is the heartless judge supposed to be God? After all, the judge is the one to whom the woman pleads. The judge has the power to bring about justice, and in the end, it's the judge who grants her what she's been asking for. Like the judge, God hears our pleas. Like the judge, God has the power to do something about our problems. But how far does it go? Is God like the judge in every way? Does God also ignore us? Does God also have no respect for people? Does God also cave in to us and answer our prayers

362

only when we've gotten on his nerves so badly that he'll do anything just to get us to stop nagging? Surely we can't believe that of God! We know that God loves us, we know that God wants good for us, and we know that God eagerly listens and answers our prayers. Surely God is nothing like the judge, and that's the point of the story. It's not a comparison. God is not likened to the unjust judge. Instead, this parable is a contrast. The judge is this ... but God is that. The judge has no respect for people. God does respect people and cares for them. The judge wants to be left alone. God want us to be with him always. The judge gives in out of exasperation. God provides for us out of love.

If a selfish and power-drunk judge, a guy who doesn't even especially like people, will give a poor widow the justice she's been begging for, then God, who loves us, will surely give us whatever good and helpful thing we request. God is not like the judge. God is better than the judge. Therefore, God will treat us better than the judge treated the widow. After the story is over, Jesus sums it up, so that no one can miss that this is a contrast. "And will not God grant justice to his chosen ones who cry to him day and night?" [asks Jesus] "Will he delay long in helping them?" (vv. 7a-8). "I tell you, he will quickly grant justice to them."

So why does this story disturb people? Why is it so tough to deal with? It's the last line that holds the answer to that. It's that last line that's the hard part. It is another question. "And yet, when the Son of Man comes, will he find faith on earth?" Jesus just told a story about how God can be trusted with our prayers; a story meant to show that God answers us and cares for us willingly. Why does Jesus ask if there will still be faith on earth when he returns? Because in spite of his assurance that God hears and answers us, it can be hard to trust that this is true. There are so many times when it seems as if God really were like the judge. So many times our prayers seem to go unanswered. It is true that some prayer is selfish. Some prayers treat God like a menu. Most people would agree that God is not Santa Claus and that praying for luxuries or for one's own glory is out of bounds. Most would agree that God is perfectly within his rights if he says, "No" to those prayers. But what about prayers said in love? What about the many just and kind and selfless prayers that don't seem to get an answer? "God please heal...." "God, please protect.... " "God, please don't let...." We pray and we beg and we plead, and people still get sick and still fall victim to crime. There is tragedy still. There is heartbreak. There is death.

It is not easy to trust. It is not easy to believe. It is not easy to pray. We do not always get what we pray for, even when what we want is a truly good thing. So how can we say that God always hears us? How can we still have faith that God says, "Yes" to us when we see "No" all around? Jesus is the answer. Jesus himself is God's "Yes." Jesus is the answer to every hope and every prayer. Jesus fell victim to crime and cruelty and evil. In Jesus, God is with us when we are victimized. Jesus was rejected and beaten and crucified. In Jesus, God is with us even when things go horribly wrong. Jesus died and was buried. In Jesus, God is with us even in death. Jesus rose from the dead. In Jesus, God gives us life and a future and a purpose. In Jesus, God answers our prayers.

God loves us. God respects us. In Jesus, God says, "Yes" to us. In Jesus, God gives peace and solace to us in times of suffering. In Jesus, God gives hope to us when we mourn. In Jesus, God gives us life when we face death. God answers all our prayers. Jesus is the answer. Amen.

Begging And Bragging

He also told this parable to some who trusted in themselves that they were righteous and regarded others with contempt: "Two men went up to the temple to pray, one a Pharisee and the other a tax collector. The Pharisee, standing by himself, was praying thus, 'God, I thank you that I am not like other people: thieves, rogues, adulterers, or even like this tax collector. I fast twice a week; I give a tenth of all my income.' But the tax collector, standing far off, would not even look up to heaven, but was beating his breast and saying, 'God, be merciful to me, a sinner!' I tell you, this man went down to his home justified rather than the other; for all who exalt themselves will be humbled, but all who humble themselves will be exalted."

— Luke 18:9-14

There were these two men who went up to the temple to pray. One of them was a Pharisee and the other was a tax collector. It's a shame, really, that one of them was a Pharisee. A shame because it spoils the surprise ending. When we hear the word "Pharisee," we know right away who the villain is. To us, "Pharisee" is just the Bible word for "bad guy." So if you have a story that starts out, "there were two men ... one of them was a Pharisee," you don't even have to get to the end of the story to know who the hero is. The hero was whoever wasn't the Pharisee. The story could go "there were two guys, one of them a Pharisee and the other an axe

365

murderer," and you'd know that in the end, somehow, the axe murderer is going to turn out not to be so bad. Sure, he might be this crazed serial killer, but at least he's not a Pharisee. Pharisees, to our ears, are worse than everybody. But that's not how it sounded to the people to whom Jesus first told this little story over 2,000 years ago.

The Pharisees, to be fair, were actually pretty good people. They did everything right. The followed the law of God to a "t." We struggle with the daunting job of keeping the Ten Commandments. The Pharisees went way beyond that. They dug through the Old Testament, from Genesis all the way to Malachi and found a whopping 613 commandments! They found 613 commandments and they kept every single one of them. They went all out to do everything that God asked them to do. And to show how serious they were, how devoted, they even went further than God asked them. The Bible says not to take God's name in vain. The Pharisees made sure that they never did, not even accidentally. They didn't even want to come close to breaking God's law, so they didn't say God's name at all. Ever. Don't boil a kid goat in its mother's milk? Well, just to be on the safe side, they wouldn't boil any goat meat in any milk, or mix any meat of any kind with any dairy product at all, not even cheese.

They studied God's law and talked about God's law and kept all the rules. This is not some evil gang of thugs we're talking about here. The Pharisees were righteous with a capital RIGHT. Jesus butted heads with another group, the Sadducees, on some pretty important issues. The Sadducees didn't believe in angels. Jesus did. The Pharisees agreed with Jesus. The Sadducees didn't believe in the resurrection of the dead. The Pharisees did (and we know whose side Jesus was on there). So why is it that the Pharisees are always the bad guys when Jesus tells his little parables? Why is it that the Pharisees were so eager to stop Jesus from teaching that they arranged for his death?

Here's the problem with the Pharisees. They were good people and they knew it. They followed the rules and wanted everyone else to see how well they did. But their problem was more than just a little misplaced pride or spiritual arrogance. They missed the point.

You know what they say about the letter of the law and the spirit of the law. The Pharisees followed every letter, but they still managed to completely miss the whole point of all those 613 commandments. The Pharisees thought that the whole thing was about following the rules, but the point of the commandments is not the commandments themselves. The point is kindness. The point is mercy. The commandments are there to teach us to love each other and be civil to each other. The point is living as God's holy people: merciful and gracious. The problem with the Pharisees is that they didn't get that.

There were these two men who went up to the temple to pray. One of them was a Pharisee. The Pharisee didn't get it. He thought that prayer was all about him. He thought that prayer was a chance to submit his résumé to God. "God, I thank you that I am not like other people: thieves, rogues, adulterers, or even like this tax collector. I fast twice a week; I give a tenth of all my income" (vv. 11b-12). It was not so much praying as it was bragging. The Pharisee's relationship with God was a total mess, and he had no idea.

There were these two men who went up to the temple to pray. One of them was a Pharisee and the other was a tax collector. The tax collector had nothing to brag about. His relationship with God was a mess and he knew it. If he was out to impress God with how holy and righteous his life was, then he didn't have a leg to stand on. His prayer was not a résumé. No amount of padding would have helped. The tax collector's prayer wasn't a résumé, it was a plea. "God, be merciful to me, a sinner!" (v. 13). It wasn't bragging, it was begging. Which is to say, it was a real prayer.

God knows how well we do, and God knows how poorly we do. There are things that we get right, but we can't get it all right all the time. The truth is that we have no hope of keeping 613 commandments and more. We can't handle ten. The truth is that we aren't always very loving. We aren't always very kind. We can be thoughtless and arrogant, uncaring and cruel. If we were to count only on our own righteousness to save us, we would be in serious trouble. But as it is, God isn't grading us on how well we follow the rules. He's not grading us on how merciful we are either. It's not our obedience that makes us holy and it's not how loving and civil and kind we are that counts in God's eyes. It's not even whether or not we really get the point. It's God's mercy that counts. It's the only thing that counts. We're in no position to brag. Praying is asking. It is begging. We need God to forgive us, to help us, to heal us, and to make us better. In Jesus Christ, in his dying and in his rising from the dead, God forgives us.

Pray for mercy and beg that God will help you to become merciful. Pray for forgiveness and beg to become more forgiving. Pray for the strength to follow God's rules, but more than that, beg for the wisdom and the faith to do God's will. Amen.

Getting Back Into Shape

*Then Jesus said to the Jews who had believed in him,
"If you continue in my word, you are truly my disciples;
and you will know the truth, and the truth will make
you free." They answered him, "We are descendants of
Abraham and have never been slaves to anyone. What
do you mean by saying, 'You will be made free'?"*

*Jesus answered them, "Very truly, I tell you, ev-
eryone who commits sin is a slave to sin. The slave
does not have a permanent place in the household; the
son has a place there forever. So if the Son makes you
free, you will be free indeed."* — John 8:31-36

It is Reformation Day. Today we mark the anniversary of the
day, October 31, 1517, that the Reverend Doctor Martin Luther —
monk, priest, and college professor, posted an invitation to a scholarly debate on the door of a church in northeastern Germany. It
doesn't sound like a very big deal, and it's doubtful that Luther
himself ever imagined it would be a big deal. But the debate Luther
hoped to schedule was on the subject of the selling of indulgences,
a practice that boiled down to some people saying you could buy
your way into heaven for cold, hard cash, and other people going
into hawk to come up with the money. Luther's sixteenth-century
Post-it® Note became such a big deal because it was the church
itself that was behind this ludicrous and harmful scam.

This minutely detailed piece of scholastic babble, known forever after as the *95 Theses*, the 95 points of argument, raised huge,
important questions about the authority of the pope, the role of the

369

church, how we are saved, what Jesus does for us, and what it means to be a Christian. In short, *everything* about it mattered. The debate never happened. Some clever, unnamed printer, with a nose for what would sell to the public, took the notice down, translated it from academic Latin into everyday German, and printed off copies as fast as he could. It was like a bomb went off. Within two weeks, the sale of indulgences in Germany, once a steady stream of income, fell off to a trickle. It is the questions raised by the 95 theses, about the power of the church, about the mercy of God, about how we are made right with God that we celebrate this Reformation Day.

You get something like Reformation Day, the Fourth of July, a birthday, or anything that marks an anniversary, and it begs the question, "Is this about something that happened a long time ago, or about what's happening now?" Does the Fourth of July just remember the founding of the country, or does it celebrate the existence of the country? Does a birthday party mark only the day of a person's birth or is it a way of celebrating that person's life?

If Reformation Day is just about what happened long ago, then what's the big deal? Put the date in the encyclopedia and on the calendars and be done with it. If it's just about what's happening now, then why are we counting off the years, remembering Luther, and singing hymns written by Luther? This day, like any anniversary is, of course, about then and now.

Today we remember what Martin Luther did centuries ago — how he questioned the practices and teaching of the medieval church and refuted the claim to authority made by the pope and the hierarchy of Christendom. Recalling how Luther and his followers got kicked out of the church for their insistence that we are saved through grace alone, through faith alone, trusting the authority of scripture alone, helps us to remember who we are and what our purpose is.

But reformation is not a once and for all deal. What God did through Luther and his followers was not the end all, but instead a rather dramatic and painful step in the ongoing process of reformation. Reformation simply means reforming — putting back into shape again. Throughout the Old Testament God is constantly whipping Israel back into shape, using prophets and foreign armies and whatever it takes. In the New Testament, our risen Lord promises that he will be with us always, until the very end, and that the Holy Spirit will guide us, to keep us from getting bent out of shape, twisted, and perverted.

The church of Christ has people in it, and they're sinful people because that's the only kind there is. For God to choose to make his holy church out of sinful people, who wear their holiness like a bad suit, would be like someone choosing to make the Statue of Liberty out of mashed potatoes. You could never let go. You'd have to hold it together every second. And you'd forever have to be working like a maniac, constantly putting it back into shape. It would need to be reformed constantly.

"Then Jesus said to the Jews who had believed in him, 'If you continue in my word, you are truly my disciples; and you will know the truth, and the truth will make you free'" (vv. 31-32). This is the truth of the gospel: Our salvation is free. We can't buy it with money or perfect church attendance or good deeds or good intentions or anything else. The death and resurrection of Jesus is our only hope. We can rely on Jesus Christ alone, even if we may want to rely on ourselves, our own efforts, our own will, and our own good character.

Reformation Day is not a celebration of the joys of being Lutheran. It's not an excuse for patting ourselves on the back and saying, "Look how right we are, too bad everybody else is wrong" or "Thank God we're Lutheran, 'cause we've got God all figured out." Self-congratulations might make us feel good, but it's arrogant and sinful. It limits the Holy Spirit for one thing, assuming the we have cornered the market on God, and that God speaks only to the likes of us. For another thing, it assumes that Lutheranism has all the answers when in fact, probably the greatest strength of the Lutheran approach to Christianity is that it knows when to say, "I don't know." It knows it needs God's help. No, Reformation Day is not a time for Lutherans to gloat over their accomplishments and insights. Instead, Reformation Day is a joyful reminder that God holds us together every second. God constantly reforms and reshapes us. God never lets go.

Reformation Day is a day to remember that we who are God's people, if left to our own devices, will drift away from the truth. It is a day to rejoice in the fact that we are not left to our own devices. God re-forms his people. God calls us back to the truth.

The Holy Spirit came to Martin Luther in northeastern Germany to bring the gospel to light against the darkness of that age. The darkness of 1517 was the lie that you could buy your way into heaven; that you had to earn God's favor. Through Martin Luther and countless others, God called the church back to the truth.

The Holy Spirit comes to us now, sending us out into the world to bring the light of the gospel to bear against the darkness of this age. Our age, like any age, has many darknesses, but chief among these is this: We are an age that does not expect resurrection. We are an age fixated with, and terrified of death. An age where we are afraid of growing older, afraid of reaching the end of life, because we are an age that thinks that death is the end of us. We are in an age that stockpiles treasure on earth, a greedy age, that doesn't know to look for greater treasure in the world to come. We are an age without hope. We are an age that is afraid. We are an age that desperately needs to hear the good news. Ours is a world that needs reformed.

Reformation Day isn't just an anniversary or just a remembrance of what God has done in the past. It is a reminder that God is working among us now, in the present; that God is calling us forward into the future. God is reforming us now, beckoning us back to the truth, back to hope and life and forgiveness we can never earn. God is sending us out to live and speak life. Through Jesus Christ, God forgives and re-forms you and calls you to be his body, his church. Through the Holy Spirit, God reforms and holds the church. And through the church, God announces the good news and reforms the world. Amen.

Saint Who?

Then he looked up at his disciples and said: "Blessed are you who are poor, for yours is the kingdom of God. Blessed are you who are hungry now, for you will be filled. Blessed are you who weep now for you will laugh. Blessed are you when people hate you, and when they exclude you, revile you, and defame you on account of the Son of Man. Rejoice in that day and leap for joy, for surely your reward is great in heaven; for that is what their ancestors did to the prophets.

"But woe to you who are rich, for you have received your consolation. Woe to you who are full now, for you will be hungry. Woe to you who are laughing now, for you will mourn and weep. Woe to you when all speak well of you, for that is what their ancestors did to the false prophets.

"But I say to you that listen, Love your enemies, do good to those who hate you, bless those who curse you, pray for those who abuse you. If anyone strikes you on the cheek, offer the other also; and from anyone who takes away your coat do not withhold even your shirt. Give to everyone who begs from you; and if anyone takes away your goods, do not ask for them again. Do to others as you would have them do to you."

— Luke 6:20-31

The whole thing started as a safety net. All Saints began as a catchall. In the old church calendar, each saint would get one day a year set aside in their honor. The feast day of Saint Mark the evangelist, just to name a saint, is on April 25. Mary, the mother of Jesus, gets August 15. Saint Andrew is remembered on November 30. Saint Philip and Saint James share the first day of May. You might not even have heard of these holidays, but there is one that most people do know — Saint Patrick's Day on March 17. It's good to remember people who lived their lives, and in some cases gave their lives, in witness to the gospel. The drawback is, of course, that you eventually run out of days. There are 365 days most years; one more in leap years. But there are way, way more than 366 people who are considered saints. There are more than that whose lives and witnesses are worth remembering. That's why there is All Saints. In the old church calendar, the first day of November was set aside for those other saints. All Saints was celebrated to make sure that no one was overlooked.

There are certain people that all Christians call saints: Saint Paul, Saint John, Saints Matthew, Mark, and Luke. These saints, and a handful of others, still have days of commemoration on church calendars. When these days of commemoration do show up on Protestant calendars, however, they are regarded as minor festivals. For example, when October 14 falls on a Sunday, Saint Luke's day gets celebrated, and the lessons for the day, maybe even the hymns and the sermon, can be especially selected to have something to do with Luke and his ministry. In years that October 18 falls on a Tuesday, good old Luke gets ignored. Many Christians recognize a dozen or so of these minor festival saints' days. There are days for the apostles, maybe a few other people from the New Testament like Mary Magdalene or Paul, and that's pretty much it. There's certainly not a whole year's worth.

For centuries, All Saints was considered one of the holiest days of the year, second only to Easter. It was far more important and a much bigger deal, than Christmas. In some places, it even marked the start of the new year. That was in the old church calendar. New calendars, the kind you'd buy at a mall or in a card shop, may not even mention it at all. All Saints has become little more than the answer to a trivia question, celebrated by few, and understood by even fewer. But All Saints is not trivial. It gets recognized in the church whether the actual day, November 1, falls on a Sunday or not. It's a big deal.

We celebrate All Saints because there are far too many saints to fit on the calendar. There are hundreds of thousands of saints — millions — billions. And those are just the ones who are walking around today. All Saints is a big deal because of who the saints are, and, more importantly, because of how they got to be so saintly. A saint is not a flawless person who does all the right things and says all the right things and never doubts and never wavers in the faith and never gives into temptation. If that was the standard, then there wouldn't be any saints at all, not even the ones from the Bible. A saint isn't a superhero, square-jawed and steady, wearing a cape and a halo. Superheroes aren't real. Saints are real.

We get the word "saint" from the Latin *sanctus*, which means "holy one." A saint is a holy person. But a saint's holiness does not come from their iron will or their unimpeachable moral character. A saint's holiness comes from the death and resurrection of Jesus Christ. A saint is a weak, flawed, normal person, who was dipped in, washed in, and lives in Jesus Christ. If you go into the ocean, you're going to get wet. If you're in Christ, you get holy. It's a big deal. Saints are sinful people who God decides must be holy, because they are soaking in the love and forgiveness and righteousness of Jesus Christ. Jesus died and rose in order to make them his holy ones.

It is All Saints and today we remember and thank God for the life and ministry of all his saints. We remember Saint Paul. We thank God for Paul's coworkers in the gospel: Joanna, Lydia, Barnabas, and many others. We remember evangelists, teachers, bishops, and martyrs. Today is a day to lift up all the saints, including you. On All Saints we celebrate the miracle of your holiness. On this day also, we remember those saints among us who have died: some of them recently, some ages ago. We don't remember them for their perfection. We don't lift you up because you get everything right. What we are doing here today is reminding ourselves that a saintly life is a life spent in coming to grips with a holiness we did not create and with love and forgiveness we do not deserve.

It's not easy living the life of a saint. Jesus talks about that life, and it just sounds backward. "Blessed are you who are poor," but "woe to you who are rich." "Blessed are you who weep," but "woe to you who laugh." "Love your enemies, do good to those who hate you, bless those who curse you, pray for those who abuse you. If anyone strikes you on the cheek, offer the other also." Oftentimes, these words get twisted. "What are we supposed to do?" we ask. "Be a doormat? Lay down and let people trample all over us?" How in the world are you blessed when things are going badly? We think we are blessed when things are going well for us and we're healthy and happy and safe. But the saintly life isn't about wealth, popularity, or comfort. It's about faith and hope, resurrection and life, compassion, love, and purpose.

The saintly life is just about staying out of trouble. It's not passive. It isn't wimpy. To live as God's holy people takes courage. Turning the other cheek is courageous. It's bold and it's tough and it's impossibly gutsy. "No," it says, "you will not win. I will not give up. Jesus died for me, rose for me, called me holy, and I will not let that go. Go ahead and hit me again. I will not let anger and vengeance and sin get the upper hand."

That's backward to our way of thinking. It's not natural. What we want to do, what we are inclined to do, is still largely our selfishness talking, our fear talking, and our sin talking. The good, the noble, the righteous, the merciful, the generous, and the loving — that is God talking. That is God calling. To live the life of a saint is to live in God's mercy. To live the life of a saint is to live in the often-uncomfortable paradox of being the sinners we know ourselves to be, and at the same time, being the holy person God says we are. Maybe you don't feel especially holy, but you are. God is calling us to be holy. God is calling us to be his. God is calling us forward. It isn't easy. It doesn't come naturally. But God is with you and will always be with you, just as God is with all the saints. Amen.

Just Deal With It

He entered Jericho and was passing through it. A man was there named Zacchaeus; he was a chief tax collector and was rich. He was trying to see who Jesus was, but on account of the crowd he could not, because he was short in stature. So he ran ahead and climbed a sycamore tree to see him, because he was going to pass that way. When Jesus came to the place, he looked up and said to him, "Zacchaeus, hurry and come down; for I must stay at your house today." So he hurried down and was happy to welcome him. All who saw it began to grumble and said, "He has gone to be the guest of one who is a sinner." Zacchaeus stood there and said to the Lord, "Look, half of my possessions, Lord, I will give to the poor; and if I have defrauded anyone of anything, I will pay back four times as much." Then Jesus said to him, "Today salvation has come to this house, because he too is a son of Abraham. For the Son of Man came to seek out and to save the lost."

— Luke 19:1-10

He gets shorter every time we tell the story. Sunday school children sing about the "wee little man." Illustrated Bibles and everything from stained-glass windows to coloring books depict a tiny elf of a man, perched bird-like in a tree. "Poor little Zacchaeus." Or maybe "rich little Zacchaeus." Either way we've got a short story about a short man who had to climb a tree to get a good view of the parade. So, how short was he? Was he fantastically tiny?

Spectacularly diminutive? Would his picture have made it into the *Guinness World Records*? To be honest, nobody knows. All we know is that he was shorter than the people standing in front of him, all eager to see Jesus, and so he had to climb a tree to get a good look. Well, maybe that's not exactly all we know. We know that he didn't ask politely to be let through to the front of the crowd, where he would have had a better view. We know that he didn't plow his way through, either. Instead of counting on the courtesy of the people who were blocking his line of sight, Zacchaeus opted for a less direct solution to his problem and climbed a tree. That was hardly the easy way to do it.

We also know why Zacchaeus chose to shimmy up a tree rather than simply asking to be let through to the front. He didn't ask because he knew what the answer would be. Zacchaeus was a tax collector. We may grin knowingly at that and agree that working for the IRS would not help to make you a big hit at parties. No one, after all, actually enjoys paying their taxes. But being a tax collector at that time and in that place was even less of a popularity booster than it is now.

It had been a long time since Israel was a truly independent country. The land of Israel had been promised, time and again, to the descendants of Abraham. It was supposed to be theirs forever. They had God's word on that. But the Babylonians invaded and took the place over and carted away a big chunk of the population. A generation or so later, the captives were allowed to return, but it was never quite the same. The Assyrians, then the Greeks — it seems that everyone had a turn at running Israel, except for the people who actually lived there.

By the time of Jesus, Israel was under the boot of the Roman empire, and nobody but the Romans was happy about that. Well, maybe not exactly nobody. There were some who found a way to profit from the Roman occupation. There were some who put personal gain or personal security ahead of loyalty to their nation, ahead of love of their own people, and ahead of respect for the promises of God. Zacchaeus was one of them. Zacchaeus was working for the wrong side. He was aiding the enemy. Zacchaeus helped those who were keeping his own people down. His job was to take money from the people of Israel, and then hand that money over to help pay for the Roman presence in Israel. Zacchaeus had made a fortune by going directly against what God had promised to do. The descendents of Abraham were to live forever in the land and God would be in charge. Zacchaeus seemed to want Caesar to be in charge. After all, the Romans paid better. Zacchaeus was a sell out and a traitor.

There were many who were offended by what Zacchaeus did; many who knew deep down in their hearts how utterly wrong his actions were. Zacchaeus was one of them. Zacchaeus didn't push his way to the front. He didn't even politely clear his throat. There, at the back of the much taller crowd, Zacchaeus found his own solution to his problem. There was one thing, however, that Zacchaeus had apparently not counted on; a grown man in a tree — a disreputable businessman at that — is rather hard to miss. Jesus didn't miss him.

We talk often about our need to invite Jesus into our hearts and into our lives. Jesus knocks on the door politely and somewhat timidly, hoping we'll open up and let him in. But it doesn't always work that way. Jesus doesn't always wait for an invitation. Sometimes Jesus just barges on in. That's what he did with Zacchaeus. Jesus didn't stand at the foot of the tree and subtly clear his throat. Jesus walked right up to the little traitor and invited himself to dinner.

"You better get down from there quick," says Jesus to Zaccheaus. "Party at your house."

Maybe it's surprising that Jesus wasn't more polite. But Jesus is in charge. He doesn't sit by demurely until we come up and ask for the dance. Jesus leads. Jesus didn't wait for an invitation. He was just there, unbidden; in Zacchaeus' face and in Zacchaeus' house and in Zacchaeus' life. There weren't any conditions. Jesus didn't say, "Okay, Zacch, if you quit working for the enemy, and if you pay people back, and if you get rid of all this dirty money, then I'll come to you." It wasn't like that at all. No, Jesus was just there, accepting Zacchaeus and loving him and spending time with him.

Zaccheaus didn't expect this. He didn't ask for it. But now Jesus was on his way over for lunch and Zaccheaus would have to deal with it. Now Jesus was in his life, and Zaccheaus would have to deal with that, too. And he did. Zacchaeus dealt with it. "Zacchaeus stood there and said to the Lord, 'Look, half of my possessions, Lord, I will give to the poor; and if I have defrauded anyone of anything, I will pay back four times as much'" (v. 8). Zaccheaus turned around. He changed his ways. He became less selfish. Did he do this to win Jesus' favor? If that were the case, he's a little too late. No, Zaccheaus cleaned up his act because he already got Jesus' favor. Zacchaeus had done some pretty rotten things, and lived a pretty rotten live; a life that Jesus couldn't have approved of. But Jesus approved of Zacchaeus.

Jesus leads. Jesus comes into our lives. Jesus offers us love and forgiveness and hope and a new chance, we don't even have to ask. All that's left for us is to deal with it. All that's left for us is to trust in that love and forgiveness; to believe in that hope and that new chance. Jesus loves you. You didn't do anything to make that happen, but he loves you. So deal with that. Live like someone who's lovable. God forgives you. You didn't do anything to earn that. God doesn't owe you a clean start, but God gives you one. God's forgiveness is honest and complete. So deal with that. Be forgiving to others; give them another chance.

Jesus rose for you. He didn't ask you first, he just did it. Deal with it. Live for your neighbor.

Jesus comes to us. Our shameful past, our dirty little secrets, our wrongheaded attitudes; none of it keeps him away. Jesus invites himself into our lives. He forgives us and he loves us and he gives us hope. May God grant us the faith to deal with it. Amen.

Trick Questions, Big Answers

Some Sadducees, those who say there is no resurrection, came to him and asked him a question, "Teacher, Moses wrote for us that if a man's brother dies, leaving a wife but no children, the man shall marry the widow and raise up children for his brother. Now there were seven brothers; the first married, and died childless; then the second and the third married her, and so in the same way all seven died childless. Finally the woman also died. In the resurrection, therefore, whose wife will the woman be? For the seven had married her."

Jesus said to them, "Those who belong to this age marry and are given in marriage; but those who are considered worthy of a place in that age and in the resurrection from the dead neither marry nor are given in marriage. Indeed they cannot die anymore, because they are like angels and are children of God, being children of the resurrection. And the fact that the dead are raised Moses himself showed, in the story about the bush, where he speaks of the Lord as the God of Abraham, the God of Isaac, and the God of Jacob. Now he is God not of the dead, but of the living; for to him all of them are alive."   — Luke 20:27-38

If you could ask Jesus a question, any question, and be promised a plain answer, what would you ask? There are a lot of big ones that have never been answered. Wouldn't it be great if you could just go up to Jesus and ask him one of life's big, profound eternal mysteries? "Why is there evil?" "What happens when we die?" "Why are we here?"

Jesus was asked a lot of questions during the time he was walking around the near east some 2,000 years ago. Some of them were pretty good questions: "What must I do to be saved?" or "Whose fault is it that this man was born blind?" Others were not nearly so profound. "Can my two sons get the goods seats in heaven?" "Can you make my brother split the family inheritance evenly?" Selfishness got in the way there. Selfishness and ambition. But however misguided those questions were, at least they actually were questions.

Members of a scholarly sect called the Sadducees had the opportunity of a lifetime with Jesus. They studied scripture most rigorously. They thought about and pondered God day and night. They dealt with life's big questions. It's pretty much all they did. So here is the opportunity of a lifetime. Here is God in the flesh walking around among them. Here is Jesus, perfectly willing to talk about the meaning of scripture. Here is Jesus, eager to shed light on the will of God. The opportunity of a lifetime and they blew it. Some Sadducees came up to Jesus and told him this big, long hypothetical story: an elaborate and drawn-out set-up. And then for the punch line, they asked a question. Only it really wasn't a question. You ask a question if you want to learn something; a fact perhaps, or someone's opinion, maybe some bit of wisdom. The Sadducees don't want to learn from Jesus. Their question wasn't really a question at all. It was a quiz, a logical trap.

"There's this woman, see, and her husband dies, which is very sad, and they have no children, which is even sadder, so the guy's younger brother marries her, which is what the Bible says to do. Then he dies. And there's still no children. So the next youngest brother marries her and it goes on that way, with no children ever being born, through seven brothers. Then finally the woman herself dies." Jesus, at this point, is no doubt nodding along with this wildly improbable story, waiting for the punch line. You can just picture the Sadducees rubbing their hands together, ready to spring the trap; and then they pounce. "So when they all rise from the dead, who is she married to?" They ran rings around him logically.

382

It's a logical trap because it involves time. You start messing with that and suddenly nothing makes sense. Those clever Sadducees thought they could show that resurrection is impossible because the time thing doesn't work.

You do things one at a time. You go through your life in order, usually not knowing what comes next. You have to deal with things as they happen. But you remember your life all at once. You can remember things in any order you want. You can connect, in your mind, something that happened this morning with something that happened fifteen years ago. The woman in the story was married to the seven brothers one at a time. One after the other. But when she's in heaven, it's a different matter. Heaven is all at once. It's about your whole life. So, who is this lady supposed to be married to?

They could have posed the same problem with a much simpler question; one that sometimes gets asked today. How old are you in heaven? If you die as an infant, are you an infant in eternity? If you die at 104, frail and confused, are you frail and confused forever?

Heaven isn't a puzzle for us to solve, and the resurrection of the dead is not a logic problem. It's a reality. It's a gift. And it's life. That's what Jesus is talking about: life. He brushes off the question about the woman and the seven husbands, by simply saying that it doesn't work that way, and then goes on to say that God is God of the living. Abraham and Isaac and all the people of God from the past are still the people of God. They might be history to us, but to God, they're real. To God, they're present. To God, it's all right now. To God, all his people are right now. Resurrection happens because our God is the God of life. The one true God is the God of *always*.

What does this mean for us? It means that it's all right now. As far as God is concerned, you are being baptized right now. You are being confirmed right now. Jesus is dying for you right now. Jesus is rising for you right now. You are forgiven right now. God loves you right now. You are a child of God right now.

What does this mean for us? It's all God's time. All at once, or one thing after the other, all our time is God's time. We talk about family time, about down time, about company time, over time, work time, and me time. But it's all a gift to us.

All our time is God's time. Sunday morning is God's and next Tuesday is God's. Every minute since the moment of our birth belongs to God, and so does all of the future. For us, things happen one after the other, day after day. But let's not forget, as we live our day-to-day lives, that Jesus is dying for the sin we are committing now. Jesus is rising to forgive us now. Jesus is calling us into the kingdom of heaven right now. God loves us now, so we must show love now. God is merciful to us now, so show it's time for us to show mercy right now. God is putting you first right this very second. It's time to put God first and our neighbors ahead of ourselves.

God is the God of the living, so we need to take the time God has blessed us with and truly see it as a time for life. Live for Jesus. Learn from Jesus. Live by scripture. Learn from scripture. Live in prayer. Learn from prayer. Live to share the good news. Learn from talking with and listening to other Christians.

We have the same opportunity the Sadducees had. Let's not waste it setting traps like they did, saying things like, "If God is there, then this will happen" or "Since this is going on, God must not care." We must keep asking questions, keep seeking knowledge and wisdom, but we have to understand, first off, that we're not going to understand everything. God doesn't owe us an explanation, and we wouldn't comprehend it if we had one. Life's big questions have answers that are too big to fit into our heads. Rather than demanding that God put everything into terms we can understand, let us look and see how God is working in the world and in our lives. Jesus is here among us. Jesus is among us and willing to show us the meaning of scripture and the meaning of our lives. Jesus is here among us eager to reveal to us the will of God. Forgiveness is ours. Love is ours. The future is ours. It's the opportunity of a lifetime. Amen.

Proper 28
Pentecost 26
Ordinary Time 33
Luke 21:5-19

Forecast

When some were speaking about the temple, how it was adorned with beautiful stones and gifts dedicated to God, he said, "As for these things that you see, the days will come when not one stone will be left upon another; all will be thrown down."

They asked him, "Teacher, when will this be, and what will be the sign that this is about to take place?" And he said, "Beware that you are not led astray; for many will come in my name and say, 'I am he!' and, 'The time is near!' Do not go after them.

"When you hear of wars and insurrections, do not be terrified; for these things must take place first, but the end will not follow immediately." Then he said to them, "Nation will rise against nation, and kingdom against kingdom; there will be great earthquakes, and in various places famines and plagues; and there will be dreadful portents and great signs from heaven.

"But before all this occurs, they will arrest you and persecute you; they will hand you over to synagogues and prisons, and you will be brought before kings and governors because of my name. This will give you an opportunity to testify. So make up your minds not to prepare your defense in advance; for I will give you words and a wisdom that none of your opponents will be able to withstand or contradict. You will be betrayed even by parents and brothers, by relatives and friends; and they will put some of you to death. You

will be hated by all because of my name. But not a hair
of your head will perish. By your endurance you will
gain your souls."   — Luke 21:5-19

Grace to you and peace from God our Father and our Lord Jesus Christ.

It seems that the people on the radio and on television who tell you what the weather will be have been getting bolder. Their predictions are becoming more specific. "The storm will affect our viewers in about eight minutes." And more times than not, eight minutes later, things are soggier. The close up stuff; an hour into the future, or maybe just a few minutes ahead can be predicted with a fair degree of accuracy. The modern science of meteorology can pretty much call whether or not it will be raining in the minutes ahead. Making predictions for hours ahead is a little less sure. And predicting the weather a week ahead, or ten days ahead is more an educated guess than anything else. So why do we have these two-week forecasts? Because people want to know, that's why. We want to know the future so badly that we're willing to pretend that we actually can know the future. The sad truth is, the only way to tell what's going to happen in the future is to wait it out. I can tell you with utter certainty, with 100% accuracy, what is going to be in the news this coming Wednesday. The only thing is, I won't be able to tell you until *Thursday.*

When you're looking for a new job, or looking for a new house, or getting ready for a first date, or waiting to see the doctor because you have a new pain that worries you — how great it would be if you could just cut to the end and know how everything is going to turn out. How useful it would be if you could come and visit yourself from five or ten years in the future. You would know what to look out for. You could brace yourself for disaster. You'd know what you had to worry about and what you didn't need to worry about.

Would we be safer if we knew ahead of time about floods and fires and earthquakes? Would our lives be better if we knew what would happen to our country, what would happen to our town, what would happen to our family and to our friends? Would it bring

386

us peace if we knew how and when our lives would end? What if we knew when and how it all would end?

People have been looking to the Bible for that last answer for close to 2,000 years. Christians and non-Christians too have been searching the Bible for signs and dates and details about the ending of history. If you just read the Bible through, you're not going to find those dates and details, so over the years, people have dug deeper, beneath the words, for hidden clues and information. They've looked for words to mean something other than what they say: weeks to mean years for instance, or certain animals to stand for nations that didn't even exist when the Bible was written. They'd connect a few words here with half a verse from there, with a couple of sentences from somewhere else. Over the millennia, people have decoded the Bible many times and figured out the exact date of Jesus' return. They've counted down and waited, and some even sat on their rooftops or gathered together in prayer on the day they knew would be the last day. Obviously, they've been wrong so far.

The Bible says that Jesus will return. It says so plainly, with no reading between the lines. The Bible promises openly, and not in secret, that the faithful will be with God forever. But cryptic symbolic messages detailing exactly when and how these things will happen just aren't there. Sorry. The Bible is not a word puzzle, and hearing the word of God is not some game for amateur detectives.

When some were speaking about the temple, how it was adorned with beautiful stones and gifts dedicated to God, [Jesus] said, "As for these things that you see, the days will come when not one stone will be left upon another; all will be thrown down." They asked him, "Teacher, when will this be, and what will be the sign that this is about to take place?" And he said, "Beware that you are not led astray; for many will come in my name and say, 'I am he!' and, 'The time is near!' Do not go after them. "When you hear of wars and insurrections, do not be terrified; for these things must take place first, but the end will not follow immediately." Then he said to them, "Nation will rise against nation,

and kingdom against kingdom; there will be great earth-
quakes, and in various places famines and plagues; and
there will be dreadful portents and great signs from
heaven."   — Luke 21:5-11

This is one of the classic "end of the world" lessons — Jesus' doomsday forecast. What's going to happen and where and when. A plan. A map. The very last page torn out of God's own personal schedule. Except, of course, that it is nothing of the sort.

First off, we have Jesus' very blunt warning about people who claim to have hacked into God's day planner: "Many will come in my name," Jesus says, "Saying, 'I am he!' and, 'The time is near!' Do not go after them" (v. 8).

Then there's the matter that the thing Jesus is predicting here, namely the destruction of the temple at Jerusalem, has already happened — a long time ago. Under order of the Roman general Titus, the temple was burned along with the rest of the city of Jerusalem on August 10, 70 AD. After that the Roman army, which really knew how to rub it in, dismantled the temple piece-by-piece until not one stone was left upon another.

The signs that Jesus gave to predict that long-ago event: nation rising against nation, earthquakes, famines, plagues, dread portents, are things that happen all the time. Pick a year, pick a week, somewhere in the world there were wars and earthquakes and plagues.

Jesus told his disciples that before all that; before the destruction of the temple at Jerusalem in 70 AD, there would be trouble. "They will arrest you and persecute you, they will hand you over to synagogues and prisons, and you will be brought before kings and governors because of my name" (v. 12). This, too, has already happened, nineteen centuries ago and more.

Clearly the gospel lesson before us now is not a doomsday forecast. It's really of no help when it comes to figuring out the exact date on which Jesus will return. But it's also not an idle history lesson, either. There are things here that speak to Christians of every time and place. No secrets. No codes. Just some things to remember in our everyday lives.

- The world is a dangerous place.
- All that stuff that fills the newspaper every day: disasters and wars and rumors of war, can become part of your own life before you know it, and there's nothing you can do to stop it.
- Your faith in Jesus can get you into trouble.
- Your friends and even your family can line up against you.

Jesus doesn't guarantee us a charmed life. It could get rough. It certainly has before. Decades before the first large-scale persecution of Christians Jesus warned that it was coming.

> *You will be betrayed even by parents and brothers, by relatives and friends; and they will put some of you to death. You will be hated by all because of my name. But not a hair of your head will perish. By your endurance you will gain your souls.* — Luke 21:16-19

But ... even when things are the darkest; even when the world is falling apart around you; even when your allies start to look more like enemies — even then there is mercy and forgiveness. Even then there is the love of God. Even then there is peace. The temple in Jerusalem was completely destroyed a long time ago. But God did not go away. Christians have been betrayed and arrested and worse many times and in many places in the last 2,000 years, but Jesus never abandoned them. Don't be afraid. Don't give up. Jesus won't give up on you, no matter how things appear to be going. God will be with you to forgive you and to show mercy to you and to show forgiveness and mercy through you. Jesus will be with you to speak his love to you and to speak his love through you. The Holy Spirit will be with you to give peace to you and to give peace through you.

Jesus does not come to bring destruction and doom. He brings peace and hope and life. Jesus has come and Jesus is here now and Jesus will come again to bring all things to a new beginning. Amen.

Christ The King
Proper 29
Luke 23:33-43

Knowing Who's In Charge

When they came to the place that is called The Skull,
they crucified Jesus there with the criminals, one on
his right and one on his left. [Then Jesus said, "Father,
forgive them; for they do not know what they are do-
ing."] And they cast lots to divide his clothing. And the
people stood by, watching; but the leaders scoffed at
him, saying, "He saved others; let him save himself if
he is the Messiah of God, his chosen one!" The sol-
diers also mocked him, coming up and offering him sour
wine, and saying, "If you are the King of the Jews, save
yourself!" There was also an inscription over him, "This
is the King of the Jews."

One of the criminals who were hanged there kept
deriding him and saying, "Are you not the Messiah?
Save yourself and us!" But the other rebuked him, say-
ing, "Do you not fear God, since you are under the
same sentence of condemnation? And we indeed have
been condemned justly, for we are getting what we de-
serve for our deeds, but this man has done nothing
wrong." Then he said, "Jesus, remember me when you
come into your kingdom." He replied, "Truly I tell you,
today you will be with me in Paradise."

— Luke 23:33-43

It sounds so old-fashioned: Christ the King. It sounds so medieval — some relic from the ancient past that the church has held on
to for all too long, like the funny old hats in the back of your

grandmother's closet. You know that at one point, long ago, those hats were all the rage, but now they sit in storage and in truth they're better off there. Couldn't they update it a little? "Christ the president"? "Christ the prime minister"? "Christ the CEO"? "Christ the leader"? Why "Christ the King"? There are hardly any kings anymore, at least not outside of fairy tales. Sure, there are a few heads of state in a few venerable countries who still use royal titles. But for the most part, those "kings" just ride around in horse-drawn carriages and cut the ribbons at the openings of new bridges, while the real work and the real power falls to the elected leaders.

If you look hard enough, you will turn up a few modern kings with true royal power, but it's hardly a good thing. Why say "Christ the King"? You wouldn't say "Christ the Dictator" or "Christ the Despot." The celebration of Christ the King Sunday is just one more way that the church shows itself to be outmoded, out of sync, and out of touch.

Except that there's this one little detail. "Christ the King Sunday" isn't old. The celebrations of Christmas and Easter, Lent and Advent, and even All Saints Day go so far back in history that it's impossible to pinpoint just when they started. The beginning of Christ the King Sunday, on the other hand, can be traced back to a letter written by pope Pius XI in 1925. That's quite a surprisingly recent origin for a celebration shared by much of the Christian faith. Maybe 1925 doesn't sound all that recent, but in the church, saying that something happened in 1925 is like saying that it happened last Thursday. Already by 1925 kingdoms were rapidly becoming a thing of the past. Democracies and republics and even communist states were pushing the idea of an inherited monarchy deep into the corner of grandma's attic. Already by 1925, the name "Christ the King" sounded old-fashioned, out-moded, and out of touch.

World War I had just ended a little more than five years before. The great empires of Russia and Austria-Hungary had collapsed. The British empire would eventually follow. Human civilization had proved to be far less civilized than it thought itself to be. Advanced communications, the wonders of technology, and the spirit of international cooperation had all failed to keep the peace. The horror of modern warfare with aircraft and tanks and chemical weapons had not acted as a deterrent. In 1925, that failure was still very raw.

Since that time, communications have advanced tremendously. Technology leaps forward and becomes more wondrous every day. Weapons are now nuclear and biological. Tanks are stronger and aircraft faster. Through the establishment of the UN, NATO, and other alliances, and the great increase in global trade, efforts at international cooperation are more serious than ever. And still there is war. Still there is terrorism and brutality and oppression. Human civilization is still far, far from civilized.

He's an odd sort of king, this Jesus. He walked around from one little town to the next, eating with sinners and talking to all the wrong people. That's not what you'd call majestic. That's not how a king lives. And being nailed to a tree between two common criminals isn't exactly a heroic way to meet your end. That's not how a king dies. If it wasn't for the sign over his head that read, "This is the King of the Jews" a passerby would never have guessed. Enthroned upon a cross, with his thorny crown piercing deep into his scalp, he looked anything but powerful. Where was the pride? Where was the fight? He just hung there, dying. There were soldiers there overseeing his execution. They were there as representatives of Tiberius Caesar. Now there's royal power for you.

The caesars were kings in the truest, most horrible sense of the word. The soldiers couldn't miss the difference between powerful Tiberius and the dying Jesus. "If you are the King of the Jews," the soldiers said, "save yourself!" (v. 37). But he didn't save himself. Even one of the criminals hanging next to Jesus, a guy who you'd think had enough problems of his own, joined in taunting Jesus. Turning his head, straining to see around his own upstretched arm, this dying felon bothered to waste his breath in ridicule, "Are you not the Messiah? Save yourself and us!" (v. 39). Jesus did not save himself. But by dying, by becoming powerless, by losing, Jesus did save us. His power was shown in weakness; his victory in his defeat.

He's an odd sort of king, this Jesus. His kingdom has no boundaries. He conquers his enemies by waging peace on them. All of his subjects are also his heirs. He rules like no other. Calling him "president" or "prime minister" or "CEO" wouldn't quite do. Christ is king. He answers to no one. There is no constitution he has to follow. There are no elected officers to veto his word. There can be no other word for it: Christ is king. He is the legislature, the judiciary, and the chief executive. He makes the rules, and he grants the pardons.

Christ is our king. Our loyalty is to him. There are other rules we have to follow. There are rules everywhere: at school, at work, on the road, at home, even at swimming pools and playgrounds. There are many rules and many people in authority over us: police and judges, politicians and officials galore. We answer to bosses and teachers and leaders of every description. These all exercise authority over us by their power to take things away. They can revoke privileges. They can tax our wages. They can levy fees and fines. They can grant or deny promotions, lower our grades, and limit our opportunities. Some of these authorities have the power to imprison us and even to take away our lives. To one extent or another, that's what it all boils down to. The many rules and rulers that govern our lives do so by the power of death: The power to take away.

He's a different sort of king, this Jesus. Jesus rules by the power of life. Jesus doesn't threaten us and cajole us and coerce us by what he can take away. Jesus leads us by giving. Jesus rules by the power of life. Jesus forgives us. Jesus is merciful. Jesus loves us. He gives us the power to be forgiving. He gives us the ability to be merciful. Jesus gives us hope and joy and life in eternity. He's an odd sort of king, this Jesus. He's the one true king and Lord of us all.

No matter who claims power, no matter what wonders and what horrors our reason and technology bring, no matter what frightens and threatens us, one thing will always be true: Christ is king. Amen.

Thanksgiving Day
John 6:25-35

Not Just Being Polite

When they found him on the other side of the lake, they said to him, "Rabbi, when did you come here?" Jesus answered them, "Very truly, I tell you, you are looking for me, not because you saw signs, but because you ate your fill of the loaves. Do not work for the food that perishes, but for the food that endures for eternal life, which the Son of Man will give you. For it is on him that God the Father has set his seal." Then they said to him, "What must we do to perform the works of God?" Jesus answered them, "This is the work of God, that you believe in him whom he has sent." So they said to him, "What sign are you going to give us then, so that we may see it and believe you? What work are you performing? Our ancestors ate the manna in the wilderness; as it is written, 'He gave them bread from heaven to eat.'" Then Jesus said to them, "Very truly, I tell you, it was not Moses who gave you the bread from heaven, but it is my Father who gives you the true bread from heaven. For the bread of God is that which comes down from heaven and gives life to the world." They said to him, "Sir, give us this bread always." Jesus said to them, "I am the bread of life. Whoever comes to me will never be hungry, and whoever believes in me will never be thirsty." — John 6:25-35

It's every year. Every year the parades, every year the football games, every year the big family get-togethers. Every year the kids are home from school, and banks and stores and businesses of all

395

kinds take the day off. Every year there are favorite foods and second helpings and third helpings and so many helpings that you have to loosen your belt and lay down and take a nap on the floor. We celebrate Thanksgiving Day every year and have been celebrating it on the same day every year since 1863, when President Lincoln declared that a national Day of Thanksgiving would be celebrated annually, on the last Thursday of November. Since then, the date has been moved to the fourth Thursday of November, but it usually works out to be the same day. If you had a perpetual calendar and enough patience you could figure out the exact date when Thanksgiving would be celebrated for the next hundred years.

So here we are, celebrating a national holiday, a day of overeating and television watching and catching up with the relatives. Here we are celebrating this holiday in church. You have to wonder why. It's not in the Bible. Jesus and the disciples didn't sit around a long table and eat yams and canned cranberry sauce every fall. It's not part of the ancient tradition of the church, either. Thanksgiving is not a religious celebration. It's a national holiday. You don't see people going to church on the Fourth of July (unless it falls on a day of the week when they'd be in church anyway). There aren't special services for Presidents' Day or Labor Day. Why are we in church on Thanksgiving?

We are in church on Thanksgiving because a day set aside for giving thanks raises an inescapable question. To whom, exactly, are we giving thanks? You give thanks to someone. We teach our children to be polite and respectful. We teach them to say, "Please" when they ask for something, and to say, "Thank you" when they get it. You can get a gift and use that gift and love that gift without ever saying, "Thank you." Giving thanks isn't about the gift. Giving thanks is about the giver. You say, "Thank you" to someone. Saying, "Thank you" acknowledges that there is another person involved. Giving thanks establishes a relationship. If we as a nation are giving thanks today, then somewhere wrapped up in all of it is the question of whom we are thanking.

On that well-known first Thanksgiving celebration in the Massachusetts Bay Colony in the autumn of 1621, there was no question whatsoever as to whom they were thanking. They were thanking God. It was a day and a feast set aside for the express purpose of thanking God. The colony was new and survival was anything but certain. Colonial settlements had collapsed or given up or just plain vanished before. But the harvest had been a good one in 1621. The colonists had learned to adapt to the climate of their new home. They were in good shape, with enough shelter and enough food to survive the harsh New England winter. The colonists were Puritans, a conservative group of Christian believers. God had clearly blessed them, and they knew it. They had been taken care of and given gifts, so they gave thanks.

What is somewhat less well known is that there was no thanksgiving celebration in 1622. The harvest was not so good the next year, and so the colonists were going into the winter with more fear and much less security. The Puritans had concluded that God had not chosen to bless them that year, and so a feast of Thanksgiving would not have been in order. To the Puritans, Thanksgiving was not an automatic celebration that happened year in and year out no matter what. They gave thanks in times of plenty. They repented in times of want.

Unlike the Puritans, we celebrate Thanksgiving annually. That, in itself, raises yet another question. If we are thankful every year, right on schedule, then what is it that we are giving thanks for? Not every year is a good year. Sometimes things are going great for ourselves, our families, and our nation. Sometimes there is health and happiness everywhere you look. Sometimes there is peace and plenty. Sometimes, but not always. There are other times when war and want dominate our thoughts and our days and our headlines. There are times, perhaps years on end, when our lives are filled with sickness and worry, dysfunction and anxiety. In those times and in those years, the fourth Thursday in November is still Thanksgiving Day.

So what is it that we are giving thanks for? Do we give thanks for our material blessings? Absolutely we should and absolutely we do, although fortunes come and go. Do we give thanks for the people that we love and that love us? Of course we do, knowing full well that families and friendships have good times and bad; that people come into our lives and people move out of our lives.

Tragedy and heartbreak can come upon us at anytime. We don't know what will happen. So what makes us so certain that there will be something to give thanks for next year? Why do calendars come already printed in the confidence that there will be reason for gratitude come November? There is, in fact, a rather simple answer to this question. We schedule Thanksgiving every year because there is no doubt that there will be something to be thankful for every year.

Even in the midst of catastrophe, there are blessings. Is this just optimism? Is this nothing more than a perky attitude? A happy, can-do outlook? No. We can say with certainty that we will always have blessings to count because we know what those blessings are. Jesus died for us. Jesus rose to give us life. Jesus loves us. Jesus forgives us. That was true last year and it'll be true next year. In Jesus Christ, God claims us as his children. Always there is hope. Always there is mercy. Always there is life. God gives us purpose. God gives us the future. We are never alone. God gives us himself. God gives us each other. God opens our eyes and opens our hearts and gives us the strength and the will to care for each neighbor.

Whether we have much or little, we always have Jesus. When our hearts are joyful and when our hearts are breaking, God always loves us.

Give thanks with your words. Give thanks with your time. Give thanks with your thoughts and your emotions. Always, every year and every day and every minute, we have reason to give thanks. Amen.

Lectionary Preaching After Pentecost

The following index will aid the user of this book in matching the correct Sunday with the appropriate text during Pentecost. All texts in this book are from the series for the gospel readings, Revised Common Lectionary. (Note that the ELCA division of Lutheranism is now following the Revised Common Lectionary.) The Lutheran designations indicate days comparable to Sundays on which Revised Common Lectionary Propers or Ordinary Time designations are used.

(Fixed dates do not pertain to Lutheran Lectionary)

Fixed Date Lectionaries *Revised Common (including ELCA)* *and Roman Catholic*	Lutheran Lectionary *Lutheran*
The Day Of Pentecost	The Day Of Pentecost
The Holy Trinity	The Holy Trinity
May 29-June 4 — Proper 4, Ordinary Time 9	Pentecost 2
June 5-11 — Proper 5, Ordinary Time 10	Pentecost 3
June 12-18 — Proper 6, Ordinary Time 11	Pentecost 4
June 19-25 — Proper 7, Ordinary Time 12	Pentecost 5
June 26-July 2 — Proper 8, Ordinary Time 13	Pentecost 6
July 3-9 — Proper 9, Ordinary Time 14	Pentecost 7
July 10-16 — Proper 10, Ordinary Time 15	Pentecost 8
July 17-23 — Proper 11, Ordinary Time 16	Pentecost 9
July 24-30 — Proper 12, Ordinary Time 17	Pentecost 10
July 31-Aug. 6 — Proper 13, Ordinary Time 18	Pentecost 11
Aug. 7-13 — Proper 14, Ordinary Time 19	Pentecost 12
Aug. 14-20 — Proper 15, Ordinary Time 20	Pentecost 13
Aug. 21-27 — Proper 16, Ordinary Time 21	Pentecost 14
Aug. 28-Sept. 3 — Proper 17, Ordinary Time 22	Pentecost 15
Sept. 4-10 — Proper 18, Ordinary Time 23	Pentecost 16
Sept. 11-17 — Proper 19, Ordinary Time 24	Pentecost 17
Sept. 18-24 — Proper 20, Ordinary Time 25	Pentecost 18

Sept. 25-Oct. 1 — Proper 21, Ordinary Time 26	Pentecost 19
Oct. 2-8 — Proper 22, Ordinary Time 27	Pentecost 20
Oct. 9-15 — Proper 23, Ordinary Time 28	Pentecost 21
Oct. 16-22 — Proper 24, Ordinary Time 29	Pentecost 22
Oct. 23-29 — Proper 25, Ordinary Time 30	Pentecost 23
Oct. 30-Nov. 5 — Proper 26, Ordinary Time 31	Pentecost 24
Nov. 6-12 — Proper 27, Ordinary Time 32	Pentecost 25
Nov. 13-19 — Proper 28, Ordinary Time 33	Pentecost 26
	Pentecost 27
Nov. 20-26 — Christ The King	Christ The King

Reformation Day (or last Sunday in October) is October 31 (Revised Common, Lutheran)

All Saints (or first Sunday in November) is November 1 (Revised Common, Lutheran, Roman Catholic)

US/Canadian Lectionary Comparison

The following index shows the correlation between the Sundays and special days of the church year as they are titled or labeled in the Revised Common Lectionary published by the Consultation On Common Texts and used in the United States (the reference used for this book) and the Sundays and special days of the church year as they are titled or labeled in the Revised Common Lectionary used in Canada.

Revised Common Lectionary	Canadian Revised Common Lectionary
Advent 1	Advent 1
Advent 2	Advent 2
Advent 3	Advent 3
Advent 4	Advent 4
Christmas Eve	Christmas Eve
The Nativity Of Our Lord/ Christmas Day	The Nativity Of Our Lord
Christmas 1	Christmas 1
January 1/New Year's Day	January 1/The Name Of Jesus
Christmas 2	Christmas 2
The Epiphany Of Our Lord	The Epiphany Of Our Lord
The Baptism Of Our Lord/ Epiphany 1	The Baptism Of Our Lord/ Proper 1
Epiphany 2/Ordinary Time 2	Epiphany 2/Proper 2
Epiphany 3/Ordinary Time 3	Epiphany 3/Proper 3
Epiphany 4/Ordinary Time 4	Epiphany 4/Proper 4
Epiphany 5/Ordinary Time 5	Epiphany 5/Proper 5
Epiphany 6/Ordinary Time 6	Epiphany 6/Proper 6
Epiphany 7/Ordinary Time 7	Epiphany 7/Proper 7
Epiphany 8/Ordinary Time 8	Epiphany 8/Proper 8
The Transfiguration Of Our Lord/ Last Sunday After Epiphany	The Transfiguration Of Our Lord/ Last Sunday After Epiphany
Ash Wednesday	Ash Wednesday
Lent 1	Lent 1
Lent 2	Lent 2
Lent 3	Lent 3
Lent 4	Lent 4
Lent 5	Lent 5
Passion/Palm Sunday	Passion/Palm Sunday
Maundy Thursday	Holy/Maundy Thursday
Good Friday	Good Friday

Easter Day	The Resurrection Of Our Lord
Easter 2	Easter 2
Easter 3	Easter 3
Easter 4	Easter 4
Easter 5	Easter 5
Easter 6	Easter 6
The Ascension Of Our Lord	The Ascension Of Our Lord
Easter 7	Easter 7
The Day Of Pentecost	The Day Of Pentecost
The Holy Trinity	The Holy Trinity
Proper 4/Pentecost 2/O T 9*	Proper 9
Proper 5/Pent 3/O T 10	Proper 10
Proper 6/Pent 4/O T 11	Proper 11
Proper 7/Pent 5/O T 12	Proper 12
Proper 8/Pent 6/O T 13	Proper 13
Proper 9/Pent 7/O T 14	Proper 14
Proper 10/Pent 8/O T 15	Proper 15
Proper 11/Pent 9/O T 16	Proper 16
Proper 12/Pent 10/O T 17	Proper 17
Proper 13/Pent 11/O T 18	Proper 18
Proper 14/Pent 12/O T 19	Proper 19
Proper 15/Pent 13/O T 20	Proper 20
Proper 16/Pent 14/O T 21	Proper 21
Proper 17/Pent 15/O T 22	Proper 22
Proper 18/Pent 16/O T 23	Proper 23
Proper 19/Pent 17/O T 24	Proper 24
Proper 20/Pent 18/O T 25	Proper 25
Proper 21/Pent 19/O T 26	Proper 26
Proper 22/Pent 20/O T 27	Proper 27
Proper 23/Pent 21/O T 28	Proper 28
Proper 24/Pent 22/O T 29	Proper 29
Proper 25/Pent 23/O T 30	Proper 30
Proper 26/Pent 24/O T 31	Proper 31
Proper 27/Pent 25/O T 32	Proper 32
Proper 28/Pent 26/O T 33	Proper 33
Christ The King (Proper 29/O T 34)	Proper 34/Christ The King/ Reign Of Christ
Reformation Day (October 31)	Reformation Day (October 31)
All Saints (November 1 or 1st Sunday in November)	All Saints' Day (November 1)
Thanksgiving Day (4th Thursday of November)	Thanksgiving Day (2nd Monday of October)

*O T = Ordinary Time

402

About The Authors

Cynthia E. Cowen is a prolific writer who has produced many volumes of worship resources for CSS Publishing Company. She serves as a rostered Associate in Ministry at Our Saviour's Lutheran Church in Iron Mountain, Michigan, and as a licensed lay minister at Calvary Lutheran Church in Quinnasec, Michigan. Cowen holds a B.A. degree in education from Northern Michigan University; she is also a graduate of the Northern Great Lakes Synod Lay School for Mission and has been certified in youth ministry at Wartburg Seminary. She has served on several synod and denominational leadership teams, including six years on the Executive Board of the Women of the ELCA.

Frank Ramirez has served Church of the Brethren congregations in Pennsylvania, Indiana, and California for nearly thirty years, and he is currently pastor of Everett Church of the Brethren in Everett, Pennsylvania. Ramirez is the author of numerous books, articles, and short stories, and he is also a regular contributor to the online service *StoryShare* (www.sermonsuite.com). His CSS titles include *Partners in Healing*, *He Took a Towel*, *The Bee Attitudes*, and three volumes of *Lectionary Worship Aids*. Ramirez is a graduate of LaVerne College and Bethany Theological Seminary.

Arley K. Fadness is a retired ELCA pastor who has served numerous Lutheran parishes in South Dakota and Minnesota. He is currently a member of Custer Lutheran Fellowship in the Black Hills of South Dakota. A graduate of Augustana College, Luther Theological Seminary, and McCormick Theological Seminary, Fadness is the author of several CSS titles, including *Blueprints for Advent* and Christmas, *Blueprints for Lent, Six Spiritual Needs in America Today, Holy Moses, Hey Joseph!*, and *Where's Noah?* He is also a contributing author to *Sermons on the First Readings* (Series I, Cycle A).

Rick McCracken-Bennett is the founding pastor of All Saints Episcopal Church in New Albany, Ohio. He is a writer, musician, songwriter, storyteller, and church planter. McCracken-Bennett is a former member of the writing team for the online service *StoryShare* (www.sermonsuite.com), and his doctoral thesis, *Future Story*, has been used by congregations in their long-range planning. He is a graduate of the University of Findlay (B.A.), St. Meinrad School of Theology (M.Div.), and Seabury-Western Theological Seminary (D.Min.).

Scott Bryte is the pastor of Berkeley Hills Lutheran Church in Pittsburgh, Pennsylvania. He is the author of *Tales of the Inner City, Beneath the Cross*, and *Dateline: Jerusalem.* He is a graduate of Thiel College and the Lutheran Theological Seminary at Gettysburg.

LaVergne, TN USA
19 August 2009

155354LV00004B/13/P